A YEAR OF RECKONING
El Salvador a Decade After the Assassination of Archbishop Romero

AN AMERICAS WATCH REPORT

March 1990

A Year of Reckoning: El Salvador a Decade after the Assassination of Archbishop Romero.

Copyright© March 1990 by The Americas Watch Committee.
All rights reserved.
Printed in the United States of America.
ISBN 0-929692-50-0.

Cover design by Deborah Thomas.

THE AMERICAS WATCH COMMITTEE

The Americas Watch Committee was established in 1981 to monitor and promote observance of free expression and other internationally recognized human rights in Central America, South America and the Caribbean. The Chairman of Americas Watch is Adrian W. DeWind; Vice Chairmen, Peter Bell and Stephen Kass; Executive Director, Juan E. Méndez; Research Director, Anne Manuel; Counsel, Jemera Rone; Consultant, Cynthia Brown; Research Associate, Mary Jane Camejo; Associates, Beryl Jacobs and Clifford C. Rohde.

Americas Watch, together with Africa Watch, Asia Watch, Helsinki Watch and Middle East Watch, comprise **Human Rights Watch**.

For more information about this and other Americas Watch reports, or concerning Human Rights Watch, please contact:

Human Rights Watch

485 Fifth Avenue
Third Floor
New York, NY 10017
(212) 972-8400
Fax (212) 972-0905
Email (PeaceNet):
   "hrwatchnyc"

1522 K Street, NW
Suite 910
Washington, DC 20005
(202) 371-6592
Fax (202) 371-0124
"hrwatchdc"

TABLE OF CONTENTS

ACKNOWLEDGMENTS i
PREFACE iii
I. INTRODUCTION 1
II. VIOLATIONS BY GOVERNMENT FORCES 9
   A. Targeted Killings 9
      1. The Assassination of the Jesuits 9
         a. The Integrity of the Investigation 11
         b. The Evidence in the Record 15
         c. The Judicial Value of the Current
             Evidence against Colonel Benavides ... 19
         d. Others Who May Have Ordered the
             Killings or Conspired in Them 20
         e. Was There a Cover-Up? 22
      2. November 1989 Murders by
         Army Soldiers in Santa Ana 24
      3. Shooting of Student by Atlacatl Battalion,
         August 1989 25
      4. Highway Assault by Sixth Military
         Detachment, August 1989 26
      5. FMLN Medical Workers Summarily Executed
         after Capture, San Vicente, April 1989 ... 27
      6. Deaths of Three Journalists and Wounding
         of a Fourth, March 1989 28
         a. Reuters Photographers Roberto Navas,
             Luis Galdamez 29
         b. Television sound man
             Mauricio Pineda Deleon 32

      c. Dutch Television Cameraman
         Cornel Lagrouw 34
  7. Killing of University Student and
     Agricultural Worker, February 1989 36
  8. Army Killing of Santos Regino Ramirez
     Perez, Fourth Military Detachment,
     January 1989 37
B. Indiscriminate Attacks 38
  1. Air Force Bombing in Morazan, March 1989 . . 38
  2. Air Force Rocketing in Chalatenango,
     February 1990 39
C. Deaths in Custody 42
  1. Yuri Edson Aparicio Campos, National
     Police, November 1989 42
  2. Lucio Parada Cea and Hector Miranda
     Marroquin Tortured and Killed, First
     Brigade, August 1989 43
  3. Julian Rosales Lopez, National Police,
     February 1990 49
  4. Jose Joaquin Gonzalez Vasquez, National
     Police, June 1989 50
D. Disappearances 50
  1. Disappearance of Six Cooperativists,
     Possibly by Seventh Military Detachment,
     December 1989 51
  2. Disappearance of Two Unionists by
     Air Force, August 1989 54
  3. Eric Felipe Romero Canales, First Brigade,
     November 1989 55
  4. Disappearance of Health Worker by First
     Brigade, November 1989 56
  5. Still Disappeared 56
     a. Miguel Angel Rivas Hernandez 56
     b. Two SICAFE Workers and Their Friend . . 57
     c. Eliseo Cordova Aguilar 57

III. VIOLATIONS BY DEATH SQUADS 59
    A. Death Squad Cases Occurring In and
        Around Santa Ana 61
        1. Sonia Elizabeth Flores Martinez 61
        2. Pablo Obdulio Vargas Carcamo 61
        3. Attempted Murder of Manuel Antonio Perez . .62
        4. Temporary Disappearance of Four Affiliated
            with the Santa Ana Campus of the National
            University and One Unionist 62
        5. Attempted Murder of Mario Roberto Alvarez . .63
        6. Unidentified Men, Found November 1989 . . .63
        7. Angel Maria Flores Aragon, Julia del Carmen
            Ponce Flores, and an Unidentified Male . . .64
        8. Jose Armando Acevedo Acevedo 64
        9. Unidentified Man 65
    B. January-February 1990 Death Squad Activities . .65
        1. Two Unidentified Young Men 65
        2. Three Unidentified Men 65
    C. Other Death Squad Cases 66
        1. Schoolteacher Maria Cristina
            Gomez Gonzalez 66
        2. Attempted Abduction of Church Worker . . .66

**IV. VIOLATIONS OF THE RULES OF WAR BY
THE FMLN AND ATTACKS ON THE RIGHT** . . .69
    A. Targeted Urban Attacks 69
        1. Miguel Castellanos 72
        2. Francisco Peccorini Letona 73
        3. Attorney General Jose Roberto
            Garcia Alvarado 74
        4. Possible Responsibility for Assassination
            of Minister of the Presidency
            Rodriguez Porth 74
        5. Possible Responsibility for the
            Assassination of Edgar Chacon 75
        6. Possible Responsibility for the
            Assassination of Gabriel Payes 76

      7. Former Supreme Court President
          Francisco Jose Guerrero 76
  B. FMLN Attacks and Attacks by Unknown
     Parties on the Right in San Salvador 78
  C. Targeted Assassinations in Rural Areas 82
  D. Indiscriminate FMLN Military Attacks 86
      1. February 21 Attack on First Brigade 86
      2. Karina Lisseth Castillo 86
      3. July 4 Attack on Cars Coming from the Beach . 86
      4. October 30 Attack on Armed Forces
         General Staff Headquarters 87
      5. November 1 Bombing of First Brigade 87
      6. November 11 Attack on National Guard 88
  E. Human Rights Violations during the
     Offensive: Update on Killing of Five
     Government Journalists 88
  F. Mines 89
      1. Killing of Nine Bus Passengers by Mine . . . 90
      2. Bus Fare Collector and Passenger Killed 90
      3. Four Peasants Killed By Explosion 90

V. THE RESURGENCE OF TORTURE 93
  A. Reina Noemi Alfaro Ramos (Atlacatl Battalion) . . 95
  B. Teenage Girl (Fourth Military Detachment,
     National Police) 96
  C. Carmen (Treasury Police) 97
  D. Pablo (Fourth Military Detachment) 98
  E. Gang Rape By Army Soldiers 99
  F. Juan (Fourth Military Detachment) 100
  G. Three cooperative members
     (Artillery Brigade) 101
  H. Torture of Seven Peasants Captured near
     Tres Ceibas (Atlacatl Battalion, First Brigade) . . 102
  I. Jose Tomas Mazariego (Treasury Police) 102
  J. Daniel Maradiaga Jovel (Fifth Brigade) 103
  K. Former Union Leader (Treasury Police) 104
  L. Jose Adolfo Lima (Probably Second Brigade) . . . 105
  M. Unionist (National Police) 107

    N. Jose Antonio Serrano (Treasury Police) 108
    O. Inmar Rolando Reyes Flores (Third Brigade) 109
    P. Andres de Jesus Sanchez Henriquez
        (National Guard) 109
    Q. Tatiana Mendoza Aguirre (National Police) 110
    R. Maria Juana Antonia Medina (National Police) . . .111
        S. Rogelio Diaz Martinez Barrera (National Police) 111
    T. Santos Faustino Fabian (Seventh
        Military Detachment) 112

VI. THE CLOSURE OF POLITICAL SPACE: VIOLENCE AGAINST CIVILIAN OPPOSITION . . .115

    A. Bombing of FENASTRAS Office,
        October 31, 1990: 10 Dead 122
    B. Bombing of COMADRES Office,
        October 31, 1989 125
    C. Other Attacks on Union Offices and September
        1989 Mass Arrest of FENASTRAS Marchers . . .125
    D. January 1990 Killing of Opposition Politician
        in Guatemala 127
    E. October Bombing of Homes of
        Opposition Leaders 128
    F. Shooting and Other Incidents at the National
        University, April 1989-March 1990 129
    G. July Bombing of UCA Printing Press 131
    H. April Mass Arrests at CRIPDES 131
    I. Recent Bombings and Other Threats to
        Religious Workers 132

VII. DUE PROCESS AND AMNESTY 135

VIII. U.S. ROLE 143

    A. Ten Years Later: U.S. Policy in El Salvador 143
    B. U.S. Officials' Interrogation of Pedro Antonio
        Andrade Martinez, Suspect in Zona Rosa Case . .160
    C. Use of U.S. Economic Assistance: Las Crucitas,
        La Estancia, Cacaopera, Morazan, January 1989 . .165
    D. Labeling Civilian Groups as FMLN Fronts 168

**APPENDIX A: LIST OF 18 PRIESTS
ASSASSINATED IN EL SALVADOR** 171
**APPENDIX B: PARTIAL CHRONOLOGY OF HUMAN
RIGHTS EVENTS IN EL SALVADOR, 1979-1990** . . 179
APPENDIX C: 1989 STATISTICS 199

ACKNOWLEDGMENTS

This report was written by James Goldston, the Orville Schell Fellow for Human Rights Watch, on the basis of research by him and Jemera Rone, Director of the San Salvador office of Americas Watch. It was edited by Anne Manuel, Director of Research, and Jemera Rone. Allyson Collins, Human Rights Watch Research Associate, provided substantial assistance in research, documentation, and the coordination of information. Americas Watch consultant Frank Howard and Americas Watch Associate Clifford Rohde provided additional research assistance.

Others who contributed research in El Salvador are Margaret Popkin of the Human Rights Institute of the Central American University Jose Simeon Canas (IDHUCA) and Kathy DeRiemer.

Americas Watch expresses its gratitude to Tutela Legal, the human rights office of the Catholic Archdiocese of San Salvador. As in the past, we rely extensively on information gathered by Tutela Legal.

We also express gratitude for all manner of assistance, particularly cooperation in publishing our reports in Spanish, that we received since 1985 from IDHUCA director Father Segundo Montes, S.J., who was assassinated on November 16, 1989.

We have dedicated this report to the memory and vision of Archbishop Oscar Romero, who was murdered ten years ago. Father Montes and his colleagues at the Central American University were continuing Archbishop Romero's work for peace and human rights when they were slain by the military last November. We are confident that other Salvadorans will carry on this important work where Archbishop Romero and the Jesuits left off.

PREFACE

THE LEGACY OF ARCHBISHOP ROMERO

This is the Eleventh Supplement to the Report on Human Rights in El Salvador. As we approach the tenth anniversary of the assassination of Archbishop Oscar Arnulfo Romero, this report is dedicated to his vision of peace, social justice and human rights, and to his courageous witness in pursuit of a society which reflects and affirms the dignity of its citizens.

It is a great sadness that, ten years after the murder of one who spoke with such passion of the need for peace, El Salvador is still locked firmly in the embrace of mutual enmity and fierce civil war. In the intervening decade, tens of thousands of innocent civilians have lost their lives, and hundreds of thousands more have been forced to leave their homes in search of a better life in new towns or strange countries far from home. Again and again the Salvadoran people have been promised democratic government, an end to political violence and swift reform of a corrupt judiciary and a bankrupt economy. And year after year, despite five national elections, the violence continues, the rule of law remains a myth, intolerable poverty afflicts the vast majority, and the thunder of military weaponry rains down upon the land.

The United States government has interjected itself into a conflict that seems to offer no resolution. During the height of Reagan era fervor, U.S. involvement in this civil war was deemed necessary to "draw the line" against "Communist advance" in "our" hemisphere. By the dawn of the 1990's, as the rationale for U.S. military involvement crumbles alongside the ruins of the Soviet empire, Americans are left to wonder what vital national interest beyond the sheer inertia of existing policy keeps us fixed on a course that has already drawn so much blood.

It is of no small moment that, ten years after the Archbishop was murdered while giving Mass, six Jesuit priests -- men who revered Romero's example for the guidance it offered in their own work on behalf of the Salvadoran poor -- were themselves brutally gunned down in cold blood. The death of the Jesuits was an incalculable loss for the Catholic Church, for the state of higher learning, and for the soul of the nation. It was also a blow to the forces urging a negotiated settlement to the conflict.

The Jesuits' assassination resonated with a painful truth about Salvadoran reality. Like Romero, the Jesuits were among the most prominent individuals in Salvadoran society; their death, like his, signalled that no one, no matter how powerful, no matter how well-loved, was safe from the assassin's bullet. Like Romero, the Jesuits were men of the cloth; the Salvadoran conflict is steeped in the blood of the clergy. Like Romero, the Jesuits were vigorous advocates of dialogue as the only way to end the war; their support for negotiations earned them the enmity of those bent on a violent solution. Finally, like Romero, the Jesuits were killed because they spoke truth to power; they refused to keep silent in the face of injustice, and for that were categorized by the undiscriminating right as the brains behind the armed insurgency, which neither they nor Romero ever were. For their unhalting courage in continuing to speak out for social justice and peace despite the invectives directed against them by the right, they gave their lives.

These two events -- the murder of Archbishop Romero in 1980 and the slaying of the Jesuits in 1989 -- stand as bookends to the decade offering harsh testimony about who really rules El Salvador and how little they have changed. Ten years later, priest-killing is still a preferred option for those who simply will not hear the cries for change and justice in a society that has had too little of either.

It was Romero's prophecy that his vision of human justice would not die with him, but would live on in the Salvadoran people. And that in fact has occurred. Despite the slaughter of thousands and the concerted attempt to exterminate opposition to government policy in the early 1980's, hundreds of unionists, cooperativists, human rights monitors, student activists, lawyers, doctors, teachers, artists and journalists have in the past decade sustained a movement capable of giving voice to popular aspirations. On the walls of offices, on signs and banners, and in the hearts of literally millions of his compatriots, the image of Archbishop Romero lives on.

Romero's example retains such potency today precisely because the conditions and injustices he decried persist. In his final sermon, delivered the day before his assassination, Romero spoke directly to those responsible for so much of the violence. The clarity of his words, and the poignancy of his plea, still ring true:

> I would like to make a special appeal to the men of the army, and specifically to the ranks of the National Guard, the police and the military. Brothers, you came from our own people. You are killing your own brother peasants when any human order to kill must be subordinate to the law of God which says, "Thou shalt not kill." No soldier is obliged to obey an order contrary to the law of God. No one has to obey an immoral law. It is high time you recovered your consciences and obeyed your consciences rather than a sinful order. The church, the defender of the rights of God, of the law of God, of human dignity, of the person, cannot remain silent before such an abomination. We want the government to face the fact that reforms are valueless if they are to be carried out at the cost of so much blood. In the name of God, in the name of this suffering people whose cries rise to heaven more loudly each day, I implore you, I beg you, I order you in the name of God: stop the repression.

Almost ten years later, six Jesuits who took up his work have suffered his fate, leaving the world to wonder at how little things have actually changed in El Salvador.

I. INTRODUCTION: A YEAR OF RECKONING

Nineteen eighty-nine was a watershed year in El Salvador, as in much of the world. After ten years of often brutal, seemingly unending civil war, and several failed attempts to negotiate a peace settlement, guerrillas of the Farabundo Marti National Liberation Front (FMLN) in November 1989 launched their most powerful and sustained military offensive to date. Two weeks of fierce ground fighting and frequent air attacks in densely populated neighborhoods brought physical misery to thousands and left whole sections of San Salvador in chaos. The offensive, and the Armed Forces' response -- including the assassination of six Jesuit priests -- dramatically transformed the Salvadoran political landscape and thrust the conflict back onto the world stage after several years on the sidelines.

The FMLN military drive visited upon the capital and other principal cities a war which had for some time been largely confined to rural hamlets lying in the shadows of Salvador's volcanoes. In November, at first the working class neighborhoods to the north and east of San Salvador, and then the wealthy enclaves to the west, became the targets of pitched street battles. A third of the nation which had previously been spared most of the war's horrors experienced first hand their full force. The country's major hospitals overflowed with incoming wounded, as domestic and international relief agencies worked courageously to recover the wounded from areas of intense conflict. As FMLN guerrillas lodged themselves in heavily populated residential areas, and Army soldiers forced them out with tank, artillery and air fire, thousands of besieged residents abandoned their homes for the crowded shelter of church-sponsored refugee centers. Many returned to find their tin or cardboard shacks damaged or destroyed and their meager possessions gone.

The crisis exacerbated tensions within the military and thrust extremist elements to the fore. The rhetoric of high officials reflected the charged intensity of the moment, and spurred some units to engage in lawless actions. Targeted killings by both the Armed Forces and the FMLN increased, and the Army went on a month-long rampage of searches and detentions directed against churches, humanitarian agencies, opposition political parties, labor unions, community groups, and others. Dozens of labor and opposition leaders and activists left the country or went into hiding, as the political space opened during the administration of the late Jose Napoleon Duarte slammed shut. Human rights conditions in the wake of the offensive deteriorated to their worst levels since the early 1980's.

The human loss may never be known with precision. Throughout November and into December, hundreds of bodies -- many of them burned, others with gunshot wounds in the head -- appeared on the sides of roads and cemeteries, some near battle sites, some not. The FMLN acknowledged 401 dead and the Armed Forces admitted to about 600. The U.S. State Department said that, as of January 2, 1990, the offensive had produced 1,706 Armed Forces wounded and 1,458 FMLN wounded. Tutela Legal estimated that more than 1,000 were killed in military operations in November and December 1989, among them both civilians and guerrillas. Since many bodies were burned before they could be identified, and fighting and checkpoints made access impossible for judicial authorities as well as human rights organizations, an accurate count of civilian victims in cross fire or targeted executions during this period will never be possible.*

This report examines human rights in El Salvador over the past year, focusing on the period since June 1, 1989, when President Cristiani came to power. The November offensive -- and the rapid deterioration in human rights conditions which followed -- looms large in any assessment of human rights in El Salvador. Abuses committed during the offensive were covered at some

---

* The U.S. Embassy in San Salvador estimated between 250 and 500 civilian dead, and between 1,500 and 3,000 civilian wounded, although conceding during the fighting that the statistics on civilian casualties were very soft.

length in two Americas Watch reports issued last year.* In this report we have updated some of the information concerning these events. We have not, however, duplicated information which may be found in our other reports.

The inauguration of President Alfredo Cristiani in June and the appointment of a new Supreme Court the following month gave ARENA, a party which has long been linked with paramilitary death squad activity, control of all three branches of government for the first time.** In the first few months of the new administration, President Cristiani, apparently with the support of the military, moved to allay fears that his government would usher in a new wave of repression and political violence. Although the number of political arrests maintained a slow if steady increase through this period, and reports of gross mistreatment of detainees by government forces soared, targeted government and death squad killings decreased slightly. (See Appendix C.) Moreover, the new government expressed a willingness to initiate a new stage of dialogue with the FMLN.

For the first half of the year FMLN killings of civilians increased to the point that, when deaths from mines were included, FMLN killings outstripped assassinations by uniformed government forces for the first time in the course of the war. The number of civilians killed by FMLN mines declined substantially in the second half of the year.*** Throughout the year, however, FMLN forces engaged in targeted assassinations of prominent civilian government officers and right-wing figures. These killings constituted violations of the rules of war. Moreover, the FMLN's failure to acknowledge responsibility for several of these crimes heightened concern that the FMLN General Command did not exert full control over all armed units operating within its military structure.

---

*   See Americas Watch, Carnage Again: Preliminary Report on Violations of the Laws of War by Both Sides in the November 1989 Offensive in El Salvador, November 24, 1989; and Americas Watch, Update on El Salvador: The Human Rights Crisis Continues in the Wake of the FMLN Offensive, December 16, 1989.

** President Cristiani received 53.82% of the votes cast on March 19, 1989. Other votes were distributed as follows: Christian Democratic Party (36.03%); National Conciliation Party (4.07%); Democratic Convergence (3.88%); Authentic Christian Movement (0.9%); and the Party of Renovating Action (0.34%). Approximately fifty percent of registered voters voted. Report of the Inter-American Commission on Human Rights (1989), at 164.

*** See Appendix C.

In the two months preceding the offensive, as the government and the FMLN met in Mexico City and San Jose, Costa Rica, in two negotiation sessions, the political climate became polarized and political violence intensified. Among the attacks in this period were the September 18 arrest and mistreatment of members of the National Federation of Salvadoran Workers (FENASTRAS), the October 10 shooting of the wife and son of a conservative newspaper editor, the October 17 murder of the daughter of an army colonel, the bombing two days later of opposition leaders' homes, and the deadly bombing of the FENASTRAS headquarters on October 31, killing 10 and wounding more than 30.

On November 2, the FMLN announced it was withdrawing from the dialogue process, and would not return until the security of popular organizations was assured. It named its November offensive in honor of a prominent union leader killed in the FENASTRAS bombing, Febe Elizabeth Velasquez. Most interpreted the FMLN's demonstration of its impressive and theretofore unsuspected capacity to bring the capital to a standstill, however, as an effort as to shake the Salvadoran government and its U.S. backers out of the illusion that the FMLN was weakening and could be forced to surrender at the bargaining table.

The offensive ultimately reaffirmed the fact of military stalemate that has been obvious for years, where neither army is able to vanquish the other. More importantly, on the political front, FMLN expectations that the offensive would spark a popular insurrection were disappointed. Most Salvadorans are weary of war, and simply want it to end.

Because of the murder of the six Jesuit priests, however, U.S. aid to the Salvadoran military was threatened for the first time in several years, leading President Cristiani to seek to assuage fears that political space had irreversibly closed and that the military, not civilians, were firmly in control. In January, the President announced that nine Army soldiers, including a colonel, were responsible for the murders of the Jesuits, and judicial proceedings commenced against the eight in custody. In early February, the indictments of two military men for the massacre of ten peasants in San Sebastian, San Vicente in September 1988 were announced.

Cristiani promised U.S. legislators and international organizations that the climate for international church and humanitarian workers would improve dramatically. By early February, several popular organizations had begun to operate above ground again. In early 1990, the head of the General Staff of the Army, Colonel Rene Emilio Ponce, met with representatives of the nongovernmental Human Rights Commission and reportedly promised to respond to all cases of human rights violations they sent him, and to meet again with them.

Both the government and the FMLN agreed to a resumption of talks under the auspices of the United Nations, although the details remain to be ironed out.

Despite these signs of marginal improvement, a pall of fear and despair hangs over El Salvador on the tenth anniversary of Archbishop Romero's assassination. By early March the Legislative Assembly had allowed some provisions of the state of siege to lapse, but maintained in force the suspension of free association; thus, peaceful marches and demonstrations are still outlawed. Although few are convinced that the full truth about the Jesuit massacre has yet been told, coup rumors within the Armed Forces upon the announcement of soldiers' arrests suggest some in the military are not at all disposed to let the investigation probe further. The disappearance of six cooperativists in December and the January killing in Guatemala of opposition leader Hector Oqueli Colindres put the popular movement on notice that dissidents, labor organizers and other non-governmental actors continue to perform their work at great risk to their lives and welfare. The February bombing which killed five and wounded 16 in Chalatenango confirmed that the Armed Forces still find it difficult to distinguish civilian from military targets. Finally the electoral defeat in late February of the FMLN's main regional ally, the Sandinista Popular Liberation Front in Nicaragua, has given rise once again to Salvadoran army predictions of the FMLN's rapid demise,* perhaps complicating renewed efforts at negotiations.

Summary of Concerns

The following pages set forth in detail a wide range of violations which reflect a worsening in the overall human rights situation in El Salvador during the past year. In summary, our concerns are as follows:

---

*   "Military commanders in El Salvador and United States diplomats there said they thought the Sandinista defeat would cripple the guerrillas of the Farabundo Marti National Liberation Front, one of Latin America's best guerrilla armies. 'They can't survive without the Sandinistas,' said Colonel Rene Emilio Ponce, chief of the armed forces high command." Lindsey Gruson, "Sandinistas' Loss to Be Felt By Other Leftist Movements," The New York Times, February 27, 1990.

* **Despite progress so far in the prosecution of the Jesuit case, there exists a real danger that the true authors of the crime may not have been identified, and that Colonel Guillermo Alfredo Benavides Moreno, the highest ranking officer yet implicated, will not be convicted or punished.** Reports of discontent and resistance within the military have surfaced ever since President Cristiani's announcement that nine soldiers were responsible for the murders. Recent revelations that the armed forces high command met twice within hours of the murders indicate that the most senior Salvadoran military officers knew far more, far earlier than has been admitted to date.

* **To date President Cristiani has failed to mention, let alone investigate, several atrocities apart from the Jesuit case committed by the armed forces in recent months.** Among these have been the November summary execution of seven young men in Cuscatancingo, San Salvador; the November murders, by Second Brigade soldiers, of as many as nine civilians and captured or wounded guerrillas just outside of Santa Ana; the November killing by soldiers of the Instruction Center of the Armed Forces (CITFA) of women's activist Norma Guirola de Herrera; and the disappearance of six cooperativists outside of Ahuachapan in December.

* **The FMLN in 1989 engaged in a series of assassinations of prominent civilian government officials and conservative figures, including the Attorney General in April and the former President of the Supreme Court in November. These are violations of the rules of war because civilians are not proper military targets.** The FMLN's failure to acknowledge responsibility in some of these attacks in addition has raised concerns about internal divisions and lack of high command control over some units.

* **The FMLN used indiscriminate catapult bombs in urban areas, which resulted in numerous civilian casualties.** The failure to exercize adequate care in the placement of contact-detonated land mines also caused the deaths of many civilians; in May nine riding a bus were killed by one FMLN land mine.

* **A series of searches, arrests, threats and attacks by government forces in the wake of the November offensive has effectively eliminated what political space previously existed.** Although the offices of some popular organizations have reopened in early 1990, opposition political parties, labor unions and cooperatives, and churches have sharply curtailed their activities.

Numerous opposition politicians have left the country or maintained a low profile.

* In the months preceding President Cristiani's inauguration on June 1, 1989, and increasingly thereafter, the government of El Salvador has engaged in more use of torture in the course of interrogating detainees. Americas Watch has in recent months noted a substantial increase in the number of reports of torture by all units of the Salvadoran army and security forces, including: asphyxiation, simulated drowning, drugging, application of electric shocks, and sexual violence.

* In the past year and one-half death squads escalated the public nature of their threats and attacks, and several new paramilitary organizations emerged. Since November 1988 death squads have murdered two leaders of the SICAFE coffee workers union in Santa Ana, and wounded two others. There have been reports of increased cooperation between Salvadoran death squads and their Guatemalan counterparts.

* The murders of the Jesuits and other crimes committed in the wake of the FMLN offensive have demonstrated the failure of U.S. human rights policy in El Salvador. Notwithstanding this, U.S. officials continue to assert that more, not less, military aid, will bring about improvements in the human rights performance of the Salvadoran military. Reacting to the initial arrests of eight army soldiers for the slayings of the priests, the U.S. government has maintained an apologetic stance: outrage that the military killed the priests has been outweighed by U.S. praise for President Cristiani's courage in acknowledging that fact and identifying the murderers. The actions of U.S. officials in the aftermath of the killings raise grave concern about their commitment to a serious investigation.

II. VIOLATIONS BY GOVERNMENT FORCES

In the past year violations by government forces increased, due largely to the extraordinary display of military power during the November offensive, but statistics-keeping was impossible under those conditions. The numbers of civilians killed in army operations or those who disappeared after last being seen in the custody of uniformed forces are believed to have increased. The most politically significant targeted killing of the past several years was the November 16, 1989 assassination by army soldiers of six Jesuit priests and two women.

Our two reports issued during the offensive* identified numerous violations of international humanitarian law on the part of government forces. These included, in addition to summary executions, instances of indiscriminate fire upon civilian targets; the failure to warn of impending attack or, in other areas, the issuance of contradictory warnings and 24-hour curfew orders; the removal of wounded guerrillas from the hospital and the arrest of health workers; attacks on Red Cross vehicles; and the misuse of the Red Cross emblem.

A. Targeted Killings

1. The Assassination of the Jesuits

On November 16, 1989, Salvadoran soldiers of the U.S.-trained Atlacatl Battalion entered the campus of the Central American University and murdered six Jesuits priests, their housekeeper and her daughter.

---

* See Carnage Again, Update on El Salvador.

In <u>Carnage Again</u> and <u>Update on El Salvador</u>, we presented the details surrounding this event as far as they were known as of December 16, 1989. Since the publication of those reports, President Cristiani has identified nine Salvadoran Army soldiers who allegedly were responsible for the murders, and eight of them, including one colonel, were restricted in their liberty by the Army (although not jailed) and consigned in January 1990 to the order of the Fourth Criminal Court of San Salvador, Judge Ricardo Zamora. (One soldier is a fugitive from justice.)

The colonel implicated, Colonel Guillermo Alfredo Benavides Moreno, 44, is a member of the powerful *tandona*, the military class of 1966 which holds the most important command posts within the Armed Forces. He is the highest ranking officer ever to be charged with a human rights abuse in El Salvador, and his arrest has sparked discontent within the *tandona*.

All eight defendants present pleaded not guilty and the court ruled on January 18, on the basis of the extrajudicial statements of the accused and other evidence gathered by the U.S.-created, trained and funded Special Investigative Unit, that there was sufficient basis to warrant judicial investigation and continued detention of the defendants on the grounds of murder in violation of Article 154 of the Salvadoran Criminal Code.

The case is now in the judicial investigatory period, lasting 120 days, during which the judge seeks evidence as well as receiving it from the parties. When this period is over, on May 22, 1990, the court must rule whether or not there is enough evidence to try any or all of the defendants.*

Notwithstanding this progress, which came in response to international outcry, recent developments have added to our suspicions that those ultimately responsible for ordering the killings may never be known, let alone punished. Whether the coverup will be punished is yet another matter.

---

* The defense has asserted that Judge Zamora lacks jurisdiction to hear the case, because the crime occurred in Antiguo Cuscatlan, which lies just outside of San Salvador, in Santa Tecla. This issue will eventually be resolved by the Supreme Court.

a. The Integrity of the Investigation

As we noted in December, actions taken by U.S. and Salvadoran investigators with respect to the lone eyewitness to come forward -- Lucia Barrera de Cerna, a cleaning lady at the university -- raised concerns about the integrity of the investigation.* Prominent among them were the reasons why Ms. Cerna's U.S. and Salvadoran interrogators badgered and threatened her in Miami until she recanted her November testimony that she had seen uniformed soldiers firing in the direction of the Jesuit residence, testimony that later, in January, was ratified by the very soldiers she saw; the alacrity and enthusiasm with which President Cristiani and U.S. Embassy officials, before the case was broken, declared worthless Cerna's initial eyewitness statement; and the active deception on the part of officials of both governments who vigorously asserted that Cerna had failed three lie detector tests, but conspicuously neglected to mention that she only failed the tests when, under pressure from U.S. and Salvadoran investigators, she changed her story and stated that she had seen nothing that night.

It is still unclear under what authority, and with whose consent, U.S. officials began to question Ms. Cerna almost immediately upon her arrival in the United States. Bernard Kouchner, the French state secretary of humanitarian action, said he had been assured by Ambassador William Walker that Ms. Cerna would be protected in the United States. Walker "never spoke of interrogation, or of lie detector tests."**

A lengthy analysis of the events surrounding Ms. Cerna's treatment by U.S. officials, prepared by the Lawyers Committee for Human Rights, indicates that U.S. officials held Ms. Cerna and her family for seven days after Jesuit officials had offered to assume responsibility for them:

> "As soon as they learned of the family's arrival in Miami [on November 23], U.S. Jesuit officials informed the State Department that they were prepared to take responsibility for the Cerna family as soon as they were released to their

---

* Ms. Cerna's interrogators were Lieutenant Colonel Manuel Antonio Rivas Mejia, head of the Salvadoran Special Investigative Unit which is funded by the U.S. pursuant to the Administration of Justice Act, and two F.B.I. agents.

** Sharon Waxman, "French official to question U.S. on Salvadoran witness," The Miami Herald, December 20, 1989.

care. When Jesuit officials inquired when the family would be released to them, State Department officials informed them that the F.B.I. needed a period of time to perform a risk assessment so that the Jesuits would know how much protection Lucia and her family required.

The family remained under the exclusive charge and control of the State Department from Thursday, November 23, to Thursday, November 30.... During the four days of their interrogation, Lucia and Jorge were not given any opportunity to consult with or obtain counsel from any priest, lawyer or other person they knew. During the entire eight-day period from November 23 to November 30, the only visitors who were allowed to see them were Spanish-speaking Jesuits living in the Miami area, with whom the family visited briefly on three occasions, the last time on November 26.

Late on the afternoon of Thursday, November 30, after Lucia had broken and changed her story, State Department officials informed the Jesuits that they could take the family into their care. When Jesuit officials asked the State Department about the results of the F.B.I.'s lengthy risk assessment, they were told that the F.B.I. was in fact not in a position to perform a risk assessment for a person in Lucia's category as a witness.... On Sunday, December 3, after the Jesuits had made arrangements for transporting the family to a secure and comfortable location in another state, the State Department formally turned the Cerna family over to the Jesuits."*

Ms. Cerna's chief interrogator and persecutor was Lieutenant Colonel Rivas, head of the Special Investigative Unit charged with the investigation. It is difficult to have confidence in the motivation of the key investigator, a military officer, when he has been shown to have coerced the only witness to step forward into retracting truthful eyewitness testimony which implicated the army.

From the moment the murders were committed, Salvadoran and U.S. officials asserted, despite persuasive circumstantial evidence to the contrary,

---

* Lawyers Committee for Human Rights, The Jesuit Murders: A Report on the Testimony of a Witness, December 15, 1989, at 33-34.

that they might have been the work of the FMLN. Several days after the murders, Colonel Francisco Elena Fuentes publicly accused the guerrillas of having committed the murders in an effort to tarnish the government's image. As late as January 2, Ambassador William Walker told congressional investigators there was no evidence to implicate the military and hypothesized that leftist rebels might have committed the act while dressed in soldiers' garb.*

The sincerity of U.S. officials' commitment to a serious investigation was further placed in question by the revelation that a U.S. major in El Salvador had been apprised of the involvement of the army, and Colonel Benavides by name, in December, but failed to tell his superiors for at least ten days.** The source of the U.S. major's information was a Salvadoran military officer, Colonel Carlos Armando Aviles Buitrago.

Inexplicably, when U.S. officials finally received this startling information from the U.S. major, they went immediately to Armed Forces Chief of Staff Colonel Rene Emilio Ponce and named Aviles as their source without

---

*   Ambassador Walker made this assertion long after a Salvadoran colonel had told a U.S. major that the Army had committed the murders. When queried as to how he could still have been asking that the FMLN might have committed the murders, the Ambassador said that, as of January 2, "there was no hard evidence to confirm the conclusion that a lot of people had jumped to: that the military was responsible." According to Walker, Salvadoran investigators made a breakthrough when they acquired "ballistics evidence" with respect to bullets and weapons a few days later. Robert Pear, "Salvador Evidence Escaped U.S. Envoy," The New York Times, January 16, 1990. However, it is not clear what ballistics evidence became available after January 2 that had not been known previously. On December 15, the Salvadoran government's Special Investigative Unit reported having conducted over 300 ballistics tests on the weapons of soldiers who were near the Central American University on November 16. Moreover, in responding to charges that they improperly revealed the name of the Salvadoran colonel who provided information implicating the military in late December, U.S. officials contended that the colonel's evidence was not key, as ballistic evidence had been uncovered implicating the army earlier. Lindsey Gruson, "Washington Criticized for Identifying Army Informant in Salvador Killings," The New York Times, January 19, 1990.

**   Lindsey Gruson, "Washington Criticized for Identifying Army Informant In Salvador Killings," The New York Times, January 19, 1990; Douglas Farah, "Army Officer Held in El Salvador," The Washington Post, January 14, 1990. In response to suggestions that the U.S. major might have known of plans to kill the Jesuits prior to November 16, the U.S. Defense Department issued a statement in mid-January that it had "no evidence" of any such advance knowledge on the part of the major. Lindsey Gruson, "Salvadoran President Announces Arrests of 8 in Killing of 6 Jesuits," The New York Times, January 14, 1990.

previously consulting with him. They now concede this was a mistake.* Aviles, who denied informing the U.S., was promptly detained by his superiors, subjected to lie detector tests, and as of this writing is still believed to be confined to the grounds of the General Staff, allegedly because he failed the polygraph. As one foreign diplomat summed it up, "The U.S. Embassy has burned the only officer who was willing to admit that the army killed the Jesuits."**

Colonel Aviles, not a *tandona* member, had a role in the October 1979 coup by reformist junior officers who overthrew a corruptly elected government and tried to initiate certain land and commercial reforms proposed by the U.S., in coalition with a range of civilian politicians. He was head of the Army press office, COPREFA, in 1985 and 1986. Ironically, he had been offered the position of head of the Special Investigative Unit when it was first being formed in 1985-86, but instead went to complete his military studies in Paraguay.

The disclosure that Colonel Aviles, who was until recently commander of psychological operations (C5) for the Salvadoran military, knew of Benavides' and the Army's involvement has led to speculation that more senior officers might also have been aware, but sought to keep that information secret. "Aviles wasn't part of the inner loop," said one official close to the investigation. "If he knew, others knew."*** There is speculation that some may have heard the confession directly from Benavides. In the investigative file forwarded to the court, however, there is no record of any admission by Benavides.

The punitive manner in which Salvadoran and U.S. officials have treated both Ms. Cerna and Colonel Aviles, two most significant early sources of information, has surely discouraged other witnesses from coming forward. Moreover, the treatment of Cerna and Aviles contrasts sharply with that afforded other witnesses and the defendants in the case.

---

*   Lindsey Gruson, "Washington Criticized . . . ," The New York Times.

** Lindsey Gruson, "Salvadoran President Announces Arrests . . . ," The New York Times.

*** Lindsey Gruson, "Washington Criticized. . . ," The New York Times.

Despite the willingness to give Cerna and Aviles lie detector tests, for example, there has been a conspicuous failure to polygraph or even question others, such as Benavides' commander Colonel Juan Orlando Zepeda, Vice Minister of Defense and fellow *tandona* member. If the government is serious about pursuing the case, it question officers close to Benavides.

The timing of events suggests that it may not have been the ordinary progress of the investigation but the leak from Colonel Aviles that moved the case forward. Shortly after his information became available, President Cristiani gave a January 7, 1990 address to the nation on the eve of visits by several congressional delegations concerned about the case, announcing, "It has been determined that there was involvement of some elements of the armed forces."* Cristiani promised that a special honor commission, composed of military officers and civilian lawyers, would work with the government's Special Investigative Unit to "find those responsible for the crime and bring justice in this reprehensible crime," and that punishment would be meted out "down to the last person implicated."**

b. The Evidence in the Record

Seven defendants gave extrajudicial statements to the National Police on January 13 and 14. Their statements, and that of Armed Forces Chief of Staff Colonel Rene Emilio Ponce, which are quoted in part in the court decision of January 18 ordering further investigation of the accused, offer the following picture of the murders of the Jesuits and the two women.

Following the start of the November 11 FMLN offensive, Colonel Ponce ordered the reinforcement of security deployment in the area around the headquarters of the Armed Force High Command, extending to and in-

---

* Associated Press, "Inquiry Shows Salvador Military Killed Six Jesuits, President Says," The New York Times, January 8, 1990.

** "Inquiry Shows...," The New York Times; Douglas Farah, "Soldiers Killed Jesuits, El Salvador Says," The Washington Post, January 8, 1990.

cluding the campus of the Central American University. Colonel Ponce ordered the formation of a Security Commando, under the direction of Colonel Benavides, to coordinate this security reinforcement. Pursuant to this order, 135 soldiers of the Commando Unit of the Atlacatl Battalion, led by Lieutenant Espinoza, were placed in reserve under the command of Colonel Benavides.*

On November 15, at about 10:15 p.m., while the Commando Unit of the Atlacatl Battalion was occupying positions in different sectors near the Battalion headquarters in *canton* Sitio El Nino, La Libertad, Lieutenant Espinoza received an order to regroup with his unit at the Military School. Lieutenant Espinoza returned to the school with four of the unit's patrols;** two other units, which had earlier been ordered to an area near the Central American University where guerrillas had been spotted,*** could not be reached by radio. About 11:15 p.m., Colonel Benavides met with Lieutenant Espinoza, Second Lieutenant Guevara Cerritos, and Lieutenant Mendoza.

Colonel Benavides told the three, according to eyewitness Espinoza: "This is a situation where it's them or us; we are going to begin with the leaders; inside the sector of ours we have the university and there is Ellacuria." Benavides pointed to Espinoza and said, "You did the search and your people know that place; use the same force as the day of the search and he must be eliminated and I don't want witnesses."****Lieutenant Mendoza was placed

---

*   Extra-judicial Testimony of Gonzalo Guevara Cerritos, reported in Order of Fourth Criminal Court, San Salvador, January 18, 1990, Congressional Research Service translation. All subsequent references to testimony in the court order are based on this translation.

** The patrols which went to the Military School were the second, headed by Sergeant Avalos Vargas; the third, headed by Sergeant Zarpate Castillo; the fourth, headed by Sergeant Molina Aguilar; and the sixth, headed by Sergeant Gonzalez Rodriguez. Extra-judicial testimony of Antonio Ramiro Avalos Vargas, reported in Order of Fourth Criminal Court, San Salvador, January 18, 1990.

*** Extra-Judicial Testimony of Angel Perez Vasquez, reported in Order of Fourth Criminal Court, San Salvador, January 18, 1990.

**** Extra-judicial Testimony of Jose Ricardo Espinoza Guerra, reported in Order of Fourth Criminal Court, San Salvador, January 18, 1990.

in charge of the operation.

Second Lieutenant Guevara testified that Benavides told the officers: "Well, gentlemen, we're staking it all, it's either us or them, since they have been the intellectuals that have led the guerrillas for a long time."*

According to Guevara, Benavides noted that "already Espinoza's soldiers know where the Jesuit fathers sleep and I don't want witnesses."

Shortly thereafter, Mendoza asked the assembled troops if anyone knew how to use an AK-47. When it was said that Private Grimaldi did, Mendoza said to Grimaldi, "Vitri, you're the key man."** Mendoza gave Grimaldi an AK-47 rifle, which Grimaldi cleaned for about 10 minutes before the start of the operation.

At about 12:10 a.m., approximately three dozen*** soldiers traveled in two Ford pickup trucks to the west side of the university, where they met up with the two Atlacatl Battalion patrols already in the area. There Lieutenant Espinoza told the soldiers that they were to "carry out a delicate mission. . . . [T]he order was to locate some priests who were in the UCA University, because they were the leaders of the delinquent terrorists."**** Espinoza explained that at the moment of withdrawal from the campus, when the operation was complete, there would be a flare and the simulation of a confrontation.

---

* Guevara Testimony. Lieutenant Mendoza, who contended that he had no knowledge, prior to or during the operation, that the objective was to kill the Jesuits, reported that Benavides simply said, "Look, Mendoza. Are you going to accompany Espinoza to carry out a mission? He already knows what it is." Extra-judicial testimony of Yusshi Rene Mendoza Vallecillos, reported in Order of Fourth Criminal Court, San Salvador, January 18, 1990.

** Espinoza contends that Mendoza made this statement before the soldiers left the Military School; Amaya reports the statement was made near the university.

*** Espinoza reported there were 36 soldiers. Others are less clear on the exact number.

**** Avalos Testimony. Avalos testified that Lieutenant Espinoza gave these orders while still at the Military School. However, several other soldiers testified that those orders were issued near the University. Corporal Perez testified that Lieutenant Espinoza told the soldiers that he had received an order to eliminate the "intellectual leaders of the guerrillas and that they were inside the UCA."

At about 1:00 a.m., the soldiers entered the south gate of the university and proceeded past the chapel to the Jesuit residence and the Monsignor Romero pastoral center. Upon reaching the residence, several soldiers beat on the doors and windows. After about ten minutes, a blond man in pajamas opened the door and "told them not to continue beating the doors and windows because they were aware of what would happen to them."* Sergeant Avalos led the man to the lawn in front of the residence. As four other priests came to the entrance, they too were brought out on to the lawn, and all five were made to lie down on the grass. Sergeant Solorzano Esquivel then entered the residence with four soldiers to look for other persons inside.

Shortly thereafter, Lieutenant Espinoza, who was standing, along with Lieutenant Mendoza, about ten meters away from the five prone priests, called Sergeant Avalos over and said, "At what time are you going to proceed." Avalos returned to the lawn, where Private Grimaldi was standing over the five priests. Avalos approached Grimaldi and said to him in a low voice, "Let's proceed." Immediately Grimaldi fired at three of the priests with the AK-47. Sergeant Avalos proceeded to fire at the head and body of the other two priests.**

As these events were taking place on the lawn, soldiers who had entered the pastoral center on the bottom level of the complex were burning documents and materials in the university offices. Corporal Perez heard the shots above as he was on the first floor of the pastoral center. He went upstairs to the second floor and entered the residential hallway. On the lawn outside, he saw the five dead priests, and then saw the sixth priest, a tall man with white clothing, go outside and view the bodies. According to one of the soldiers, the sixth priest appeared at the door and begged, "Don't kill me because I don't belong to any organization."*** The priest went back inside the residence and entered a room, where he was apparently shot and fell to the ground. As Perez

---

*   Avalos Testimony.

**   Avalos and Amaya Testimonies.

***   Extra-judicial Testimony of Oscar Mariano Amaya Grimaldi, reported in Order of Fourth Criminal Court, San Salvador, January 18, 1990.

went inside the room, the priest grabbed at his feet, and Perez shot him four times.

Sergeant Zarpate, who had been stationed outside the door of the housekeeper and her daughter while the operation proceeded, fired at them several times shortly after the priests were killed. Minutes later, as the soldiers began their withdrawal from the facility, Sergeant Avalos and Private Sierra heard moaning sounds as they passed by the room where the housekeeper and her daughter had been shot. Avalos "lit a match, observing that inside of [the room] there were two women spread out on the floor . . . who were embracing, moaning, so that he ordered the soldier Sierra Ascencio to finish them off, so that the soldier with his M-16 fired a round . . . of 10 cartridges toward the body of those women until they no longer moaned."*

As the troops left the area, several soldiers shot at the windows of vehicles in a nearby parking area and fired a LOW anti-tank weapon. A fire was burning in the first floor of the pastoral residence. A 40 mm. grenade launcher fired a flare as a signal to all the troops that the operation was over.

c. The Judicial Value of the Current Evidence Against Colonel Benavides

Colonel Benavides cannot be tried or convicted unless evidence in addition to that outlined above is produced, according to Salvadoran legal experts. Unlike the other defendants, he gave no incriminatory statements, either judicially or extrajudicially. There is no record of any admission he may have made to fellow officers.

The major stumbling block to keeping Benavides in the case on the basis of the current record is the provision in Salvadoran law that makes the testimony of co-defendants inadmissible in a criminal prosecution. Therefore, the eyewitness statements of the junior officers, Lieutenant Espinoza and Second Lieutenant Guevara, that he ordered the killings cannot be used to convict him, because they are also defendants in the case.**

---

*   Avalos Testimony.

**   Plea bargaining or dropping one defendant from the case in exchange for his testimony against another is not an alternative in the Salvadoran system.

In a 1986 partial reform to this antiquated law and in order to facilitate the just-commenced prosecution of kidnappers of the rich, the Christian Democrat-dominated Assembly made admissible the testimony of co-defendants in kidnapping and extortion cases. The Church and others urged at the time that the reform be extended to cover cases of murder, but the Assembly refused.

It therefore remains extremely difficult to prosecute an officer who orders a killing, as long as the officer makes sure that the witnesses to his order get blood on their hands as well, or at least their fingerprints on the weapons.

An additional problem with the evidence against Benavides is that the lieutenants did not ratify in court those portions of their extrajudicial statements that implicated him, although the extrajudicial statements are still valid if they are ratified by the police agents who witnessed and signed them.

d. Others Who May Have Ordered the Killings or Conspired in Them

Congressman Joe Moakley, the leader of a U.S. congressional committee created by the Speaker of the House of Representatives to monitor the Jesuit investigation, stated at the close of a February 1990 trip to El Salvador the congressional committee's belief:

> that the investigation is not over and that important leads and allegations remain to be fully investigated -- namely reports which suggest that the intellectual authors of the murders may not have been identified and suggestions that there may have been a cover-up of this crime by some in the armed forces. We note in this connection that Colonel Ponce told us that not one person in the military -- not one -- came forward to report to him the complicity of the Army in the murders.

There may well have been a conspiracy to kill the Jesuits that reached beyond Benavides and the lieutenants. It is known that top Salvadoran army commanders met twice within hours of the murders, once the night before and once the night after, "indicating several officers may have been in a position to know who was involved in the killings long before that information became public January 6."*

---

* Ana Arana, "Salvadoran officers met before, after Jesuits slain," The Miami Herald, February 4, 1990.

According to news reports, 30 high-ranking officers, including Chief of Staff and *tandona* head Colonel Ponce, met three hours before the killings on the night of November 15.

At that meeting the officers, panicked by the strength of the FMLN offensive in the capital, decided on a plan which included the elimination of guerrilla leaders and the destruction of rebel command posts, and a stepped-up use of aerial bombardment on guerrilla positions. Colonel Benavides left that meeting about 10:30 p.m. Just after that, Lieutenant Espinoza and the other Atlacatl soldiers were, according to the extrajudicial testimony of lieutenants, summoned to the Military School, where Benavides ordered them to execute the Jesuits.

There is reason to doubt that Benavides ordered the killings completely on his own, without the complicity of higher authorities. There is nothing in the colonel's past which indicates any pre-existing disposition to murder the Jesuits. He has not been associated with the most extreme elements in the Armed Forces who could have had an interest in undertaking this act, which would threaten the stability of the existing Armed Forces hierarchy. Nor is it likely that Benavides would have taken advantage of the crisis atmosphere prevailing during the first week of the offensive in order to murder the priests simply because it was then possible.

If the murder was neither the product of political calculations among discontented hard-liners, nor the consequence of a uniquely anarchic situation, Benavides is still an unlikely candidate to have made such an important decision alone. Benavides is not known to have commanded the authority, within the military inner circle, to issue an order of such magnitude without at least tacit prior*re senior military officers.

Other factors suggest more extensive involvement and planning than has been acknowledged. On Monday, November 13, two evenings before the murders took place, soldiers of the Atlacatl Battalion meticulously searched the Jesuits' residence, paying more attention to the location of particular rooms and persons than to potentially objectionable writings or other papers. This prior search by soldiers from the same Atlacatl unit that carried out the executions* indicates that the soldiers were casing the Jesuit residence in preparation for the murders.

---

* Ana Arana, "Cristiani accuses colonel of ordering priests killed," <u>The Miami Herald</u>, January 17, 1990.

The greater the prior planning, the more likely it is there was a conspiracy among Benavides' peers and superiors, none of whom, as far as we know, have been submitted to the lie detector tests that seem to be the stock in trade of the Special Investigative Unit.

Nevertheless, following the identification in early January of the nine soldiers implicated in the murders, President Cristiani said that his announcement "marked the end of an investigation by a special commission of military officers and civilian lawyers he had appointed to look into the killings."* It was reported several days later that the "[p]ossibility of other top army commanders['] involvement has been ruled out for now, according to investigation sources."**

The results of this "Honor Commission" investigation have never been made public, however, leading to the predictable speculation that it might have uncovered evidence of wrongdoing by other high officers. In particular, the evidence gathered by the "Honor Commission" does not form part of the court record, and the military and civilian members of that Commission have not been identified publicly, as far as we know.

e. Was There a Cover-Up?

As Congressman Joe Moakley observed, Colonel Ponce stated that "not one person in the military -- not one -- came forward to report to him the complicity of the Army in the murders." Yet in an officer corps as small and as tightly-knit as in El Salvador, it is difficult to believe that such knowledge did not move with the speed of light through trusted circles.

A meeting was held at the National Intelligence Directorate the morning of November 16, a few hours after the murders. At this intelligence meeting, Salvadoran officers cheered when a junior officer interrupted the session with news that Father Ignacio Ellacuria had been killed.***

---

*   Douglas Farah, "Army Officers Held in El Salvador," The Washington Post, January 14, 1990.

** Ana Arana, "San Salvador judge charges soldiers with Jesuit murders," The Miami Herald, January 20, 1990.

*** Ana Arana, "Salvadoran officers met . . . ," The Miami Herald.

At the very least, these revelations suggest that the highest Salvadoran military officers may have known more about the Jesuit case far earlier than has been admitted to date. U.S. officials may also have known as of this November 16 meeting.*

There is little evidence that the Army High Command wholeheartedly supports thorough investigation and prosecution in the Jesuit case, and indeed certain sectors within the military are bridling at the detention of fellow officers and soldiers. Junior officers are reported to be unhappy with the prospect that a colonel who ordered lieutenants to commit murder may walk, while the lieutenants go to jail because of forensic evidence against them. Meanwhile, *tandona* officers are demonstrating the loyalty to their military class for which they have long been famous, accompanying Benavides to court in a show of solidarity. By mid-January, divisions within the military and opposition to the arrests from the far right had reportedly led to "some serious talk of a coup for the first time since Cristiani took office eight months ago."**

Reports that Colonel Benavides has been accorded special treatment -- although officially confined to National Police headquarters, he was seen in February in a luxury hotel owned by the military and has been given special food -- and has been visited regularly by senior army officers, raise additional questions about the military's commitment to the judicial proceeding.***

Americas Watch has called for an independent investigation of the actions of U.S. officials in the aftermath of the killings in order to clarify whether there was any effort to hide Army responsibility for the crimes until public and congressional pressure forced a turnabout.**** We await the

---

* CIA representatives usually attend such intelligence meetings but it is not known now if the CIA was absent from this meeting. It seems unlikely that the CIA, long involved in intelligence work with the Salvadoran army, would skip such a crucial meeting, held at the height of the guerrilla offensive when the army was fighting for its life.

** Douglas Farah, "Army Officers Held in El Salvador," The Washington Post, January 14, 1990; Lindsey Gruson, "Tensions Rise in Salvador After Arrests," The New York Times, January 15, 1990; and Douglas Farah, "Salvadoran Colonel Said to Order Killing of Jesuits," The Washington Post, January 17, 1990.

*** Douglas Farah, "Colonel Charged in Jesuit Killing Lives in Luxury," The Washington Post, February 22, 1990.

**** James A. Goldston and Anne Manuel, "Are We Shielding the Killers of Salvador's Priests?" The New York Times, January 21, 1990.

replies to Freedom of Information Act requests we filed with a number of federal agencies involved in the investigation.

We call on the Salvadoran government not to consider the investigation closed, but rather to continue working until all military officers and any others who might have been involved in the killings of the Jesuits, or in the coverup, have been identified and criminally sanctioned.

2. November 1989 Murders by Army Soldiers in Santa Ana

In the December 16, 1989 Update on El Salvador, Americas Watch reported on its investigation of the summary execution of between five and nine persons -- several of whom appeared to have been non-combatants -- by soldiers of the Second Infantry Brigade on November 12, 1989. Further investigation has clarified that some of the killed were wounded or captured guerrillas who were no longer taking part in hostilities, others were civilians who were assisting the guerrillas in non-combatant roles, and other civilians. Summary execution after capture of civilians and guerrillas is strictly prohibited by the Geneva Conventions.*

A woman resident who was there on November 12 when the November FMLN offensive began testified that a male non-combatant (who was executed later that morning) drove a red truck, with firearms and equipment for the guerrillas, into *Colonia* La Union while it was still dark. The firearms were unloaded and placed in the community center. In response to guerrilla exhortations, some people began to distribute corn and dig barricades. Some villagers were inside the community center.

At about 8:00 a.m., a man was carried in a hammock into the community health clinic, located in a small building between the community center and the witness's house. The man, an FMLN combatant, had a bullet wound in his left thigh. After he received medical treatment, he left the clinic and began walking. A corporal in command of the Second Brigade unit at the site,

---

* Common Article 3 to the four Geneva Conventions of 1949 provides: "In the case of armed conflict not of an international character occurring in the territory of one of the High Contracting Parties, each Party to the conflict shall be bound to apply, as a minimum, the following provisions: (I) Persons taking no active part in the hostilities, including members of armed forces who have laid down their arms and those placed hors de combat by sickness, wounds, detention, or any other cause, shall in all circumstances be treated humanely.... To this end, the following acts are and shall remain prohibited at any time and in any place whatsoever with respect to the above-mentioned persons: (a) violence to life and person, in particular murder of all kinds, mutilation, cruel treatment and torture..."

reportedly known to some of his soldiers as "El Loco" (The Crazy One), and another soldier approached the wounded guerrilla, grabbed him, and took him away. A woman ran up to the corporal, pleading with him to respect the wounded man. His body was later found, stabbed in the throat.

Later that morning, the witness saw the man who had driven the truck lying mortally wounded at the bottom of a dirt path which leads on to the main field in town, on which the community center is situated. The corporal approached the man, lifted his head and let it fall. She heard the corporal say, "Why should we let these people live? If we let them live, they'll be put in prison and then human rights [groups] will let them out." The man died shortly thereafter.

At some point on November 12, another wounded FMLN combatant sought refuge inside the community center. Soldiers tossed a grenade inside, ripped off the corrugated tin roof and crawled into the building. Once inside, soldiers put a megaphone to the mouth of the wounded guerrilla to magnify his screams as they killed him.

Americas Watch has received as-yet unverified allegations that Army soldiers executed, in summary fashion, as many as thirteen persons in La Union on November 12. As many as four persons may have been knifed in the neck. Americas Watch calls on the Salvadoran Armed Forces to investigate the actions of its forces in the area on November 12, and prosecute those responsible for these incidents.

3. Shooting of Student by Atlacatl Battalion, August 1989

On August 22, 1989, Miguel Ernesto Miranda Reina, 17, was returning home from a friend's house where he had gone to study after school, when a soldier from the Atlacatl Battalion stopped him in the Residencial Claudia, San Salvador. After Miranda had identified himself and allowed the soldier to check his bag, the soldier would not permit him to pass. Finally, Miranda walked away. The soldier fired at the ground near Miranda's feet. Miranda pleaded, "No, please, no," and continued walking rapidly. The soldier followed Miranda, but tripped and fell. Furious, the soldier lifted himself up and shot Miranda, killing him immediately, according to Tutela Legal.

According to Colonel Elena Fuentes, when the soldier stopped the student to ask for identification, the student pushed the soldier down, "and the soldier in his confusion, thinking that he was being attacked by a terrorist, shot him."* Witnesses disputed the contention that the soldier was pushed. The soldier is reportedly under investigation.

4. Highway Assault by Sixth Military Detachment, August 1989

In the early morning of August 29, 1989, fifteen college friends from the town of San Julian, Sonsonate, left a party and drove to the port of Acajutla, Sonsonate to celebrate in a restaurant. The group left Acajutla at about 2:30 a.m. to return to San Julian in a green Datsun pick-up. They had driven five kilometers when their car ran out of gas. The young people pushed the car past two closed gasoline stations to the La Campana Farm, where an employee suggested the farm administrator might sell them gas.

Unable to locate him, the sub-group of eight who had gone to look returned to the pick-up, at which point a white and green Hiace microbus approached on the highway, and three students tried to make it stop. The microbus was driven by uniformed soldiers of the Sixth Military Detachment, who, without saying a word, opened fire on the young people as they passed by. Another car, a white Toyota pick-up, pulled up soon afterward and stopped.

Uniformed soldiers of the Sixth Detachment disembarked and shot at the young people, as well as at the farm employee, injuring six, according to Tutela Legal.

As several screamed that they were unarmed civilians, the Hiace microbus returned, and soldiers came out and began to beat those who had not been injured by gunfire. When the beating stopped, the soldiers, after some persuasion, consented to take six of the wounded to the Hospital San Juan de Dios in Sonsonate. One of the injured, Rafael Mauricio Garcia Sermeno, 23, died shortly after arriving at the hospital.

Seven others were taken to the headquarters of the Sixth Detachment in Sonsonate, where four were interrogated and struck. A soldier put a rope around the neck of one of the four and held him in mid-air until he began to asphyxiate, at which point he let him down. They were freed at 5:00 p.m. on August 29.

---

* Diario Latino, August 30, 1989.

Following this incident, COPREFA issued a statement asserting that the event originated when a taxi driver telephoned the Detachment to let them know that a group of heavily armed subversives was on the highway. According to COPREFA, when the gravity of the incident became apparent, the soldiers gave help to the injured.

5. FMLN Medical Workers Summarily Executed after Capture, San Vicente, April 1989

On April 15, 1989, in San Ildefonso, San Vicente, the Argentine doctor Gustavo Ignacio Isla Casares and the French nurse Madeleine Languedec, along with a 16-year-old Salvadoran paramedic health worker, Maria Cristina Hernandez, a patient being treated in an FMLN field hospital, Carlos Gomez, and a school teacher, Clelia Concepcion Diaz Salazar, were killed after capture by Air Force soldiers at an FMLN field hospital in hacienda Catarina, San Ildefonso, department of San Vicente.

COPREFA said that the dead, including the two foreign medical persons, were among nine armed combatants from the Central American Revolutionary Workers party, PRTC, one of the five FMLN groups, who died in combat against the Air Force in *canton* La Guaza, San Ildefonso.

On April 27, 1989, representatives of the attorney general's office, the judge's secretary, Tutela Legal and several other organizations and the press attempted to attend the judicial recognition of the bodies. Fifth Brigade soldiers blocked the entry into the zone of all but the judge, the forensic doctor, representatives of the Embassies of France and Argentina, and the ICRC. The soldiers explained that this was a conflictive zone and all others needed permission from the General Staff to enter. The bodies of the two foreigners were finally recognized in the morgue in San Vicente.*

On April 27, 1989, the body of the French nurse was repatriated to France, and an autopsy performed in Brest, France. The forensic report based on the autopsy was released on August 16, 1989. The Christian Association for the Abolition of Torture made the report available to human rights organizations.

The forensic report shows that the nurse was killed by six high caliber bullets, probably from M-16 rifles, fired from a vertical position at close range. The bullet wounds were in the left shoulder, upper chest, pelvis and legs. Judg-

---

* Recognition is the judicial procedure for registering the death of persons.

ing from the angle and site of the wounds, the medical experts stated that it was improbable that the victim was in a vertical position when she was shot.

She was killed while wearing only a blouse, although army photographs show her body fully dressed. The brassiere, shoes and pants did not have any signs of bullet impacts; it was deduced that she was not wearing those clothes when shot and killed. The wounds in her throat, shoulders and the amputation of her left hand indicate she was tortured before she was assassinated. The forensic doctors concluded that in all likelihood, she was also raped.

The French human rights group concludes that "The most probable scenario is that Madeleine was assassinated by a group of soldiers, armed with M-16s of 5.5 mm. caliber, who surrounded her while she was bent over and wearing no more than a shirt. The injuries to the thorax, shoulder and the left hand, which was amputated, leads one to think that she was also tortured."

A Belgian medical doctor responsible for medical services of the FMLN in San Vicente, Marc Ingelbercht, sent a letter to French President Francois Mitterand on April 20, 1989. He described the aerial attack, the disembarkation of troops, and the arrest of the five victims. He said the five were alive and uninjured when they were arrested by army soldiers, except the Salvadoran paramedic who was injured. He wrote that following cruel torture to extract information, which they would not give, the five were assassinated.

6. Deaths of Three Journalists and Wounding of a Fourth, March 1989

Within a period of less than twenty-four hours on March 18-19, 1989 -- the evening before and day of presidential elections in El Salvador -- members of the Salvadoran Armed Forces were involved in the shooting deaths of two journalists -- Roberto Navas Alvarez, a Reuters photographer, and Mauricio Pineda Deleon, a television sound man with Salvadoran Channel 12 -- and the wounding of a third, Luis Galdamez, a Reuters photographer. In addition, when Dutch cameraman Cornel Lagrouw was gravely injured in cross fire, an Air Force plane and helicopter strafed and rocketed the press vehicle attempting to take him to the hospital, forcing the vehicle off the road and delaying Lagrouw's arrival at the hospital. These incidents occurred in the midst of a nationwide guerrilla traffic stoppage imposed to impede the elections. To date, despite clear evidence linking members of the Armed Forces to these crimes, no one has been tried or convicted, although three Air Force soldiers are said to be awaiting trial for the Navas killing.

a. Reuters Photographers Roberto Navas, Luis Galdamez

The undisputed facts of this case are that Air Force soldiers located around the 7.5 kilometer mark on the Boulevard del Ejercito running between San Salvador and Ilopango shot and killed Roberto Navas and wounded Luis Galdamez at about 9:00 p.m. on March 18 as the two were on a motor bike heading for San Bartolo, where Galdamez lives. Navas, who was driving, was killed instantly by two bullets. Galdamez was badly injured by one bullet which shattered his left arm and entered his lung. Galdamez received medical attention in El Salvador and later in the United States. Twenty-two spent 5.56 mm shells were found at the scene that night.

Three Air Force soldiers* implicated in the shootings have been confined to a military base pending further investigations. In recent months, however, the judicial investigation has slowed. Galdamez has not been called to testify in court regarding what happened on the night of March 18. On February 9, 1990, Navas' body was exhumed at the request of defense attorneys for soldiers charged in the case in order to determine which soldier shot the fatal bullet. Forensic specialists were unable to locate a bullet but it was established that Navas had only one bullet wound.**

The Air Force has offered the following version of events. COPREFA (the Armed Forces press office) issued a statement shortly after the shootings which alleged that the journalists ignored signs to stop at two successive checkpoints, and, when they failed to heed signals to stop given by soldiers at a third checkpoint, were fired on by soldiers. Air Force officials contended that both the second (at the 6.5 kilometer marker on the Boulevard del Ejercito) and third (at the 7.5 kilometer marker) checkpoints were clearly denoted by cones and barrels in the road, and that the bikers accelerated at the third checkpoint despite a soldier's waving of a flashlight. The Air Force cited a TACA airlines

---

* Lieutenant Nelson Saul Solano Reyes, Benjamin Caballero Pleitez, and Nicolas Rodriguez Huezo. Diario Latino, February 12, 1990.

** Diario Latino, February 12, 1980.

employee who was in the vicinity at the time as having seen a soldier wave a red light in front of the motor bike.*

Thus, according to the Air Force, soldiers were never given an opportunity to identify the riders of the bike. Air Force officials contended that only the second and third roadblocks were manned by Air Force soldiers, that soldiers at the first roadblock never communicated with their counterparts up the road, and thus that Air Force soldiers at the second and third roadblocks had no way of knowing the bikers were journalists.** On the evening before elections, in the midst of a nationwide traffic stoppage, with the Armed Forces on alert following a series of FMLN attacks in preceding days, soldiers had reason to be suspicious of such blatant disregard of their stop signals.

Indeed, the Air Force claimed, soldiers would have had good reason to suspect that the two were urban commandos of the guerrillas carrying explosives in their camera bags. Accordingly, after the bikers passed the second checkpoint without pausing, an order was issued to fire to stop the bike if necessary at the third checkpoint. It is not known who gave the order to shoot. Lieutenant Solarno Reyes told the justice of the peace that the soldiers were under specific orders of Captain Angel Roman Sermeno Nieto to act in special cases.

However, there is reason to doubt the military's contentions that soldiers were shooting to stop a speeding vehicle, and that the journalists openly defied clear signals to stop. First, it appears the soldiers did not fire any warning shots. Galdamez has told friends that he heard only one burst of shots, the burst which hit him and Navas. Thus, the soldiers either employed excessive force to stop the bike, or they intentionally shot to kill.

Second, the notion that soldiers were trying only to stop the motor bike is put into doubt by the physical evidence and the statements of Galdamez, which together suggest that the bike was either stopped or almost stopped at the time the shots were fired. When the justice of the peace, Bachiller Manuel

---

* The military reported that the Air Force soldiers on duty at the 7.5 marker checkpoint the night of March 18 were Lieutenant Nelson Saul Solano Reyes, sub-Sergeant Efrain Guardado Prada, and soldiers Cesaer Caballero Pleitez, Francisco Gonzalez Perez and Felix Rivas Gomez.

** Committee to Protect Journalists Interview with Air Force General Rafael Bustillo, April 1989.

de Jesus Aguilar Hernandez, arrived at the crime scene that night, Navas' body was face up on the divider in the middle of the road, about one meter from the motorbike. According to Justice Aguilar, the motorbike looked as though it had come to a stop exactly parallel and immediately next to the divider, then fallen over on its side. It did not look as though the bike had spun out of control after Navas, the driver, had been shot. Justice Aguilar noted that neither Navas' body nor the bike itself had any scratches or dirt on it, and asked Lieutenant Solano Reyes how it could be that, if they were going so rapidly when the soldiers fired, the bike and the body could be in that position, with no scratches or stains. The Lieutenant had no answer.*

Press who visited and filmed Galdamez in the hospital the following morning noted that his body was similarly devoid of any abrasions which might have been expected to result from a spill at high speed.

According to Galdamez, there simply was no "second" roadblock at the 6.5 kilometer marker. He said he was aware there were soldiers all along the road in that area, but no soldier made any motion or displayed any light for them to stop until the soldier waved his hand at the 7.5 kilometer marker. Galdamez said there was no red light at the 7.5 kilometer roadblock.

Justice Aguilar saw only chest-high metal structures pulled half-way out into the road, no cones or barrels, at both the 6.5 and 7.5 kilometer markers when he investigated following the shootings. At about 2:00 a.m., Reuters journalists found no sign of any roadblock at all at the 6.5 or 7.5 kilometer points, although Air Force officials claim the roadblocks remained throughout the night.

The actions of the military in this case are put into further question by the fact that Air Force soldiers on the scene may not have immediately secured medical attention for Galdamez, despite his grave condition. For some time, perhaps an hour after the 9:00 p.m. shooting, Galdamez was apparently lying unconscious on the ground, his arm shattered. Air Force officials alleged that their soldiers took Galdamez to the hospital at 10:32 p.m. However, Reuters was told by officials at the hospital that Galdamez was not brought there until

---

* The justice of the peace also discovered that the soldiers had removed the journalists' camera bags and other property to the Air Force base, and he required them to turn the victims' property over to the custody of the court.

11:30 or 11:45 that night. It should have taken no longer than 15 minutes to drive from the site of the shooting to the hospital that night. What happened in the interim is not clear. When soldiers dropped him off at the hospital, one reportedly remarked, "Here's another corpse for you."

While in the hospital, a military official reportedly sought to have Galdamez sign a blank paper and alleged that he and Navas had been drunk. Galdamez refused to sign and rejected the accusations.

The likelihood that Air Force soldiers shot Navas and Galdamez after their bike had come to a virtual stop, and the efforts by military officials to blame the journalists in the aftermath of the killings, paint a most unfavorable picture of the military's role in these events.

b. Television Sound Man Mauricio Pineda Deleon

Mauricio Pineda went to San Miguel on March 18, 1989, with other journalists to report on the elections there. With him were Raul Beltran and Mauricio's brother Wilfredo Pineda, also of Television Channel 12, and Sergio Rodriguez and Carlos Alvarado, of YSKL radio. The journalists hoped to cover conflictive areas where the guerrillas might attack. They rode in a light blue Datsun pickup truck with a camper shell, which was clearly marked on all sides with the insignia of the press and TV. The truck also carried a white-colored flag by the cabin.

The journalists in Pineda's group all checked in with the Third Infantry Brigade in San Miguel on the afternoon of March 18. At their request, they were provided military helicopter passage to towns in northern Morazan, and returned to the garrison at 6:00 p.m. At 7:00 p.m., they met with and interviewed the Third Brigade commander, Colonel Mauricio Ernesto Vargas.

During the night, the journalists learned by telephone from San Salvador of the shootings of Navas and Galdamez. As a result of this call, they decided to delay their morning departure from San Miguel, originally scheduled for about 5:00 a.m., to 6:00 a.m., after daylight.

At about 6:05 a.m., the five drove to the TAES air taxi company to drop off videotapes for shipment to San Salvador. On the way, they passed by the road turnoff known as Shell Palo Blanco, where there is a Shell gasoline station along the highway which runs from San Miguel to La Union. All five noted that there was an army checkpoint at the turnoff, and the soldiers saw the journalists pass by in the pickup.

At 6:15 a.m., they left Carlos Alvarado with the videotapes at the runway. The four remaining journalists returned the way they had come, with Mauricio Pineda riding in the back of the truck, sitting on a mattress with his back to the rear of the vehicle.

They drove along the highway and, at about 6:20 a.m., reached the Shell Palo Blanco turnoff for the highway to La Union, their destination. About 200 meters before the turnoff, the journalists could see that there was still a military checkpoint with eight to ten army soldiers there. The soldiers were from the Arce Battalion, they learned later. As they approached the fork in the road, before turning onto the highway to La Union, the driver, Beltran, made a brief stop. None of the journalists saw any soldier at the checkpoint signal for them to stop. Beltran then turned onto the road to La Union.

They had gone about 75 meters when the journalists heard several shots followed by a cry coming from the back of the truck. Beltran looked through the rear view mirror to see Mauricio Pineda falling to his right. Sergio Rodriguez and Wilfredo Pineda, the other two journalists, shouted to Beltran, saying they were being shot at and that Mauricio had been injured.

The car stopped about 50 meters from where they had heard the shots. The three journalists in the cabin got out and examined Pineda, seeing he was seriously injured. Two bullets perforated the back of the truck; one had penetrated Pineda's back and the other had passed through his right hand. As Wilfredo Pineda and Rodriguez filmed the scene, Beltran turned the truck around and drove back to the Shell station, where the soldiers were. By that time, Pineda was dead.

When the journalists asked to be taken to military superiors for an explanation, one of the soldiers replied, "It was because *you* shot at the gasoline station." Soldiers searched the vehicle, but found no arms. After the soldiers left, one of the journalists phoned Colonel Vargas, who said he would come right over. In the meantime, the same soldiers who had been at the checkpoint returned and said they were going to detain the journalists, because they had been armed and were members of a guerrilla urban command unit. When told that Vargas was coming, the soldiers left again.

Colonel Vargas arrived one half hour later and offered his help with the transfer of Pineda's body. Shortly thereafter, a legal medical inspection of the body was performed.

The markings of the car and the light conditions were such that the soldiers would almost certainly have known that the vehicle was carrying journalists. On neither occasion in which the journalists passed by the checkpoint did any soldier signal them to stop, or, when they did stop, not to proceed. Indeed, a videotape taken by two of the journalists after the shooting disproves the soldiers' original contention that the truck's occupants were armed and establishes convincingly that the vehicle was clearly identified as carrying journalists. It appears undeniable that the soldier who fired his weapon knew he was shooting at a press car.

A corporal of the Arce Battalion who was identified as having fired the fatal shots was arrested shortly after this event. The Armed Forces contended, however, that the corporal intended only to stop the car, and that poor aim was responsible for the tragic results.

c. Dutch Television Cameraman Cornel Lagrouw

Two groups of journalists arrived in San Francisco Javier, department of Usulutan in the morning of March 19, 1989 to cover guerrilla activity in the area. Scott Wallace, a CBS Radio correspondent; Arturo Robles, a journalist with JB Photos; and a driver were in a Suzuki jeep marked with "TV" and "International Press" insignia, and a white flag. Cornel Lagrouw, a Dutch television cameraman; Kees Elenbaas, a Dutch television technician; William Gentile, a U.S. Newsweek photographer; Analise Helwegen, Lagrouw's wife; and a driver were in a station wagon car, which similarly carried insignia of "TV" and "International Press" and a white flag.

Lagrouw and the others were interviewing guerrillas in the town when the Army attacked. The journalists were caught in the middle of a firefight. Lagrouw was shot in the chest as he stood up in the line of fire to film the events. Gentile and Robles dragged Lagrouw, who was still alive, out of the shooting and, with the assistance of Elenbaas, put him into the back of the Suzuki jeep, Wallace's car. The journalists drove down the block to where the larger station wagon was parked, and transferred Lagrouw inside. Gentile and Elenbaas climbed into the station wagon next to the body. The driver and Elenbaas sat in front.

In the Suzuki car, Wallace, Robles and their driver drove ahead along the ten-kilometer road leading to the coastal highway to Usulutan, the provincial capital, and site of the nearest hospital. As they were heading south towards the highway, they came under attack from an Air Force O-2 reconnaissance plane and an Air Force helicopter flying overhead. Machine-gun strafing and rockets fell all around their vehicle, finally forcing them to stop. They entered the house of a peasant family, and the helicopter and airplane withdrew. Shortly thereafter, Wallace and those accompanying him continued on to Jiquilisco in search of an ambulance.

The station wagon carrying Lagrouw was also attacked as it left San Francisco Javier. The Air Force helicopter followed it and strafed it repeatedly. First forced off the road for several minutes, the occupants tried to drive again, only to be compelled after twenty minutes of pursuit and attack from above to seek refuge in a house near the side of the road. After forty minutes inside, they resumed their journey. An ambulance sent from Jiquilisco met the party at the turnoff to the coastal highway, and they rushed to the hospital in Usulutan. LaGrouw was pronounced dead on arrival.

Colonel Inocente Orlando Montano, then-commander of the Sixth Infantry Brigade (since promoted to Vice Minister of Defense for Public Security), appeared at the hospital and rejected the journalists' version of what had happened. He offered to have the pilots of the helicopter and the airplane speak with the journalists. Although some journalists accompanied Colonel Montano back to the Brigade garrison, the pilots never showed up.

Although Lagrouw's fatal injuries were sustained in cross fire, Americas Watch believes the repeated firing on the civilian vehicles, clearly marked as press, was a violation of the rules of war.

The Armed Forces have consistently asserted that neither the ground troops nor the soldiers firing from the air knew that the objects of their fire were press vehicles. A Salvadoran Joint Chiefs of Staff report contended that the helicopter never flew below 3,000 feet, and said its occupants were acting on information from ground troops that "civilian-dressed terrorists armed with a rifle" had placed the evacuee into one of the cars.

However, one of the journalists with Lagrouw reported having seen the eyes of the helicopter pilot; a resident in the area said he had seen the pilot's head. Others said they saw the helicopter flying just above the trees.

Whether or not the Air Force knew these were press vehicles, they were still civilian vehicles. Objects normally dedicated to civilian use, such as cars, are not proper military targets.

The guerrillas, by requisitioning a car and using it for military purposes, could convert it to a military target. There is no evidence nor any assertion by the Air Force that the vehicle had been converted to military use by the guerrillas, however. They never contended that the soldiers were receiving fire from the vehicles. Instead, they suspected that the vehicles were being used to transport wounded guerrillas, a protected humanitarian activity. Transporting wounded ex-combatants does not convert a civilian vehicle into a proper military target for either side.

The Army report maintains that "the helicopter began to fire at the sides and in front [of the vehicle], without attacking it directly at any time, since there was no guarantee whether innocent persons were being transported...."

This Army statement concedes that there was doubt about the identity of the persons in the vehicle. In cases of doubt, combatants are required to hold their fire, under the Geneva Conventions.

In a meeting with Americas Watch in April 1989, Colonel Rene Emilio Ponce, head of the General Staff, said that no action would be taken against the helicopter pilot. According to Colonel Ponce, the pilot violated no regulation by shooting at the vehicle, no matter who was inside. Colonel Ponce hastened to add that new regulations were being drafted to cover such situations and prevent such shootings in the future.

7. Killing of University Student and Agricultural Worker, February 1989

Mario Antonio Flores Cubas, a 32-year-old economics student at the National University campus in San Salvador, and Jose Gerardo Gomez, agricultural worker, were arrested by uniformed soldiers on February 2, 1989. Their bodies were found the next day in a ravine over 100 kilometers from the place of capture. According to witnesses, on February 2, five heavily armed soldiers wearing green camouflage uniforms and riding in a red Datsun pickup truck, went to the house of Gomez in Barrio Santa Lucia, San Salvador, and arrested him, forcing him to take them to the house of Flores, also in Barrio Santa Lucia. Flores was captured while sitting on the sidewalk outside, talking to a group of friends. They forced him into the red pickup and drove away.

On February 3, the bodies of both Flores and Gomez were found at the bottom of a cliff in *canton* El Suncita, Acajutla, Sonsonate. The bodies were initially buried as unknown persons, and exhumed and identified on February 7 and 8.

Flores's body had a bullet wound in the back of the head. His right wrist was crushed, and there was a 3-centimeter wide wound made by a sharp object in the left part of the thorax. The victim's genital organs were bruised and purple. Cuts made by a sharp object were found on the lower third of both legs, the right leg was fractured, and there were signs of heavy beatings to the thighs of both legs.

Gomez's body had a bullet wound in the left eye. There were stab wounds in his hands, legs, arms, face, chest, lower abdomen and crotch, and his fingernails were dark purple.

8. Army Killing of Santos Regino Ramirez Perez, Fourth Military Detachment, January 1989

Army soldiers of the Morazan Battalion of the Fourth Military Detachment based in San Francisco Gotera, Morazan arrived at the house of Santos Regino Ramirez Perez in *caserio* El Rodeo, *canton* La Estancia, Cacaopera, Morazan at 1:00 a.m. on January 23, 1989. They took Ramirez out and shot him dead.

Eyewitnesses told Americas Watch that the soldiers were pretending to be guerrilla combatants, and called for Ramirez -- to whom they referred as *compa* or comrade -- to come out of the house. They shot at and kicked in the front door of the house. Upon entering, the soldiers said they knew very well that Ramirez was keeping weapons, that they wanted him to turn over his weapons, and that if he refused to turn them over, he would give them his life. Ramirez and his wife replied that the only arms in the house were his farming knife, a *cuma*.

The soldiers wanted to take Ramirez away immediately, but his wife demanded that he be allowed to put on some clothing, which the soldiers permitted. About a dozen soldiers took Ramirez from the house, while another dozen or so stayed with his wife and their three children in the house, looking for arms and questioning her. They called her a "whore" and accused her of collaborating with the guerrillas. The soldiers stayed in the house about one hour, and then left.

Within minutes after the soldiers took Ramirez away, his wife heard gunfire. The next morning, she and some neighbors found Ramirez's body face down at the edge of the Torola River. The body had gunshot wounds in the stomach and thorax. The intestines were falling out of a wound in the abdomen. The third, fourth and fifth fingers of the right hand had been cut off. The right wrist was broken, and one of the feet had been cut. That afternoon, with the assistance of neighbors, Ramirez's wife buried the body where it was found.

B. Indiscriminate Attacks

1. Air Force Bombing in Morazan, March 1989

Five civilians, including four children, were killed and five others were seriously injured when Air Force planes bombed and strafed villages in northern Morazan province on March 8, 1989. The incident occurred in the midst of a cease-fire by government troops declared by then-President Duarte.

According to neighbors who witnessed the attack, at 9:00 a.m. on March 8, a bomb from an A-37 plane fell one and one-half meters from the house of Vicente Sanchez in *caserio* El Junquillo, *canton* Tijeretas, jurisdiction of Torola, department of Morazan. Thirteen people were huddled inside. The house was destroyed by flying shrapnel. Five of those inside -- Carmen Rivera, 3, Brigida Valeriana Rivera, 2, and Lorenzo Rivera, 11, all siblings; and Leonor Sanchez, 7, and Baudillo Hernandez, 51 -- died instantly. Five other persons in the house were seriously injured.* The five were carried in hammocks to San Isidro, about twenty kilometers away. From there, they were taken in a car to the hospital in San Francisco Gotera.

Residents of El Junquillo said there had been a guerrilla ambush and subsequent combat between soldiers of the Third Infantry Brigade's Leon Battalion on March 7 in nearby villages, but there were no soldiers or guerrillas present in El Junquillo, where the bombing occurred. At about 5:00 p.m., after the skirmishes were over, two A-37 Air Force planes and four helicopters appeared and began firing rockets and bombs. The bombing and rocketing lasted through the night until the next morning, when the house of Vicente Sanchez was hit.

We have no evidence that Sanchez's house was deliberately targeted. Rather, this seems to have been a classic example of indiscriminate fire upon

---

* These victims were: Maria de la Paz Rivera, 35; Concepcion Martinez, 40; and two of her children, Natividad, 8, and Santos Digno, 10; and Juan Jose Sanchez, 14.

the civilian population, which is outlawed by the Geneva Conventions and the Additional Protocols.

2. Air Force Rocketing in Chalatenango, February 1990

Between 9:00 and 9:30 a.m on February 11, 1990, two rockets fired from a Salvadoran Air Force helicopter hit a house in which 21 civilians had taken refuge, killing five and wounding sixteen, in Corral de Piedra, Guancorita, San Jose Las Flores, Chalatenango.*

After initially denying responsibility and blaming the explosion on the FMLN, the Army admitted that its helicopter had rocketed the house. It promised to indemnify the families but those responsible for ordering and performing the rocketing of a house in the middle of a village will not be punished.

The victims were members of four family groups, all officially registered as repatriatees by the United Nations High Commissioner for Refugees (UNHCR). Four of the five dead were children between two and eleven years of age. The dead adult was a 30-year-old father who held his two-year-old daughter, also killed, in his arms.** Eleven of the wounded were children between four months and twelve years of age.

The Army was well aware that civilians lived in the village. On October 29, 1989, Corral de Piedra was repopulated by 520 repatriatees from the Mesa Grande refugee camp in Honduras with the full knowledge and approval of the government and the assistance of the UNHCR. Soldiers had passed through several times since then, searching the houses. Colonel Jorge Antonio Medrano at the nearby First Military Detachment in Chalatenango had recently denied villagers permission to transport more zinc to rebuild the roofs of houses.

Combat started outside of town about 6:00 to 6:30 a.m. the morning of February 11. Sounds of battle could be heard for several hours from a location just east of town, so many villagers who lived in flimsy shacks congregated in more substantial houses for protection.

---

*   Americas Watch visited the site on the afternoon of February 11 and the following day.

**   The five persons killed in the attack were Anibal Guardado, 28; his daughter Blanca Lidia, 2; Dolores Miranda Serrano, 10; Isabel Lopez, 11; and her sister Ana Beatriz, 2.

At about 8:40 a.m., three Air Force helicopters arrived at the battle scene, firing machine guns and more than a dozen rockets over the next hour. Residents also heard two A-37 planes drop what sounded like nine bombs nearby. In total there may have been as many as five helicopters and three A-37's used in the attack. A C-47 plane was observed circling the area as well, although it did not fire on the village.

Some guerrillas fled from the battle site through the village, with the helicopters in hot pursuit, shortly before the house was rocketed. One neighbor of the attacked house saw three guerrillas run by, but they were gone when the house was rocketed. Residents denied that there were guerrillas inside the house; nor were there any injured or dead guerrillas found in the house.

The house that was hit by two rockets was one of a cluster of six adobe or brick houses, four shacks and another semi-finished house. The houses are in an open area on a side road that is visible from the main road running from Chalatenango to San Jose Las Flores. All of these structures had zinc roofs, clearly visible from the air; no trees or other vegetation nearby block the view.

According to those interviewed in nearby houses, at the time of the rocketing, there were 75 civilians hiding in houses within 50 meters of the rocketing, including the 21 in the house that was hit.

Those hiding in nearby houses, some of whom were relatives of the victims, learned of the disaster when one of the wounded women, who was pregnant, ran out of the house bleeding, screaming and crying, with part of a child in her arms. Fifteen minutes after the rockets hit the affected house, with helicopters still flying low overhead and machinegunning, relatives of the victims emerged with white flags overhead from nearby adobe houses and helped move the injured to safer houses. Residents said the helicopters were low enough for them to see the pilots and the machine guns. Soldiers were seen in the area.

Bullets from helicopters perforated zinc roofs and struck the dirt floors of nearby houses. Four holes -- each no more than six inches deep, with pieces of shrapnel in them -- were left in the ground within a few meters of nearby houses by what residents described as rockets from helicopters.

U.S. nuns in the village went to investigate and church vehicles took the most seriously wounded to the hospital in Chalatenango. Later in the morning soldiers went house to house looking for guerrillas. Numerous items -- including blankets, sugar, money, shoes, and a radio -- were taken in the course of these searches. Three men -- Juan Javier Cordoba, Abel Serrano and Abel Dubon Chavarria -- were detained and taken away in an Army helicopter at about 1:00 - 2:00 p.m., along with a dead soldier, Julio Cesar Molina, 22. Three wounded uniformed soldiers were evacuated by the Salvadoran Red Cross.

On the day after the attack, February 12, the Armed Forces press office, COPREFA, stated that there was combat from 6:20 a.m. to 2:00 p.m. on the outskirts of San Jacinto Guancorita, San Jose Las Flores. The army found 60 "terrorists" from the Popular Forces of Liberation (FPL), one of the five FMLN groups, near Corral de Piedra. As a result of the combat, 15 civilians were wounded; six "terrorists" died, others were wounded, and three were captured, according to COPREFA.

Also on February 12, the Salvadoran military refused to permit Tutela Legal and the press from getting to the site on the grounds that there was ongoing combat. There was in fact no combat in the area at the time Tutela and the press were denied permission to enter. The UNHCR received permission to visit later in the day, but others were not permitted to enter for several days.

The following day, February 13, the government published a communique lamenting the death and wounding of civilians, and announced that the Special Investigative Unit would exhume the dead and conduct an autopsy to determine responsibility for the attack.

On February 17, the Salvadoran Armed Forces reversed prior statements after investigation by the Special Investigative Unit and interviews with the pilots and other military present, and accepted responsibility for the deaths of the five civilians,* promising to indemnify the victim's families. Two days later, however, the Armed Forces characterized Tutela Legal's call for prosecution of those responsible for the killings as a "malicious . . . effort to create a criminal case which does not exist against those who were complying with their duty."**

---

*   "Army admits blame in refugee deaths," The Miami Herald, February 18, 1990.

**   El Mundo, February 21, 1990.

On March 6, the bodies of the five victims were recognized by a judge at an exhumation at the Guarjila cemetery.*

Under the rules of war, the armed forces of both sides have the obligation to take care to avoid civilian casualties and to refrain from indiscriminate attacks, that is, attacks which may be expected to cause incidental loss of civilian life which would be excessive in relation to the concrete and direct military advantage anticipated.

Soldiers on the scene defended the air strike to relatives of the victims on the grounds that guerrillas were hiding in the house which was hit. Even if there were guerrillas inside the one-room building, which we do not believe, rocketing the civilian structure was still an indiscriminate attack in violation of the rules of war. The army does not have *carte blanche* to use helicopter rockets against guerrillas in populated areas under the rules of war.

The rocketing of a civilian structure surrounded by other homes in the middle of a populated area could be expected to, and in fact did, cause incidental loss of civilian life. That loss was clearly excessive in relation to the direct and concrete military advantage anticipated -- the killing or capture of guerrillas fleeing through the village.

C. Deaths in Custody

1. Yuri Edson Aparicio Campos, National Police, November 1989

Yuri Edson Aparicio Campos, 23, a student at the University of El Salvador, left home in Soyapango near San Salvador on November 8 and was not heard from by his family until November 22, when he was located in Hospital Rosales under police guard. He had been taken there on November 19 at 10 p.m. by the National Police, as a prisoner, with internal injuries that were about three days old at the time. He was unconscious when he arrived at the hospital, dehydrated, and had trauma to the head, and a cut in the stomach.

---

* En route to the exhumation in a military helicopter, the Attorney General Dr. Mauricio Eduardo Colorado and two assistant attorneys general for Human Rights were wounded when the guerrillas fired at the helicopter. Also wounded were four journalists in the helicopter and the two military pilots; the helicopter gunner was killed. Diario de Hoy, March 7, 1990; La Prensa Grafica, March 7, 1990.

He died in the hospital on November 25, as a result of beatings by the National Police.

2. Lucio Parada Cea and Hector Miranda Marroquin
Tortured and Killed, First Brigade, August 1989

Between July 1 and 3, 1989, a patrol from the Atlacatl Battalion accompanied by two soldiers from the First Brigade arrested seven young men from the Tres Ceibas and Camotepeque farming communities around Apopa, a northern San Salvador suburb. They beat them severely enough to cause the deaths of two of the detainees: kicking them, hanging them from trees, whipping them with branches, smothering them with *capuchas*, stabbing them with bayonets, and dunking them in a river.

Lucio Parada Cea, 20, died in the field on July 2 and his body was secretly buried there by the soldiers to hide the crime.

Hector Joaquin Miranda Marroquin, 20, also brutalized in the field, was taken with the other captives to the First Brigade. There, despite constant inquiries by family members, Tutela Legal, and the ICRC, the First Brigade refused to acknowledge their presence, said they were "cooperating" with the army, and then finally let the ICRC see Miranda on July 11; at the ICRC's insistence, he was taken to the hospital on July 12, where he died the next day from internal injuries.

After his arrest and severe beating on July 3, Miranda was held incommunicado in the First Brigade from July 3 to 11; the law in El Salvador at that time was that no detainee could be held longer than 72 hours before being consigned to the judge. The other prisoners were held even longer in the First Brigade, where they all received some superficial medical treatment to cure their wounds to make them presentable upon release. Although his cell mates kept telling the medical and military authorities that Miranda was very sick, he received no care. At best, the First Brigade is guilty of criminal negligence, and at worst of deliberately permitting Miranda to die.

There are charges pending against only two persons, however, and neither of them was responsible for the gross negligence of Miranda in the First Brigade; the commander of the First Brigade, Colonel Francisco Elena Fuentes, seems to have escaped all scrutiny in this matter.

The two defendants who have been charged in the crime, accused of intentional murder under section 152 of the Salvadoran criminal code, are Corporal Alcides Gomez of the Atlacatl Battalion and Cesar Vielman Joya Martinez, a soldier assigned to the intelligence unit of the First Brigade. Gomez is accused of allowing the murders to take place and of helping to bury Parada's body. Gomez was ordered detained and placed in the Quezaltepeque prison in August. Joya Martinez is accused of murdering both Parada and Miranda. He was ordered detained in July, but escaped and subsequently left the country.

Joya Martinez is now seeking political asylum in the U.S. He has alleged publicly that he participated in a death squad operating out of the First Brigade's military intelligence section, under the noses of U.S. military advisors who provided cars, money and safe houses but preferred not to know about certain intelligence operations.

Joya Martinez denies guilt in the Parada and Miranda killings, blaming Parada's death on soldiers from the Atlacatl Battalion and noting that Miranda was alive when turned over to the First Brigade. Joya Martinez's testimony is not in the court record.

The following account is based on an examination of the court record as of October, 1989, as well as on interviews with victims, family members, government and military officials, and the Tutela Legal report, and others.

Early in the morning of July 1, seventy-three soldiers of the Sixth Infantry Company of the Atlacatl Battalion, commanded by Lieutenant Herbert Antonio Soriano Romero, accompanied two soldiers from the intelligence section (S2) of the First Brigade -- Cesar Vielman Joya Martinez and Humberto Rodriguez -- on a mission from San Salvador to the Apopa-Nejapa suburbs to the north. The First Brigade soldiers were seeking FMLN members in the area. They were divided into three patrols, one under the command of Atlacatl Battalion second sergeant Elmer Ernesto Moran Martinez, one under the command of Atlacatl Corporal Alcides Gomez, and a third under another command.

Moran's troops went to *canton* Tres Ceibas, Apopa in the afternoon of July 1. At about 3:00 p.m., they arrested Fausto Funes Garcia, 23 (nickname "Chicharron"), at his house and took him under a tree for interrogation. They accused him of possessing arms and of being involved with the FMLN, which he denied. At about 6:00 p.m., Funes's friend, Andres Hernandez Carpio, 23 (nickname "Cangrejo"), a member of the El Angel cooperative, came by the house and was also detained. Soldiers tied both men's thumbs behind their backs, tore up their identification cards, and marched them off. They pulled off Funes's shirt, tore it up and took his shoes.

The soldiers walked the men for three hours to *canton* Camotepeque, Nejapa, where they met up with the other soldiers. They camped out at a farm called Barba Rubia. Lieutenant Soriano ordered that security precautions be taken and sentinels posted so that the two detainees would not escape.

The next morning, July 2, several of the Atlacatl soldiers, accompanied by the two First Brigade soldiers and the two detainees, went to Loma El Jute. At about 7:00 a.m. Moran and some soldiers left Loma El Jute for Hacienda Mapilapa, a government-sponsored cooperative, taking Hernandez with them. Funes was left with the soldiers at Loma El Jute under Corporal Gomez's control all day.

Around 11:30 a.m., about twelve uniformed soldiers (presumably from Moran's patrol) arrived at the house of Lucio Parada Cea (known to the soldiers as "Edwin") in Camotepeque. They grabbed Parada and tied his thumbs behind him. One soldier, "El Diablo," pulled Parada by the neck while other soldiers punched and kicked him and struck him with sticks and rifle butts.

After detaining Carlos Antonio Romero Martinez (nickname "Cusuco"), also a member of the El Angel cooperative, the soldiers continued on their search. At about 1:30 p.m., they stopped a pickup along the road from Camotepeque to Quezaltepeque, in which were riding Maria Ana Funes, 43, and her son, Jose Catalino Melendez Funes, 21. Melendez, another El Angel member, was identified by his nickname, "Cafe Amargo," and beaten as he was pulled off the truck. His thumbs were tied behind him with a nylon tie, and untied only when he arrived at the First Brigade two days later. He was not given any food in the field; soldiers occasionally dribbled some water to him from their canteens.

At about 3:30 p.m., the same soldiers returned to the house of Lucio Parada, bringing Parada in tow. They said they were looking for arms. Parada's parents could see that their son had been hit repeatedly in the head and stomach. Upon not finding any arms, the soldiers once again took Parada away, saying they were heading to the nearby Barba Rubia farm.

All three persons arrested that afternoon (Parada, Romero, and Melendez) denied the soldiers' charges that they were FMLN members and had blown up posts and buses. They were all interrogated in the field, blindfolded, and beaten with clubs before they were brought back to the soldiers' camp at Barba Rubia. Soldiers covered Melendez's head with a green army poncho, twisting it closed at the neck, and interrogated him while cutting off his breath. They said he would go free if he turned in other people or arms.

That evening, at 7:15 p.m., soldiers captured Emilio Martinez Guevara, 22, who is mentally ill, in Camotepeque. They tied his thumbs behind his back and took him to Barba Rubia with the other detainees.

At about 5:15 the next morning, July 3, Monday, soldiers walked Martinez around and questioned him, while kicking and hitting him. They forced him to lie down and jabbed him in the stomach with a bayonet. They applied the *capucha* twice so that he could not breathe.

On Moran's orders, about twelve soldiers under the command of Corporal Gomez, including the two First Brigade soldiers, took Funes and Martinez that morning and walked them to Tres Ceibas. The purpose of the trip was to detain Hector Joaquin Miranda Marroquin, also of Tres Ceibas. On the way, they passed over a hammock bridge of rotting wood, fifty yards long, over the Azalguate River. The two detainees were still tied up. Funes had a rope around his waist with a soldier holding one end to prevent him from escaping. Funes apparently fell, jumped, or was pushed off the bridge, dropped 25 meters, and landed on some rocks on the bank, badly scraping his left shoulder and arm.

Nonetheless, the soldiers forced Funes and Martinez to continue on to Tres Ceibas. There the troops apprehended Joaquin Miranda, known to the soldiers as "Tres Pesos" or "Ever," at his home. Soldiers pushed, shoved and beat Miranda as they took him away. When Miranda's mother protested, she was told, "Shut up, old woman." According to testimony of other soldiers, First Brigade soldier Joya Martinez and other soldiers beat Miranda fiercely and placed a poncho on his head in the form of a *capucha* to stop his breathing.

In nearby coffee fields, soldiers found a Claymore mine, two M-67 grenades, blocks of TNT, some aluminum, electric detonation capsules, five nylon ponchos, five camouflage uniforms and three olive green uniforms, all with First Brigade or Fifth Military Detachment insignia.

Upon returning to Barba Rubia, the soldiers beat the detainees with clubs and kicked them. Several of the detainees were hung from a tree, one at a time, with a rope under one arm. Each was hung for twenty minutes while being questioned, beaten with clubs, and kicked.

Again according to statements given to the court, Joya Martinez was accused by other soldiers of interrogating Miranda, hitting him and applying the *capucha*. Under his orders, Atlacatl soldier Eugenio Mendez hung Miranda from a tree by his knees and waist, while hitting him with sticks.

When Miranda finally told Joya that Parada was the leader of a local guerrilla band and knew where rifles could be found, some soldiers went to look for the guns, but found nothing.

It was then Parada's turn to be beaten. Upon returning from the unsuccessful search for guerrilla guns, the soldiers took Parada away to an unknown site, where they beat him, hung him and applied the *capucha*. As the soldiers were walking him back to Barba Rubia, Parada collapsed and died. Joya Martinez and Atlacatl Corporal Gomez borrowed a shovel from a nearby house and dug a grave, where they buried Parada.

In the evening of July 3, the six remaining detainees were taken to the First Brigade in San Salvador. Soldiers carried Miranda because he could not walk.

In the First Brigade, soldiers beat one of the detainees and tortured him with a *capucha* during interrogation the first two nights, while he continued to deny accusations of guerrilla involvement. On their first day there, and once or twice a day afterward, the detainees were visited by a doctor called "Linda," who gave penicillin injections and dressed their wounds. When she entered the cell, they were blindfolded so they could not see her.

Miranda's cell mates saw that he was very sick and could neither move nor eat; he kept them awake at night calling out for water and groaning. Miranda complained that he felt as though his insides were burning up. His friends and fellow cell mates complained to the soldiers on Miranda's behalf, and said that he should be taken to the hospital, that he would not live. "Let him die," the soldiers replied. Although they complained to the army "doctor," little was done for Miranda.

The ICRC and Tutela Legal, which on July 3 had been alerted by family members of the detentions, could not get in to see the detainees; the First Brigade would not even admit that they were in custody.

In the meantime, on July 6, family members found Parada's body on a hill. On July 7, it was recognized by a Justice of the Peace. The body was half-buried, with stones on top of the head and stomach. The face had been beaten in, the eyes were bulging out, and part of the tongue had been removed. A firearm wound perforated the head. The body was bruised and bloody.

It was not until July 10 that the First Brigade even acknowledged holding the remaining detainees. Family members were told that the detainees were not being released because they were "cooperating" in investigations. All the detainees interviewed later denied any cooperation.

On July 11, when the ICRC saw Miranda's condition, it sought his transfer to a hospital, according to relatives. Miranda was admitted to the Hospital Rosales on July 12 at 4:40 p.m. At the time of his transfer Miranda was very weak, had difficulty breathing, and had bruises on his head and both legs from what appeared to be beatings with blunt instruments. He also had deep lacerations on both wrists, was malnourished, and could barely talk or move. He had difficulty eating and drinking, and his urine was red. He died in the hospital the next day, July 13, at 4:15 p.m.

Soldiers released the five remaining detainees on July 18. None was brought before a judge, and no charges were pressed. At least two of the detainees said they affixed their thumb prints to documents which accused them of being guerrilla members and engaging in acts of terrorism, and which said they had not been mistreated. Identification documents which had been taken from some of the detainees were not returned.

Most of the detainees who returned to their homes left shortly after receiving death threats from the FMLN, which accused them of having collaborated with the army.

Army officials have offered evasive and contradictory responses to inquiries about this matter, and their actions in the weeks after the events indicate an attempt to cover up what took place. Colonel Elena Fuentes, commander of the First Brigade, told Americas Watch that the second sergeant in command of the Tres Ceibas mission, Moran, reported the death of Lucio Parada to the First Brigade as soon as he learned of it on July 3. According to Elena Fuentes, upon being notified, he immediately ordered the mission to return to the Brigade and called upon the National Guard to investigate.

The sincerity of high Army officials' desire to get to the bottom of this case is put into question by a number of factors. First, U.S. Embassy officials told Americas Watch that Army Chief of Staff Colonel Ponce ordered the National Guard to investigate, but that he did not do so until July 25, after the international press had begun to ask questions about the case.*

That First Brigade officials were interested in seriously investigating Parada's case as early as July 3 is not credible in light of their confinement and mistreatment of the other detainees for two weeks thereafter, their refusal to acknowledge those detentions for about a week, and their denial of medical attention to Miranda until July 12, by which point it was too late.

Finally, Colonel Elena Fuentes maintained as late as November, against the weight of all the evidence, that Parada's death was caused, not by army mistreatment, but by having fallen from a truck. Nowhere in the court record does any witness -- soldier or detainee -- mention that Parada fell from a truck. Instead, the court record, compiled before November, makes it clear he was beaten to death by soldiers.

3. Julian Rosales Lopez, National Police, February 1990

At about 9 a.m. one morning in early February 1990, Lopez, 42, went to a parcel of land near *canton* San Jose Cortez, Ciudad Delgado, San Salvador. Soldiers of the Atlacatl Battalion stopped him, tied his thumbs behind him, and covered his face with his shirt. They took him to San Jose Cortez church, where another 30 persons were being held. When a relative of Rosales came for him, soldiers refused to turn him over. They said they would not torture him, and added that they would free him if he were not involved with any political organization. At 11 p.m. two trucks with soldiers arrived; soldiers put Rosales in one of the trucks and left for an unknown destination.

Relatives looked in many different military and security force posts, but could not locate Rosales. On February 8, they were informed he was dead and his body was in the Isidro Menendez Judicial Center in San Salvador. When they arrived there, officials told them Rosales had died in the National Police.

An autopsy determined that Rosales had been bruised in the left temple and lower lip, the right chest, the left part of the rib cage, both wrists,

---

* See Ana Arana, "Pushed by U.S., Salvadoran army probes 2 deaths," The Miami Herald, July 27, 1989; Douglas Farah, "Salvadoran Colonel Admits Troops Killed 2 in Detention," The Washington Post, July 26, 1989.

both thumbs, the left lower arm, the left leg, and the intestines and head. His death had been caused by torture. Tutela Legal held the National Police responsible.

4. Jose Joaquin Gonzalez Vasquez, National Police, June 1989

Jose Joaquin Gonzalez Vasquez, 50, a member of the agrarian cooperative La Esperanza de R.L., died June 20, 1989 in the custody of the National Police in San Miguel. Gonzalez was captured on June 15 by Third Brigade soldiers at his home in Lote El Amatal, Hacienda La Esperanza, *caserio* Santa Lucia, *canton* Las Lomitas, San Miguel. The soldiers said they needed him for only two hours. When he did not return, his wife located him at the National Police, where she was told he had been sent June 17 from the Third Brigade. When she went to the governmental Human Rights Commission on June 20, she was told Gonzalez had hanged himself with his shoelaces in his National Police cell.

The National Police handed his body over to her the same day. It had a blow to the back of the head, and the cranium was broken. There had been blows to the right eye, near the nose and on the chin. There were burns evident on his palms and the backs of both hands. He had suffered a blow to the right temple, and had a mark around his neck from hanging, according to Tutela Legal.

Gonzalez, who had been a member of the civil defense of Las Lomitas for three years, had been captured twice previously by the Third Brigade, and accused of being a guerrilla collaborator.

D. Disappearances

Four persons connected with the Santa Ana campus of the National University and one local union activist disappeared in July and August, 1989. Most were held for periods of over a month and then, after an international campaign had been mounted on behalf of some of them, they were reappeared in late August; some had been tortured. Some accused the Army Second Brigade, based in Santa Ana, of kidnapping and holding them against their will. The commanding officer denied responsibility for the disappearances, and there was never an official record that they had been detained. (See Chapter on Death Squads)

These events gave rise to the hope that other disappeared persons might be freed if enough pressure were brought to bear on the military and security forces, some of whose intelligence units have historically been the locus for death squad operations.

1. Disappearance of Six Cooperativists, possibly by Seventh Military Detachment, December 1989

In December 1989, six cooperative members at the San Cayetano El Rosario cooperative, *canton* Llano de la Laguna, city and department of Ahuachapan, disappeared after their abduction by soldiers in two separate incidents, according to testimonies given to Americas Watch. The leaders of the co-op were among those disappeared.

Uniformed soldiers captured co-op members Julio Cesar Juarez Vasquez, 18, and his brother, Juan Antonio Juarez Vasquez, 23, from their homes at the cooperative in the presence of family members about 9:00 p.m. on the night of December 5, 1989.

The day before, two truckloads of soldiers had conducted a fruitless search for weapons at the cooperative offices and all the surrounding houses. Cooperative members estimate that about 200 troops were in and around the cooperative during the search. The other four victims, co-op treasurer Leonardo Perez Nunez, 23, and three brothers -- co-op president Gerardo Saldana Salazar, 23, secretary Juan Saldana Salazar, 25, and driver Jose Eladio Saldana Salazar, 33 -- were captured at 8:30 a.m. on December 29, 1989, in front of the coffee processing plant Beneficio Ausoles, near the cooperative.* They were traveling with eight other people in a co-op truck, which was stopped by four soldiers in olive green uniforms. Four men in civilian clothes with pistols got out of a white jeep nearby and asked the driver for his identity papers and the registration of the car.**

---

*   The co-op officers had been asked to attend an appointment at the bank that held the co-op loan in Ahuachapan. However, other co-op members visited the bank and found it was closed for the Christmas holidays. It is not known how the message regarding the appointment was delivered to the disappeared men.

** The jeep, with lightly tinted windows, had been seen passing the co-op at about 6:00 a.m. that same morning. It turned around, stopped briefly at the co-op gate, and then drove off in the direction of the coffee plant.

The plainclothesmen forced Jose, Gerardo and Leonardo, who were all in the cabin of the truck, to show their papers and get into the white jeep. They then made those riding in the bed of the truck get down. All the men were required to show their identification papers. The plainclothesmen singled out Juan Saldana and made him get into the jeep. Two of the plainclothesmen got in as well and drove off.

The other two plainclothesmen drove to Ahuachapan in the co-op truck with the other eight passengers, and then left the truck with the keys in and the motor running. The passengers found a driver to bring the truck back to the co-op, where they informed the others of what had happened.

That same day, relatives went to the Seventh Military Detachment in Ahuachapan to inquire, and were told that the captured men were not there. The Seventh Military Detachment in Ahuachapan is headed by Colonel Roberto Staben, a *tandona* member who was implicated in 1986 in a band that was kidnapping the rich; at the time Colonel Staben was head of the U.S.-trained counterinsurgency Arce Battalion and, after a brief interrogation, was absolved and restored to his position.*

Family members have exhausted all means of locating the disappeared men, and have reported the case to all possible agencies, to no avail. Colonel Staben has met several times with cooperative members to tell them to stop saying he has captured the six missing men. He denies that he ever captured the men or that he knows anything about the case. At a meeting with the members February 6, Colonel Staben accused some cooperative members of collaborating with the guerrillas. There has been no known FMLN activity in the area.

The 128-*manzana* co-op originally belonged to Maria Clementina Pineda, a relative by marriage of Colonel Elmer Gonzalez Araujo, implicated in the Las Hojas massacre in Sonsonate in 1983; that case has been amnestied. The cooperative was formed on the day of Archbishop Romero's assassination, March 24, 1980, and a government agency issued provisional title to the

---

* Captain Lopez Sibrian, who was implicated in but never tried for the 1981 assassination of the head of the agrarian reform institute and two U.S. labor advisors at the Sheraton Hotel, still remains in custody in connection with that band of kidnappers.

land to the cooperative on July 28, 1982. Pineda has since been pressing to get the land back.

In May 1982, supposedly at Pineda's prompting, the National Guard came to the co-op in search of guerrillas, threatened to kill everyone, and arranged an "agreement" whereby all the land was given back to Pineda. But in 1983, the government agency FINATA restored the cooperative to the peasants, except for 10 *manzanas* given to former tenants. Shortly thereafter Pineda again sought the intervention of military authorities, but Colonel Maravilla, then commander of the Seventh Military Detachment, declined her request to oust the cooperativists.

Problems cropped up again this past year. In February 1989, soldiers captured co-op member Reyes Coronado Martinez, tortured him and held him for three days. As noted above, soldiers searched the co-op on December 4, following allegations that a recently completed water tank was being used to store arms for the FMLN. Nothing was found.

On December 26, a woman claiming to have purchased the property from Pineda appeared at the co-op and gave the farmers one month to vacate, making veiled threats. The four cooperativists were disappeared three days later. She later claimed not to have known the co-op had title to the land, and has decided not to pursue the matter further.

Colonel Staben pledged to help find the disappeared persons, and at another meeting he called for the co-op members on February 12 denied again participating in their capture. Pineda also denied having the men.

One week later, the Federation of Agricultural Production Cooperative Associations of El Salvador (FEDECOOPADES) reported in a newspaper advertisement that, at 9:40 a.m. on February 12, residents of *canton* Los Magueyes, Ahuachapan saw a truck pass by containing uniformed men along with two of the disappeared co-op officers, Gerardo Antonio Saldana Salazar and Leonardo Perez Nunez.

Following this report, soldiers from the Seventh Military Detachment came to the cooperative and took one of the witnesses to the Detachment, where she was interviewed. When she returned home, she was unwilling to give any further statements.

The military visited the co-op again and pressured members to sign statements saying that the advertisement had been taken out by FEDECOOPADES and that they had no responsibility for it. On March 1,

Colonel Staben again visited the co-op, this time with members of the National Guard. Colonel Staben continued to maintain that the military had nothing to do with the disappearances and reiterated his desire to help solve the case. He also insisted that co-op members stop taking out ads saying the military was involved.

Despite the professed desire of the military to solve the case, the most elementary steps to obtain proof, such as taking fingerprints from the co-op vehicle that two of the captors drove, have not been done.

2. Disappearance of Two Unionists by Air Force, August 1989

On August 19, 1989 Juan Francisco Massin, member of the SELSA bakery union at the Pan Lido factory, and Sari Cristiani Chan-Chan, a photographer for FENASTRAS, disappeared after last being seen in the custody of Air Force soldiers. They have not been seen since.

One witness told Americas Watch that on August 19 he was in a van coming west from Santa Lucia toward San Salvador along the Boulevard del Ejercito when the vehicle stopped in traffic at the 2-1/2 kilometer point opposite the entrance to the Reprocentro Factory. It was about 6:30 p.m. The witness looked through the van window and saw, across the Boulevard, directly in front of the main gate of the Factory, two civilians surrounded by a group of five uniformed Air Force soldiers.

The two civilians, whom he recognized as Massin and Chan-Chan, were standing next to each other, facing the street, with the five soldiers forming a semi-circle in front of them. The witness also saw two groups of two Air Force soldiers standing nearby, closer to the Boulevard. One of these soldiers was examining some documents, which, from the positions of the parties, the witness took to be the identity papers of Massin and Chan-Chan.

During the approximately two minutes that the van was stopped in traffic, the witness could see Massin respond to questions from the soldiers. Chan-Chan said nothing.

Another witness reported to Americas Watch having seen Massin and Chan-Chan in the custody of Air Force soldiers along the Boulevard del Ejercito early that evening.

In the first few days after the disappearance, Maria Juana Antonia Medina, 37, Chan-Chan's mother, visited the Treasury Police, the National

Guard and the National Police, asking for her daughter's whereabouts. None of the officials with whom she spoke knew anything. Finally, on August 23 a Treasury Police official told her that the Air Force had arrested Chan-Chan. Shortly thereafter, this information was confirmed by a friend of the family.

On August 28, Captain Flores of the Air Force received Medina, and told her to look among the dead for her daughter. He denied that the Air Force had arrested her, and told her to bring to him anyone who said the Air Force had done so, so he could arrest those persons for lying.

Medina later saw the governmental Human Rights Commission, where an official told her the guerrillas had captured her daughter. Medina's letters to the Minister of Defense and President Cristiani went unanswered. In November, rumors circulated that both Massin and Chan-Chan were still alive in a safe house in San Salvador. These were not confirmed.

Medina was herself arrested and severely mistreated by the National Police following the FENASTRAS march of September 18. She is the widow of Jorge Eduardo Chan-Chan, First Secretary of Conflicts for the SETA water workers union, who she said was killed by a death squad in 1980.

3. Eric Felipe Romero Canales, First Brigade, November 1989

Romero, 17, was captured by soldiers of the Libertador Battalion of the First Brigade, under the command of Captain Eric Samayoa Leiva, about 4:30 p.m. on November 18, 1989, two blocks from his house in *Colonia* La Hermita, Apopa, San Salvador. Last seen in army custody on November 19, his current whereabouts are unknown, according to an Americas Watch interview with his mother.

When Romero's mother went to the local command post on the day of her son's capture to see him, Lieutenant Oscar Sanabria explained that Romero had been arrested on Captain Leiva's orders because a local informant, whose identity is known to the family, had denounced Romero for helping the FMLN build barricades during the offensive. (On November 13, at the height of the offensive, Romero had been forced by guerrillas to help them dig trenches. He declined their suggestion that he join them, and pleaded with them to let him go, which they did.)

Romero's mother visited him in army custody in Apopa after his capture on November 18 and again the next morning, November 19, being allowed to bring him food both times. However, when she returned to see him in the afternoon of November 19, a soldier told her that Romero had been sent to the First Brigade and then to the National Police for a 15-day investigation.

The First Brigade and the National Police both denied that they had ever had custody of Romero. His mother has made the rounds of all the possible places of detention and all the humanitarian agencies several times, but could not find him. Romero has not been seen since, although his mother has a photograph from a local newspaper showing a group of young men arrested by the First Brigade during the offensive. One of the men in the photograph, she believes, is her son.

4. Disappearance of Health Worker by First Brigade, November 1989

In <u>Carnage Again</u>, we reported the November 19 capture by First Brigade soldiers of five health workers at the Church of San Francisco de Asis, in Mejicanos, San Salvador.* Although four of the workers were released within two days, David Alexander Hernandez Amaya has not to date reappeared. His whereabouts remain unknown. When a *habeas corpus* petition proved unsuccessful, a petition was filed with the Inter-American Commission on Human Rights.

5. Still Disappeared

Few of the thousands who have been disappeared in prior years have reappeared. The victims' relatives are still searching for these and many others:

a. Miguel Angel Rivas Hernandez, disappeared by the Air Force in November 1986, was seen surreptitiously by relatives in the custody of the National Guard in March 1988. His detention has never been acknowledged, and a complaint on his disappearance is pending before the Inter-American Commission on Human Rights.

Rivas was just 19 when he disappeared; he would be 23 now. His father, who had vigorously pursued his case, was arrested by the Air Force and released in 24 hours during the first days of the November 1989 offensive, after

---

* See <u>Carnage Again</u> pp. 72-73.

well-connected foreigners intervened with the Air Force. He was rearrested by the Treasury Police shortly thereafter and consigned to prison, accused of collaborating with the FMLN. He was freed by the court on January 31, 1990. His son remains disappeared.

    b. Two SICAFE workers and their friend were disappeared in Santa Ana returning from an antigovernment union march on May 1, 1987. Despite a sit-in by their mothers in the Cathedral that month, they remain disappeared.

    c. Eliseo Cordova Aguilar, member of the Social Security Institute Workers Union (STISSS), was disappeared after capture near San Salvador in July 1988. The two men captured with him were released. A source reported seeing him inside the Treasury Police, which denied his detention. He has not been seen again.

III. VIOLATIONS BY DEATH SQUADS

Throughout most of 1989, the number of civilians killed by death squads declined from 1988. Tutela Legal recorded 43 death squad killings in 1989, down from 60 in 1988.* Nonetheless, in 1989, death squads adopted a higher public profile for the first time in several years, adding to the impression that they could operate freely without fear of apprehension or prosecution. In total, nine death squads issued communiques in 1989, including older groups such as the Maximiliano Hernandez Brigade and the Ghost Busters Command, and new organizations, such as the Central American Anti-Communist Hand (MACA), the Eastern Solidarity Committee (COSOR) and the Democratic Defense Commands (CDD). The links between uniformed government forces and the death squads were demonstrated in the case of two students of the Santa Ana campus of the National University who were abducted from their house near Cine Colon in Santa Ana at 6:30 p.m. on January 15, 1989, by seven armed plainclothesmen and another man in a black uniform. Jacqueline Astrid Hernandez, 21, a law student, and Victor de Jesus Ramos Urrutia, 22, general secretary of a students' organization (SECUO), were taken to the Second Infantry Brigade barracks in Santa Ana, and transferred to Treasury Police headquarters for "investigations." They were charged with being part of an urban guerrilla command unit. On January 17, then-Minister of Defense General Carlos Eugenio Vides Casanova and two other high military officials told the university rector that the students were in the custody of the security forces. Shortly thereafter, two local radio stations broadcast a

---

* See statistics at Appendix C.

communique from ARDE, the Revolutionary Anticommunist Action for Extermination, asserting that ARDE was holding the two students and might kill them.

In March 1989, an anti-communist organization called the "Democratic Defense Commands" threatened members of the FMLN-FDR and stated,

> For every case in which a civilian or a military non-combatant is assassinated... we will respond by executing a collaborator or an ally of the FMLN from among the leaders of the UNTS, the National University and similar groups.... And similarly, for every act of sabotage against public offices and services, private businesses and private homes, we will respond with an act of sabotage against the buildings of the UNTS, the National University and the homes of persons allied with the FMLN.*

On September 7, 1989, ARDE issued a death threat over _Radio Chaparrastique_ in San Miguel against several persons, including Inmar Rolando Reyes Flores, 32, Treasurer of the Association of Treasury Ministry Employees (AGEMHA). Eight days later Reyes was captured by Cavalry Regiment soldiers and brought to the Third Brigade, where he was tortured and later released. (See Chapter on Torture)

In October 1989, Cesar Vielman Joya Martinez, formerly a soldier with the intelligence section of the First Infantry Brigade, asserted publicly that he had participated in a death squad which operated out of the Brigade. Joya Martinez, who is a fugitive from justice and is charged with murder in the Tres Ceibas case reported above, alleged that the work of the death squad, which undertook numerous murders, was facilitated by U.S. advisors' funds for cars, safe houses, and payments to informants. These contentions were denied by the Salvadoran military.

The apparent death squad killing in Guatemala of Salvadoran opposition leader Hector Oqueli in January 1990 sparked concern that paramilitary

---

*   Tutela Legal Report, Mar. 10-16, 1989.

forces were operating with impunity beyond the Salvadoran border. In November 1989, Guatemalan President Vinicio Cerezo and Guatemalan Defense Minister General Hector Gramajo told reporters that Roberto D'Aubuisson and other ARENA officials had arranged weapons shipments to Guatemalan rightists from El Salvador.*

A. Death Squad Cases Occurring In and Around Santa Ana

Santa Ana always has had the reputation as an area where the death squads and right-wing paramilitaries are particularly strong. Many persons targeted in the last 18 months are unionists associated with the coffee industry, the source of great wealth -- for the owners -- in this western part of El Salvador.

1. Sonia Elizabeth Flores Martinez

On November 16, 1988, an armed plainclothesman fatally shot Sonia Elizabeth Flores Martinez, 27, Secretary of Assistance and Social Planning of SICAFE, the coffee workers' union. The man followed Flores as she left work at the Santa Ana INCAFE coffee processing plant with a friend about 5:00 p.m. and shot her. She died at the Social Security Hospital in Santa Ana about an hour later. Coworkers reported to Tutela Legal that Flores had previously received warnings to leave her work, and questions which asked which she preferred, her life or the union. They said she had been followed home from work previously.

2. Pablo Obdulio Vargas Carcamo

Pablo Obdulio Vargas Carcamo, 29, was secretary of organization of the SICAFE (coffee workers union) local in Chalchuapa, Santa Ana, and secretary of organization of SICAFE's western regional board. On April 8, 1988, Vargas began receiving frequent telephone death threats against himself and other SICAFE members from a voice identifying itself as ARDE, the Revolutionary Anti-Communist Extermination Action. Because of these threats, SICAFE members did not hold an assembly on April 16, as planned, to elect a new board.

---

* "Guatemala Chief Links Salvador Party to Attacks," San Francisco Chronicle, reprinted from The Baltimore Sun, November 11, 1989.

After April 16, Vargas received four more telephone death threats from the same voice, directed at him as secretary of organization. The caller threatened to kill Vargas and his family and told him to leave the country. The caller accused SICAFE of being an FMLN front group.

Vargas told his fellow union members that he was thinking of leaving the country because of these threats, as soon as the new oard was elected. On May 11, 1989, Vargas was shot and killed on a street corner in Barrio Las Animas, Chalchuapa, Santa Ana, by two young men who were just shooting in the air until they spotted him walking toward them, according to Tutela Legal.

Later that evening another SICAFE member received an anonymous call inquiring if Vargas was dead or alive. When the respondent said he was dead, the voice signalled approval.

3. Attempted Murder of Manuel Antonio Perez

On May 11, 1989, the same day that Pablo Obdulio Vargas Carcamo was killed by a death squad in Chalchuapa, Manuel Antonio Perez, Press Secretary of SICAFE's Santa Ana local, was shot and injured in Santa Ana, in front of the same INCAFE processing plant where Sonia Elizabeth Flores was killed in November 1988. Perez, interviewed by Americas Watch, reported that a witness to his shooting was later threatened.

4. Temporary Disappearance of Four Affiliated with the Santa Ana Campus of the National University and One Unionist

Four persons connected with the Santa Ana campus of the National University disappeared in July and August 1989. Cecilia del Carmen Rodriguez, a professor, was abducted on July 11 by unknown armed persons; she was freed on August 29. David Antonio Guevara Toledo, a student, was kidnapped on August 6 and reappeared on August 31.

Jose Adolfo Lima, a student at the university and son of UNTS leader Marco Tulio Lima, and Santiago Martinez Centeno, a university driver, disappeared on August 11. They reappeared on August 31, after an international campaign had been mounted on their behalf. Lima claimed he had been beaten and threatened with death. (See Chapter on Torture)

Jose Antonio Chavez Lafaro, a member of ASTIRA, an association of workers at the government's food supply and price control institute, was arrested in late July and released in late August. Many accused the Army Second

Brigade, based in Santa Ana, of kidnapping and holding them against their will. The commanding officer denied responsibility for the disappearances.

5. Attempted Murder of Mario Roberto Alvarez

Mario Roberto Alvarez, 31, Secretary General of the Santa Ana local of the SICAFE coffee workers union, left work December 5 at about 5:00 p.m. and rode home on his bicycle. He was one block away from his house in *Colonia* Santa Marina, Final 6a Calle Oriente, when, Alvarez told Americas Watch, a man in civilian clothing and a red baseball cap carrying a briefcase approached him, pulled out a gun, and told him to stop. The man appeared to be alone. Neighbors later told the family he had been waiting for a while in the neighborhood that afternoon.

Pointing the gun at Alvarez's head, the man said, "Show me your documents." Alvarez showed him a Social Security card with his name and photograph on it. The man looked at the card, briefly took off his sunglasses to compare Alvarez's face and the photograph, then said, "You're the one." As Alvarez raised his right hand in defense, the man shot at Alvarez. A bullet entered his hand, and Alvarez fell off the bicycle and lay on the ground. The assailant continued to shoot. Alvarez was hit by a total of six 9 mm. bullets -- in the right hand, the left testicle, the right knee (fractured), and the left foot (fractured).

Alvarez told Americas Watch that he faked being dead but never lost consciousness. During hospitalization, a doctor told him his life was saved by his girth, that most other men would have died from the attack. Alvarez has been Secretary General of the SICAFE local in Santa Ana for the past three years.

6. Unidentified Men, Found November 1989

The bodies of two unidentified men, both about 24 years old, were found on November 28, 1989, in canton Monte Largo, about 500 meters from the highway from Santa Ana to Chalchuapa, in the jurisdiction and department of Santa Ana. Both had bullets in the head and burns on the body and head. The second had thumbs tied behind him. Tutela Legal blamed a death squad.

7. Angel Maria Flores Aragon, Julia del Carmen Ponce Flores, and an Unidentified Male

Angel Maria Flores Aragon, 25, was shopping in Chalchuapa, Santa Ana, with Julia del Carmen Ponce Flores, 24, an employee of FEDECOOPADES in Chalchuapa, when four plainclothesmen captured them at 12:10 p.m. on December 31, 1989. Their unidentified bodies were found on January 10, 1990, at kilometer 55-56 and kilometer 56, respectively, of the Panamerican Highway from Santa Ana to San Salvador, in Coatepeque, Santa Ana. His body had two bullet wounds and it appeared that his wrists had been tied. Coagulated blood stains were found 100 meters from the body. The victim had been killed elsewhere and dumped where it was found. The body was exhumed and identified on January 26, 1990.* The body of Ponce Flores had been shot twice and had lacerations around the nipple, thorax and umbilical region. It was exhumed and identified on January 29.** Tutela Legal held a death squad responsible.

On the same day, the body of an unidentified man, about 45, was found nearby, at kilometer 54-55 on the Panamerican Highway from Santa Ana to San Salvador. The wrists showed signs of having been tied for a long time. There were two bullet wounds. The body, which had been killed elsewhere and dumped there, had a burn mark on the inside of the left forearm. Tutela Legal held a death squad responsible.

8. Jose Armando Acevedo Acevedo

Acevedo Acevedo, 48, a teacher and resident of *canton* Cojucuyo, Texistepeque, Santa Ana, was shot and killed by armed men in civilian clothing on January 30, 1990. Acevedo was at home watching television in the evening, when two armed men in plainclothes entered the house, each carrying a 9 mm. caliber firearm. The two men grabbed Acevedo by the arm, dragged him out of his house and headed toward the street. One of Acevedo's daughters clung to her father with her arms around his neck and pleaded with the men not to take him away. One of the men suddenly shot Acevedo in the

---

*   Tutela Legal Report, January 5-11, 1990; Diario Latino, January 30, 1990.

** Diario Latino, January 30, 1990.

head, killing him. and left him in front of the house. A pickup truck pulled up in front of the house, the two men jumped inside, and the vehicle drove off towards the city of Santa Ana. Tutela Legal held a death squad responsible.

9. Unidentified Man

The body of an unidentified man, 21, was found on February 3, 1990, at kilometer 57-56 of the Antigua Carretera Panamericana from Santa Ana to San Salvador, near canton Conacaste, known as Las Vueltas Del Pezote, jurisdiction of Coatepeque, department of Santa Ana. The body was found about two meters from the road covered with dry trash, and had been shot in the left eye, no exit wound, with blows to the forehead. He was killed in another place, according to the investigation by Tutela Legal.

B. January-February 1990 Death Squad Activities

Ten bodies found in a period of four weeks in early 1990 were the victims of death squads, according to Tutela Legal.

In addition to the five Santa Ana bodies (three, including two FEDECOOPADES associates, on January 10; a teacher in Texistepeque, on January 30; and an unknown man near Coatepeque on February 3), there were another two unidentified bodies found together in La Paz and three in San Vicente within two days in late January, attributable to death squads.

1. Two Unidentified Young Men

The bodies of two unknown boys approximately 15 and 17 years of age were found on January 31, 1990, in a cane field near kilometers 50-51 of the Autopista Sur highway running from San Salvador to Zacatecoluca, in *canton* San Jose Obrajito, Santiago Nonualco, La Paz. Both bodies had been burned; an odor of gasoline remained. Marks and scabs were visible on the neck of each cadaver. The bodies were dressed only in underpants. The younger boy had three bullet wounds and had apparently been beaten about the mouth. The victims were apparently dead when tossed into the ditch and burned there. Neighbors said no guerrillas had been seen in the area for several days. Army soldiers had been seen patrolling the area. Tutela Legal held a death squad responsible.

2. Three Unidentified Men

The bodies of three unknown men, two about 30 and one about 22, were found on the morning of January 31, 1990 in an empty field in *canton* San

Isidro, Villa Verapaz, San Vicente. The bodies were dressed only in underpants and bore burn marks and signs that they had been tied with a rope around the neck. The body of the youngest man had a .38 caliber bullet wound in the mouth. The second body had a .38 caliber bullet wound near the left ear. The third body had a .38 caliber bullet wound in the back of the head. Tutela Legal held a death squad responsible.

C. Other Death Squad Cases

1. Schoolteacher Maria Cristina Gomez Gonzalez

Maria Cristina Gomez Gonzalez was a 41-year-old mother of four children, a second-grade schoolteacher, a women's rights activist and a member of the ANDES *21 de Junio* teachers' union. Precisely because she was not a prominent opposition figure, her abduction and murder by death squads in broad daylight was seen as a signal that involvement in popular organizations at any level is dangerous.

Gomez was abducted by two heavily armed men in civilian clothes at 11:25 a.m. on April 5, 1989, as she was leaving the morning session of classes at the John F. Kennedy elementary school in Ilopango, on the outskirts of San Salvador. In front of a multitude of students and teachers, Gomez was pushed into a grey Cherokee car with polarized windows, and the vehicle sped away.

An hour later, on the opposite side of town, she was tossed from the same car and was shot in the back and the head as she fell to the street. Her mouth was gagged, leading many to conclude that this action was undertaken not to obtain information, but to terrorize the civilian population. Acid on her back and markings around her left eye indicated she might have been tortured.

2. Attempted Abduction of Church Worker

About 11:20 A.M. on January 23, 1990, a male employee of the Social Communications office of the Catholic Church and of the YSAX church radio station left the Archdiocese building in Urbanizacion La Esperanza, two blocks from the U.S. Embassy, and saw National Guardsmen on the street. When the man began to walk in the direction of the Embassy, a brown Nissan vehicle with darkened windows drove against the traffic on the one-way street and pulled up alongside him. Two men in civilian clothing, armed with pistols, jumped out, and one said, "Here is the son of a bitch; we've been looking for you." Two other men in camouflage uniform stayed inside the car. One, pointing his pistol at the church employee, said, "Don't run." The employee nevertheless took off running down the street, and escaped by boarding a nearby bus. He was not pursued.*

---

*   Churchworker Report, "Attacks on the Churches in El Salvador," December 16, 1989 - February 10, 1990.

IV. VIOLATIONS OF THE RULES OF WAR BY THE FMLN AND ATTACKS ON THE RIGHT

A. Targeted Urban Attacks

Civilians are not proper military targets under the rules of war. In the course of 1989, however, the FMLN engaged in a series of targeted killings of prominent civilian government officials and right-wing figures, in violation of these rules.*

While the FMLN has excused these killings on the grounds that the FMLN tries persons for crimes and imposes the death penalty only following due process, we have found little evidence that the FMLN procedures meet the due process criteria of common article 3 of the Geneva Conventions or Article 6 of Protocol II additional to the Geneva Conventions, applicable in El Salvador and binding on the FMLN. In many, if not most, of the cases of killings by the FMLN, as the examples below illustrate, there is little, if any, time between the capture of the victim and his execution. Therefore there is no time for the victim to defend himself and be heard, one of the most fundamental aspects of due process.

Perhaps because the targets chosen were not proper military targets, in many cases of FMLN assassinations in 1989, the FMLN did not acknowledge responsibility publicly. For instance, the FMLN publicly denied responsibility for the Francisco Peccorini Letona killing on March 15, 1989, and never commented on the assassination of the Attorney General Roberto Garcia Alvarado

---

* The total number of civilian victims of FMLN targeted and indiscriminate attacks (not counting land mines) in the first ten months of 1989 was 34. See Appendix C.

on April 19, 1989. In meetings with Americas Watch in May and June, 1989, FMLN officials categorically denied that the FMLN was responsible for either action.

However, Americas Watch confirmed that the Armed Forces of Liberation (FAL), the armed wing of the Communist Party and one of the five FMLN groups, committed both of these assassinations. In a July 7, 1989 interview with Lindsey Gruson of The New York Times, FMLN Commander Ana Guadalupe Martinez conceded that FMLN forces were responsible for the assassinations of Peccorini and the Attorney General. Douglas Farah wrote in The Washington Post on May 25, 1989:

> two knowledgeable leftists said the spate of killings of well-known rightists, including that of former attorney general Roberto Garcia Alvarado April 19, were carried out by commandos of one guerrilla faction without prior approval of the high command. The murders reportedly angered the four other factions, who feared a political backlash.*

It appears that the General Command of the FMLN did not order the assassinations and did not take credit for them because it retroactively did not approve of them. This creates the impression that the FMLN is unable to agree internally on strategy, leaving at least one of the five political-military groups to commit illegal assassinations of civilian political figures while others abstain from and disagree with that policy.

The FMLN is said to have had a series of internal meetings in May 1989 after the public backlash caused by the killing of the Attorney General, as a result of which the FMLN broadcast a communique outlining new instructions for its combatants on its clandestine Radio Venceremos on May 25, 1989. These instructions said that FMLN "actions should be publicly admitted in order to avoid confusion with the proceedings of dirty war that the enemy conducts." It also emphasized that in executions (*ajusticiamientos*), an exhaustive investigation should be conducted to confirm that the target is an enemy of the people.

---

* Douglas Farah, "Salvadoran Rebels Apologize for Civilian Deaths," The Washington Post, May 25, 1989.

Shortly after this communique was published, Jose Alejandro Antonio Rodriguez Porth, just named Minister of the Presidency in the nine-day-old ARENA administration, was assassinated. After a delay, the FMLN denied responsibility.

When the former Supreme Court President Francisco Jose Guerrero was assassinated by the FMLN in late November, one of his alleged assailants was killed and the other wounded, and their guns captured. The Attorney General, Mauricio Eduardo Colorado, claimed that that the gun that killed Guerrero has been shown by ballistics tests to be the same gun that was used in the earlier 1989 killings of conservatives Edgar Chacon, Gabriel Payes, and Francisco Peccorini,* the last of whom the FMLN privately admits killing. The government accuses the wounded prisoner of belonging to the Popular Forces of Liberation (FPL) of the FMLN; it was our understanding that the FAL carried out the Peccorini killing.

The Treasury Police captured an alleged FMLN commander on December 29, 1989, conveniently attributing to him every assassination of any importance in 1989: Castellanos, Peccorini, Rodriguez Porth, Chacon, Payes, Guerrero, and the daughter of Colonel Casanova Vejar. The accused, Pablo Salvador Carcamo Centeno, 27, refused to make any statement while in administrative detention and denied guilt when charged before the military judge, according to the press.** Although it is our information that the FAL carried out the Peccorini killing, Carcamo is accused of belonging to the FPL.

Over the past two years, Americas Watch has met with FMLN officials on several occasions, and at each meeting different officials have put forth a different conception of FMLN policy with respect to attacks on civilians. They have said, alternatively, that 1) since 1984, the FMLN has required that there be consultation with the "nearest command" before any execution could be undertaken; 2) such a policy requiring approval of executions by the next-highest level of authority was implemented beginning in January 1988; 3) after the assassinations of Peccorini and the Attorney General the FMLN estab-

---

* El Diario de Hoy, December 6, 1989; La Prensa Grafica, December 7, 1989.

** Diario de Hoy, January 13, 1990 (name given as Pablo Salvador Medrano); Diario Latino, January 10, 1990; El Mundo, January 10, 1990.

lished a policy which prohibits the assassination of civilian figures absent opportunity for trial in accord with internationally recognized standards of due process; 4) such a policy has been in force since 1988; and 5) no such policy exists or has ever existed.

If FMLN policy with respect to the killings of civilians remains unclear, international law on the subject is unequivocal: such summary executions of civilians are illegal. We call on the FMLN to abandon such tactics and punish all offenders.

We expect that such executions will not continue to occur at this time; as a gesture of good will and in order to encourage the opening of the political space in El Salvador, the FMLN announced that as of March 16, 1990, it would no longer target civilians or government employees who did not participate in military activities.

At the same time the FMLN announced it would cease sabotage of public transport, commercial establishments, and telephone lines. Such sabotage is a violation of the rules of war insofar as none of these objectives are military, with the exception of certain telephone lines.

The following cases are the most prominent of the targeted urban attacks occurring in 1989.

1. Miguel Castellanos

Miguel Castellanos (whose real name was Napoleon Romero Garcia), 39, a commander of the FPL who switched sides after his capture by the army in 1985, was shot dead by the FMLN at 6:30 p.m. on February 16, 1989, as he was leaving his office in the Center for Studies of the National Reality (CEREN) in *Colonia* Flor Blanca, San Salvador. He was an editor of the journal *Analisis* at the time of his death. One of Castellano's bodyguards was seriously injured.

The FMLN took credit for having killed "the traitor to the people's interests." The FMLN claimed that Castellanos was a military target because he had collaborated with the army and caused the deaths of many people. He undeniably collaborated with the army and the government, no doubt providing extensive intelligence on people and methods used by the FMLN.*

---

* He even participated on behalf of the government (and the U.S. administration) in the debate over U.S. aid to the Nicaraguan contra rebels by testifying to members of the U.S. administration, as a former FMLN commander, about the aid sent from the Nicaraguan Sandinista government to the FMLN.

However, he was not a military target because he was not a member of the armed forces of a party to the conflict nor was he participating in hostilities at the time of the ambush.

2. Francisco Peccorini Letona

Peccorini, 72, a conservative public figure, was shot in his car as it was nearing the Deluxe Cinema in San Salvador at 11:00 a.m. on March 15, 1989; he died later in the Military Hospital. The FMLN admitted privately that a FAL unit was responsible, although denying any FMLN involvement publicly.

Peccorini was a dual U.S.-Salvadoran citizen who had returned to live in El Salvador. A Jesuit priest from 1949 to 1964 when he retired in order to marry, he was an academic who had written numerous books and was Professor Emeritus in Philosophy at California State University in Long Beach.* He was often featured as a panelist on Salvadoran TV, usually defending the most extreme right-wing position.

Peccorini was also a member of the Committee for the Rescue of the University of El Salvador, a committee created to rid the University of communist influence.His assassination occurred only days after the March 10, 1989 shooting at the car of Antonio Rafael Mendez, also a member of the Committee to Rescue the University of El Salvador, wounding his colleague Gladis Larromana and a bodyguard. It appears that this was the responsibility of the FAL as well.**

The government claims that it has recovered the FMLN gun used in the killing and that it separately captured one of the FMLN planners of the assassination.

---

* El Mundo, March 17, 1989; La Prensa Grafica, March 16, 1989.

** This was the second attack on Mendez, the first being a grenade attack on his son Jose Maria Mendez Llort, 19, injuring him and a woman on November 25, 1988.

3. Attorney General Jose Roberto Garcia Alvarado

On April 19, 1989, at 7:30 a.m., Attorney General Garcia Alvarado was killed at an intersection in San Salvador when unknown men placed a powerful explosive on top of his armored vehicle, just above the place where he was sitting. The explosion ripped through his body, killing him instantly. It was so precisely targeted that it only slightly injured his driver and bodyguards. The FMLN privately admitted the killing, again the responsibility of the FAL.

Garcia was the second attorney general to be murdered in El Salvador in the last decade. Christian Democrat Attorney General Mario Zamora was assassinated in March 1980 by death squads.*

4. Possible Responsibility for Assassination of Minister of the Presidency Rodriguez Porth

Jose Alejandro Antonio Rodriguez Porth, 74, Minister of the Presidency, was killed with his driver, Juan Gilberto Clara Carranza, and orderly, Benjamin Perez Jimenez, by shots a man fired at Rodriguez Porth in front of his home in San Salvador at 8:15 a.m. on June 9, 1989. The three victims, all of whom were unarmed, were preparing to leave for the Presidential Palace. The assailant escaped on a motorbike.**

Rodriguez Porth was a founder of ARENA and one of its most important leaders; he was one of the few in the incoming administration with prior government experience and was regarded as a senior figure and valued counselor. A staunch supporter of free enterprise, he was also known as a proponent of dialogue between the government and the FMLN, and had been designated to be the ranking government representative at any such negotiations.

He was probably best known to the public during the Duarte presidency for his frequent denunciations of Duarte as a Communist dupe. Rodriguez Porth was a close friend of Peccorini.***

---

*   His brother, Ruben Zamora, and others in the Christian Democratic Party left the party to form the Popular Social Christian Movement (MPSC) partly in reaction to the inability of the Christian Democrats in the junta to protect against such human rights abuses. Mario Zamora's widow, Aronette Diaz, is now president of the National Democratic Union (UDN).

**   Kenneth Freed, "Chief of Staff . . . ," The Los Angeles Times.

***   Kenneth Freed, "Chief of Staff to Salvador's New Leader Is Slain," The Los Angeles Times, June 10, 1989.

The top-level assassination severely shook the new administration of President Cristiani, then only nine days old.

After a delay of several days, the FMLN publicly denied responsibility for this crime. In connection with the denials, FMLN spokespersons privately admitted the previous killings of Peccorini and the Attorney General and said that as a result of FMLN meetings held after those killings, the strict policy of the FMLN was promptly to admit all assassinations.

Based on the pattern of assassinations before and after this killing, however, it appears likely that the FMLN is indeed responsible. A military court is now trying Pedro Carcamo Centeno, accused of being the FMLN planner of the killing, a charge he denies.*

5. Possible Responsibility for the Assassination of Edgar Chacon

Edgar Chacon, 38, a well-known anticommunist and president of the Institute of International Relations, was shot on June 30, 1989, at 2:50 p.m. in his car at a traffic light in San Salvador; his wife, at his side, survived.

An extreme rightist, Chacon had broken with ARENA because he believed it had abandoned its anticommunist principles. He had helped form the Patriotic Civil Defense, which was sworn in in May 1989 at the First Brigade. Amid controversy about the arming of right-wing paramilitary groups, potential death squads, by the army, the Patriotic Civil Defense was then supposedly deauthorized by the army.**

The FMLN denied the army's accusations that it was responsible for the assassination.*** As noted above, the government claims that it has recovered the FMLN gun used in the killing and that it separately captured one of the FMLN planners of the assassination.

---

*   Diario de Hoy, January 13, 1990 (name given as Pablo Salvador Medrano); Diario Latino, January 10, 1990; El Mundo, January 10, 1990.

** El Diario Latino, July 1, 1989; La Prensa Grafica, July 1, 1989.

*** El Diario Latino, July 3, 1989.

6. Possible Responsibility for the Assassination of Gabriel Payes

Gabriel Payes, 38, a computer specialist and president of the Association of Professionals of El Salvador, was shot on July 19 when he was entering the Moore Business Center in San Salvador. He unsuccessfully attempted to defend himself with his gun. He was taken to the Hospital Zaldivar, and later transferred to the Military Hospital, where he died of his wounds on August 22, 1989.*

Payes was a close friend and associate of Chacon in the formation of the Patriotic Civil Defense. He was also a member of Chacon's Institute of International Relations.**

As noted above, the police claim that the gun used by the FMLN in the assassination of Dr. Guerrero was shown by ballistics tests to be the one that killed Payes as well, and FMLN member Pedro Carcamo Centeno is now accused before the military court of planning this assassination.

7. Former Supreme Court President Francisco Jose Guerrero

On November 28, 1989, Francisco Jose (Chachi) Guerrero, 64, former president of the Supreme Court (1984-89), presidential candidate (1984) and Foreign Minister, was shot in his car at an intersection in San Salvador on the Boulevard Los Heroes near the Biggest fast food restaurant. Three of the six bullets that hit the car struck him.*** He died shortly thereafter, as did one of the attackers.****

---

*   La Prensa Grafica, August 23, 1989.

**   Diario de Hoy, July 20, 1989; El Mundo, July 19, 1989.

*** El Mundo, November 28, 1989.

**** Ana Arana, "Politician killed in Salvador," The Miami Herald, November 30, 1989; Lindsey Gruson, "Prominent Rightist Slain in El Salvador," The New York Times, November 29, 1989.

His bodyguard and a driver were wounded, as was one of the alleged attackers, Ernesto Erazo Cruz, from whom the police later took a statement implicating the FMLN. Erazo Cruz, in jail awaiting trial, is said by the police to be a University of El Salvador student and member of the FPL.*

We have testimony from an eyewitness that indicates that Guerrero's killing was a targeted assassination. According to the eyewitness, who was in a raised four-wheeled drive vehicle with a clear view of the intersection, Guerrero's car was the first car at the stoplight, followed by a car that seemed to belong to his security, followed by a taxi, followed by this four-wheeled vehicle. It was Guerrero's car that was targeted; the assailants approached it and shot the driver, who was Dr. Guerrero. Then the second car started shooting at the assailants. Because of the rapidity with which the assailants shot the driver, the impression of the eyewitness was this was not a robbery. Persons having their car stolen rarely resist and robbers rarely if ever resort to shooting the driver to complete a car robbery in a busy intersection.

The FMLN, while not admitting that the person in custody committed the act, has claimed to various people that the Guerrero killing was an accident and that the intention was to requisition another automobile for military use, a common FMLN practice. The car which was sought for guerrilla expropriation was stopped at a traffic light. (According to this version, which contradicts the eyewitness testimony, the car carrying Guerrero was not the first car at the light but the one right behind it.) As one of the guerrillas stood guard at the side of the road, the other one approached the targeted car and, pointing a gun in the side window, made the request. Upon seeing this, a Guerrero security man in Guerrero's car behind the targeted car got involved in the robbery attempt by shooting and killing the guerrilla making the demand. The guerrilla standing guard then fired at Guerrero's car and killed Guerrero. The man now in custody was wounded by a shot fired by one of Guerrero's bodyguards.

The FMLN claims that the guerrillas involved in the auto requisition operation did not know Guerrero was in a nearby car. Even if this were a botched holdup, it is a violation of the rules of war. A traffic intersection is not

---

*   El Diario de Hoy, December 6, 1989.

a combat zone and civilian casualties there are foreseeable. The killing of a civilian in a civilian zone is indiscriminate under the facts of this case and shows a failure to take proper care to avoid collateral civilian casualties.

B. FMLN Attacks and Attacks by Unknown Parties on the Right in San Salvador

The ARENA party started in 1981 as a paramilitary response to the communist threat about to engulf El Salvador, and metamorphosed after electoral setbacks into a party that with stunning success incorporated the business and propertied classes into politics. Despite U.S. backing for the people and the centrist-right reform programs of the Christian Democrats, who controlled the Assembly from 1985 to 1988 and the Presidency from 1984 to 1989, ARENA in 1989 won control of all three branches of government. In the March 1988 legislative and municipal elections, ARENA won a one-person majority in the 60-person Legislative Assembly and a majority of the municipalities, all three-year terms. In the March 1989 presidential elections, ARENA won the six-year presidency. In July 1989 the ARENA-dominated Assembly named a new Supreme Court to serve for the constitutional five-year period, the new magistrates being more conservative, among them prominent ARENA members.

But control of the three branches of government was no guarantee that ARENA could govern the country nor even that its members and other conservatives could sleep in peace. Although the right did not have to fear arrests or assassination by the army or security forces, searches and destruction of its offices, or prohibitions on marches (these remain a significant problem for the left and continue to impede legitimate organizational activities), the right did face continued violence from the armed left, as well as common crimes directed at property.

In addition to the targeted attacks above, there also have been bombings and machinegun attacks on family members of the military and rightists. Attacks on these civilians and civilian structures such as homes and businesses are violations of the rules of war. They are not military targets.*

---

*   Export industries such as the coffee industry, whose earnings significantly contribute to the defense budget, are an exception to this prohibition on military attacks on commerce.

The FMLN has not taken responsibility for all of the attacks listed below. The insecurity they provoke nevertheless has lead many in the targeted classes to justify and some actively to foment violence against the unarmed left. Particularly chilling in view of the recent assassinations of the Jesuits is a tendency to blame priests for stirring up the poor and being the cause of the war.

January 9, 1989: FMLN commandos threw explosives into the Santa Tecla houses of two Armed Forces officials, Captain Vladimir Roberto Iglesias of the Arce Battalion, and Captain Miguel Angel Mojica, of the Air Force.

January 10, 1989: an FMLN bomb was placed in the house of Lieutenant Jose Alirio Sibrian in *Colonia* Las Cumbres, Antiguo Cuscatlan, La Libertad, which damaged the house and injured one person inside.

January 19, 1989: an FMLN bomb damaged the home of an Army official in the *Colonia* La Sultana, San Salvador.

January 21 and 22, 1989: the Urban Commandos of the FMLN dynamited a house of Lieutenant Hugo Vasquez Penate of the Air Force in *canton* Lourdes, Colon, department of La Libertad.

January 27, 1989: The house of the 75-year-old mother of General Eugenio Vides Casanova, Minister of Defense, was bombed by the FMLN in the *Colonia* Atlacatl, San Salvador, producing extensive damage but no injuries.

January 28, 1989: Club M nightclub in Escalon, San Salvador, frequented by foreigners, was the scene of an FMLN Urban Commando bomb explosion at 10:30 pm, injuring two people.

February 2, 1989: at 3:00 p.m., FMLN Commandos threw a bomb at the house of Francisco E. Granadino, director of the Electric Commission of the Rio Lempa, in the *Colonia* San Francisco, San Salvador.

February 3, 1989: unknown men in a car without plates or lights placed a powerful bomb in the door of the house of Gloria Salguero Gross, outspoken ARENA deputy for Santa Ana, which seriously damaged the house. No persons were injured.

February 7, 1989: two official cars and one private car in front of the Office of Rural Development of the Ministry of Agriculture in *Colonia* San Jose, San Salvador, were damaged by a bomb placed by unknown persons.

February 16, 1989: a bomb was thrown from a moving taxi by the FMLN at the house of an Army officer in *Colonia* La Sultana, San Salvador.

February 16, 1989: Miguel Castellanos, assassinated by FMLN. (See above) March 10, 1989: FMLN shot at car of Antonio Rafael Mendez, wounding two. (See above)

March 15, 1989: Francisco Peccorini Letona, 72, assassinated by FMLN. (See above)

March 28, 1989: the FMLN placed a bomb at a beauty parlor which had earlier been a house of prostitution. On March 29 the FMLN launched a LOW at a house of prostitution.

April 5, 1989: Carlos Ernesto Mendoza, like Miguel Castellanos an editor of the magazine *Analisis*, was gravely wounded in San Salvador when an unknown man placed a bomb in his car, parked at his house. His right forearm was destroyed and he had serious wounds to the head, thorax and abdomen. The University of New San Salvador decided the next day in an emergency session to suspend publication of *Analisis*, in order to avoid new losses of intellectuals. *Analisis* had been published since January 1988 by the Institute of Scientific Investigations of that university.* April 14, 1989: Vice President-elect Jose Francisco Merino Lopez's home in *Colonia* Maquilishuat, San Salvador, was bombed at 5:30 a.m. when men in two cars threw three pieces of dynamite at the house, slightly injuring a niece and seriously damaging the house. The men who threw the bomb opened fire on the armed guards of the house. Merino and his wife were not home, but four of their minor children and three nieces and nephews were asleep inside. The FMLN publicly denied but later privately admitted the act.

April 19, 1989: at 7:30 am, Jose Roberto Garcia Alvarado, Attorney General, assassinated by FMLN. (See above)

May 2, 1989: a bomb was thrown on the roof of the warehouse of the U.S. Embassy, in San Salvador.

May 16, 1989: in an attack on the San Salvador residence of ARENA Assembly President Ricardo Alvarenga Valdivieso one guard was killed.

June 9, 1989: Jose Alejandro Antonio Rodriguez Porth, Minister of the Presidency, assassinated, probably by FMLN. (See above)

---

*   Diario de Hoy, April 8, 1989; Diario de Hou, April 7, 1989.

June 30, 1989: Edgar Chacon, 38, well-known anticommunist promoter of paramilitary groups and president of the Institute of International Relations, was shot in his car in San Salvador and died shortly thereafter. The FMLN denied responsibility but is the likely author.

July 3, 1989: the FMLN attacked an urban area where military families live, killing one armed officer defending his home.

July 4, 1989: Jose Victor Montova, watchman at the Banco de Fomento Agropecuario in San Salvador, was shot dead by the FMLN which claimed that death squad vehicles left from those offices.

July 4, 1989: bodyguard Serapio Antonio Mata and Violeta Eugenia Posada Urrutia were killed in an indiscriminate FMLN attack at an FMLN roadblock on the road from the beach, wounding at least three other civilians, one of who was the recently-named President of the Supreme Court Mauricio Gutierrez Castro.

July 7, 1989: The security personnel of the office of ANEP (private enterprise association) were machinegunned, for which the FMLN took credit.

July 13, 1989: A car bomb was detonated by the FMLN at 6:00 a.m. at the Torre Democracia, the tallest building in San Salvador and one of the newest, blowing out the glass walls. The FMLN declared the capital a "zone in dispute."

July 19, 1989: Gabriel Payes fatally shot; he died on August 22. (See above)

September 26, 1989: 50 combatants of the FMLN attacked the command post in Planes de Renderos near San Salvador in the evening, after which they asked for and located the house of the family of Colonel Mauricio Ernesto Vargas, head of the Third Brigade in San Miguel. They shot at and damaged the house but injured none of the relatives inside.

October 10, 1989: Edelmira Sanchez de Fuentes, 45, the wife of an editor of the rightist daily _El Diario de Hoy_, was killed and her son and mother wounded when their car was machinegunned by unknown persons in San Salvador. COPREFA blamed the crime on the FMLN saying that another son is an army officer.* The son, Oscar Rene Fuentes, 21, later died. The FMLN

---

* El Mundo, October 10, 1989; El Diario de Hoy, October 11, 1989; Reuters, "Journalist's wife killed in El Salvador," The Miami Herald, October 12, 1989.

denied responsibility and later the National Police said that possibly common criminals were responsible.

October 17, 1989: the daughter of Colonel Edgardo Casanova Vejar, Ana Isabel Casanova Porras, was killed on her 23d birthday when her car was hit with 60 bullets by unknown men in Santa Tecla. The army blamed the FMLN* and the FMLN denied responsibility, although a local radio station received a call a half hour after the killing, in which the FMLN Comandos Urbanos Modesto Ramirez took credit for the killing.**

November 28, 1989: Francisco Jose (Chachi) Guerrero, former president of the Supreme Court, killed by FMLN. (See above)

C. Targeted Assassinations in Rural Areas

For years prior to the November 1989 FMLN offensive in the cities, the war was waged in the rural areas. Targeted assassinations are used there by the FMLN as a way of combatting army infiltration and spying by civilians paid for information, and are usually admitted for the purpose of setting an example.

Many of the victims are civil defense members accused of abuses. Although the FMLN claims that it investigates and fairly tries those it sentences to death, it does not seem possible that the accused have any meaningful opportunity to establish their innocence. In most of the assassinations investigated by Tutela Legal listed below, there is simply no time after capture of the victim for due process. Such killings violate the requirements for due process of the Geneva Conventions and Protocol II.

January 1, 1989: Julio Martinez, 44; Demesio Santos, 58; and Walter Nelson Osorio Rivas, 16, all campesinos, in *canton* San Antonio, jurisdiction of Metapan, department of Santa Ana. On January 3, the bodies of the three were found nearby, with signs on the wrists of having been tied. On January 4, the FMLN held a meeting for the residents and told them that the three had been killed because they were paid informers for the military. The FMLN played a casette of the voices of the three men.

---

*   El Diario de Hoy, October 18, 1989.

**   El Diario de Hoy, October 19, 1989.

January 4, 1989: Orlando Orellana, 45, day laborer, in *caserio* Los Castro, *canton* Santa Rosa, Sesori, San Miguel, shot in the head after he failed to heed guerrilla summons to meet with them.

January 18, 1989: Jose Orlando Martinez Gutierrez, a 28-year old student, in *caserio* El Centro, *canton* Sitio Viejo, jurisdiction of Ilobasco, department of Cabanas.

January 26, 1989: Santiago Elias Pineda, 54, campesino, in Barrio Las Delicias, jurisdiction of El Carrizal, department of Chalatenango. When the guerrillas came for him, he asked them not to kill him in front of his children, but they hit him, ordering him to lie down on the ground. He refused, grabbed the gun of one of the guerrillas, and began to back out into the street. The guerrillas shot him, thinking he was escaping.

January 27, 1989: Ernesto Antonio Flores Serpas, 37, governor of Usulutan, in *canton* Llano Grande, jurisdiction of Jucuapa, department of Usulutan. He was captured at his home and shot outside immediately afterward, with a bullet in the head, two in the back, and one in the right arm. The FMLN took responsibility on Radio Venceremos. He had been mayor of Villa El Triunfo, Usulutan from 1985 to 1988, although the FMLN had asked him to resign from that position in 1986.

January 30, 1989: Hilda Portillo Pineda, 19, housewife, at 1:00 a.m., in Barrio El Carmen, jurisdiction of Dulce Nombre de Maria, department of Chalatenango. She had been shot in the neck, cheek, abdomen, and her right arm was completely destroyed by an explosive. Family members believed she was killed because she was too friendly with soldiers.

February 15-16, 1989: Simeon Tobar, 59, and Noel Tobar Rivas, 24, his son, in El Coyolito, Barrio Santa Rita, San Pedro Masahuat, La Paz, both farmers. Captured on February 15 in front of witnesses, their bodies were found on February 18 with bullets in the head and signs of having been beaten in the chest and other parts of the body. They had been civil defense patrollers.

March 29, 1989: Alfonso Mendez Peraza, 48, campesino, near *canton* Tahuilapa, jurisdiction of Metapan, Santa Ana. He was shot twice in the head and had signs of torture on his thumbs. The FMLN believed he was an informant for the Treasury Police in Metapan, and had caused many crimes. His body was found with a note from the FMLN taking responsibility for the killing.

April 10, 1989: Jose Alcides Romero Orellana, 23, member of the civil defense of Chapeltique, San Miguel, in San Sebastian, Sesori, San Miguel.

April 18, 1989: Eulalio Sibrian Lemus, age 60 and the commander of the civil defense patrol in *canton* Palacios, jurisdiction of Jutiapa, department of Cabanas, and two of his sons Antonio Sibrian Pena, age 25, and Jose Sibrian Pena, age 23, also members of the civil defense patrol, were killed by the FMLN after capture, their bodies found the next day three kilometers from their houses.

May 10, 1989: Jose Reyes Bolanos, 56; Encarnacion Perez Perez, 58; Simeon Parada, 38, all peasants. Reyes was the first cantonal commander of the canton Hacienda Vieja, San Pedro Nonualco, La Paz, and Perez was the second in command. They were captured on May 10 and the bodies of Bolanos and Perez were found the same day, shot with high caliber bullets. Later that day, after a clash with the army, the guerrillas came to the house of Parada, who had been obliged to participate in the civil defense of San Pedro Nonualco. The guerrillas made his wife cook tortillas, and lend them a hammock to move a wounded combatant. Parada brought back the hammock but then cried when he told his family he had to go off with the guerrillas and would return soon. The guerrillas brought him back briefly the next day; shortly thereafter the soldiers came in pursuit of the guerrillas but did not find them. His body was found on May 14. He had been decapitated and his thumbs amputed, with the hands tied behind. He had been shot in the back with firearms.

May 10, 1989: Hugo Samuel Bolanos Lopez, 20, ex-soldier, also killed in canton Hacienda Vieja, San Pedro Nonualco, La Paz. He was discharged in 1987 after he stepped on a guerrilla mine and incurred a foot injury. On May 10 at 8:00 a.m., he left home with his mother to go to a doctor's appointment. The guerrillas encountered him resting outside a neighbor's house and, in view of his mother, shot him three times, killing him.

May 22, 1989: Alejandro Torres Melara, 39, peasant, captured by name at his house during a guerrilla attack on the town at 4 am in Barrio El Calvario, Guazapa, San Salvador. His body was found the next morning.

June 6, 1989: Jose Plutarco Garcia Quintanilla, 19, student, and Hector Orlando Quintanilla Chavez, 25, peasant, killed five minutes after capture on June 6, 1989 in canton Piedra Azul, San Rafael Oriente, San Miguel. They were accused by the FMLN of raping five girls. Hector's family said he had been a soldier in Military Detachment Number 4 in San Francisco Gotera, Morazan, for seven years and that was the cause of his death.

June 7, 1989: Jose Antonio Morales Rosales, 38, civil defense member, killed near his home in barrio La Vega, Tamanique, La Libertad. He was captured on June 7, 1989 after a guerrilla attack on the local civil defense post. His body was found on June 10, with the hands still tied behind, with signs of having been strangled (no bullet holes, bruises on the neck), with the right arm badly broken. He belonged to the civil defense of Tamanique.

June 11, 1989: Juan Dario Echegoyen Leiva, 57, peasant, member of ARENA and ex-commandant of the civil defense patrol of the *canton* Concepcion, jurisdiction of Santa Maria Ostuma, La Paz, killed on June 11, 1989, by the FMLN. They gave his captured son the chance to embrace his father once, then released the son on the condition that he leave town within 72 hours. Echegoyen was then shot in the head.

June 14, 1989: Carlos Antonio Ayala Guzman, 39, farm administrator, captured on June 14 by the FMLN near Berlin, Usulutan. On June 15, his body was found near Berlin, with a bullet in the heart and a paper that said the FMLN killed him because he did not pay war tax, complained about it to the army, and robbed and mistreated the workers.

July 2, 1989: Manuel Antonio Martinez, 42, peasant, killed after he was captured by the FMLN on July 2, 1989, in *canton* San Sebastian, Zaragoza, La Libertad. The body was found on July 6 in Tablon Las Mesetas, *canton* El Barillo, Zaragoza, partly devoured by buzzards, with a bullet in the chest. He had just resigned from long time service as commander of the civil defense of Zaragoza.

August 17, 1989: Tomas de Jesus Velado Barillas, 27, farm worker, killed five minutes after capture by FMLN in Ochupse Abajo, Santa Ana; he had left the Second Infantry Brigade seven months before. August 23, 1989: Ricardo Regalado Morales, 66, municipal employee, and Rodrigo Zuniga Serrano, civil defense collaborator of Villa de Zaragoza, La Libertad. The FMLN, posing as Army, captured them the evening of August 23, shots were heard 10 minutes later, and the bodies were found nearby the next day.

December 5, 1989: Jorge Atilio Navarrete, 26, member of the Sixth Brigade, killed admittedly after capture by the FMLN while on leave in *canton* Vado Marin, El Transito, San Miguel, with a shot in the head. The FMLN, which delivered the body to the family for a wake, had been looking for Navarrete for a month.

D. Indiscriminate FMLN Military Attacks

Americas Watch has previously condemned the FMLN for using catapult bombs launched from vehicles, directed at military targets, but often resulting in loss of civilian life.* These homemade devices had an unreliable track record and often misfired, killing civilians in the vicinity rather than hitting the military target. While the FMLN, on February 27, 1989 announced a suspension of the use of these devices in cars in concentrated urban areas, other types of explosives have been used to devastating effect for nearby civilians. Americas Watch reiterates its call for the FMLN to abandon the use of such explosives in civilian areas, a practice which violates the laws of war.

These are some of the cases of civilian casualties caused by indiscriminate FMLN fire investigated by Tutela Legal.

1. February 21 Attack on First Brigade

Pedro Mauricio Hernandez, 75, and Maria Teresa de Hernandez, 70, were killed when a catapult bomb left by the FMLN urban commandos misfired near the barracks of the First Brigade, in San Salvador, on February 21, 1989.

2. Karina Lisseth Castillo

Karina Lisseth Castillo, 11, was killed on April 7, 1989 when a LOW rocket fell on her house during a FMLN attack on the National Police Battalion Zacamil in the neighborhood of the same name.

3. July 4 Attack on Cars Coming from the Beach

The FMLN stopped about 200 cars on the main highway from the beach to San Salvador on Sunday July 4, in order to talk about the revolution.

Some of the people coming from the beach had their bodyguards with them, and the FMLN in some cases shot at the bodyguards. The president of the Supreme Court, Dr. Mauricio Gutierrez Castro, was wounded, although it did not appear to be a targeted attack against him; as his car caught sight of what was going on and turned around, the FMLN caught sight of the armed bodyguard, Serapio Antonio Mata, and shot him dead.

---

*   See Americas Watch, Human Rights in El Salvador on the Eve of the March 1989 Elections, at 9.

Violeta Eugenia Posada Urrutia was killed in another car. She was also traveling with bodyguards who did not heed the order to halt. Two others in that car were wounded.

Americas Watch considers this incident, as described by Tutela Legal, an indiscriminate attack because the overwhelming number of people stopped at this FMLN roadblock were unarmed civilians. Bodyguards who are not members of the armed forces and who are not actively participating in hostilities are not military targets. It does not appear that these bodyguards shot at the FMLN.

There is no acceptable rationale for using deadly force against the occupants of a civilian car that backs away from a roadblock.

4. October 30 Attack on Armed Forces General Staff Headquarters

On October 30, 1989 FMLN guerrillas fired at least 16 shells from homemade mortars at the headquarters of the Armed Forces General Staff in San Salvador. These mortars were fired from two trucks parked in a shopping center. Most of the shells exploded in nearby streets, killing a gas station attendant and wounding at least 15 people. Colonel Ponce said that 30 unfired shells were found on two trucks from which the other shells had been launched, about 300 yards from the General Staff headquarters.*

5. November 1 Bombing of First Brigade

At 3:10 p.m. on November 1, 1989 two explosives were launched from a passing vehicle at the headquarters of the First Infantry Brigade in San Salvador. A civilian, Jose Hermogenes Martinez, 59, who was sitting in a parked car in front of the barracks, was killed. Another civilian, Maria del Carmen Perez, 36, was injured.**

---

* "Salvadoran Rebels Launch Mortar Attack," The Washington Post, October 31, 1989.

** El Rescate Chronology, Volume IV, No. 11, November 1989.

6. November 11 Attack on National Guard

The first military action of the FMLN November offensive was an attack early on November 11 on the National Guard headquarters in San Salvador. Guerrillas launched six homemade mortars at the National Guard barracks. One struck the installation, injuring three soldiers. Another mortar landed outside the barracks in a poor neighborhood surrounding it, killing two children and injuring five civilians. The mortars had been placed in three vehicles at the barracks' perimeter; one was deactivated before it exploded.*

E. Human Rights Violations during the Offensive: Update on Killing of Five Government Journalists

Our two reports issued during the November offensive identified numerous violations of international humanitarian law on the part of the FMLN. These included, apart from summary executions in violation of the right to life: illegally using civilians as shields in isolated instances; attacking Red Cross vehicles; misusing the Red Cross emblem on vehicles not employed primarily for medical purposes; and launching military attacks on hospitals and endangering patients and medical staff.

Our December 16 report described the November 29, 1989 operation in which an FMLN force attacked the offices of the National Center of Information (CIN) and five government journalists disappeared.** We noted that an exhumation of seven corpses discovered shortly thereafter had proven inconclusive,*** and called on the FMLN to account for the whereabouts of the missing newsmen.

The FMLN has since confirmed to Americas Watch that it did attack the CIN offices that day, after two guerrilla combatants were killed when they approached the building and one other guerrilla was shot and injured by someone inside the building. The FMLN concedes that its forces killed six persons

---

* "Salvadoran Rebels Attack in Capital," The Washington Post, November 12, 1989; Marjorie Miller, "Battle Rages in Salvador Capital," The Los Angeles Times, November 13, 1989.

** The five journalists were Anibal Dubon, Alfredo Melgar, Alibardo Quejado Lopez, Jose Ceballos and Oscar Herrera. See Americas Watch, Update on El Salvador, at 22-24.

*** At a second exhumation conducted January 26, 1990, forensic specialists concluded that none of the journalists were among the corpses described above.

in the course of this attack, all of whom were killed in or near the CIN offices. The FMLN says it does not know the identity of the six killed.

International journalists who saw five bodies together near the CIN offices shortly after the events in question, however, noted that some appeared to have been shot in the head at close range. At the time, the FMLN still controlled the zone. It appears they were not killed in combat but were captured and then executed. It appears to us from the circumstances set forth here and in our prior report, including the position of the bodies, the head wounds, and the discovery of a missing journalist's identity papers of one of the bodies, that these were in all likelihood the five journalists, and that they were executed after capture by the FMLN.

The FMLN says it does not know whether the six persons killed were armed. Until it is sure that they are armed combatants or actively engaging in hostilities, the FMLN must presume persons to be civilians, and refrain from targeting them in combat.*

Even if the six were combatants, however, the Geneva Conventions strictly prohibit their execution after capture.

F. Mines

In the first half of 1989, the guerrillas' use of land mines increased substantially over that of 1988. Whereas Tutela Legal attributed 11 civilian deaths to FMLN mines in all of 1988, 25 civilians reportedly died from FMLN mines in the first six months of 1989. Indeed, by May 1989 the number of civilian deaths caused by guerrilla mines was so high that it shifted the overall balance of civilian deaths in the war. For the first time, as we noted in July 1989, FMLN guerrillas caused more civilian deaths than did uniformed government forces. Perhaps as a result of the public outcry which the killing of nine bus passengers generated, the FMLN dramatically reduced its use of mines in the second half of 1989.**

---

* "In case of doubt whether a person is a civilian, that person shall be considered to be a civilian." Article 50, Protocol Additional to the Geneva Conventions of 12 August 1949 (Protocol I).

** See Appendix C.

1. Killing of Nine Bus Passengers by Mine

At 8:30 a.m. on May 22, 1989, nine bus passengers were killed by an FMLN mine, which exploded under the bus at El Leon Pintado, *canton* Nancintepeque, Santa Ana, Santa Ana.* Passengers heard a bomb go off under the rear of the Dodge van in which they were riding, leaving them all wounded with shrapnel. The bomb was on the left side of the road, at a wall. In addition to the nine people who were killed, many others were wounded.

A few moments after the bomb went off, passengers saw two guerrillas standing on a wall over the road. The two went to join about 23 guerrillas on a nearby hill after the explosion. Two were in camouflage uniforms; the rest wore olive green. Shortly after the guerrillas left, civil defense members were seen shooting at the hill where the guerrillas had been.

In a statement broadcast on *Radio Venceremos*, the FMLN publicly apologized for the incident and vowed "to avoid those situations in the future as a matter of principle and to keep the enemy from using its mistakes in its plan for a dirty war."**

2. Bus Fare Collector and Passenger Killed

Only a few weeks before that incident, Jose Alexander Hernandez Velasco, a 16-year-old employee who collected bus fares, and Eusebio Corvera Servellon, 76, a passenger, died when the public bus they were riding ran over a bomb placed along the highway by the FMLN, according to Tutela Legal. A number of other bus passengers were also injured by the explosion, which occurred at about 3:00 p.m. on May 1, 1989, in *canton* Izacatal, San Isidro, Cabanas, at kilometer 66 of the highway from Sensuntepeque, Cabanas to San Salvador.

3. Four Peasants Killed By Explosion

Nilton Gonzalez, 16; Marvin Eliberto Gonzalez, 8; Maria Concepcion Orellana, 18; and Victor Manuel Contreras Orellana, 15 died when a bomb left

---

* The nine killed were Manuela de Jesus Vasquez, 47; Juan Mexpucemo Rivas Magana, 71; Juan Jose Colocho Espinoza, 39; Acadio Antonio Ramos, 40; Jose Jaime Vasquez Garcia, 20; Santos Martinez Escobar, 50; Miguel Angel Castro, 9; and Maria Celia Rivas Nerio, 18.

** Douglas Farah, "Salvadoran Rebels Apologize for Civilian Deaths," *The Washington Post*, May 25, 1989.

by the guerrillas exploded. The incident, investigated by Tutela Legal, occurred in the morning of May 4, 1989 in *caserio* La Zorra, *canton* Guadalupe La Zorra, La Herradura, La Paz.

Residents heard a loud explosion, followed by gunshots, at about 10:00 p.m. on May 3. At about 6:00 a.m. the following morning, residents learned that the guerrillas had blown up an electrical light post. Two cloth banners, separated from each other by about 25 meters, were left near the electrical post. One of them said that the area's residents should not support the civil defense; the other said that because May is mothers' month, the people should stop supporting the soldiers, and was signed "FMLN" in red letters.

A group of about 50 villagers went out to look at the downed electrical post and the banners. No one touched them until a resident named Jose Batres Moreno, saying nothing would happen, said he could use a blanket and grabbed one of the banners. As he grabbed the banner, there was a loud explosion. Two of the dead died instantly, and two died on route to the hospital.

V. THE RESURGENCE OF TORTURE

In the months preceding President Cristiani's inauguration June 1, 1989, and increasingly thereafter, the government of El Salvador has engaged in more extensive use of torture, which had not been commonly employed since the early 1980s'.* Methods now applied during many interrogations include asphyxiation, simulated drowning, drugging, application of electric shocks, and sexual violence. The new trend has been evidenced in all three branches of the security forces -- the National Police, the Treasury Police and the National Guard -- as well as in the Armed Forces, under whose authority the security forces operate.

By emphasizing the resurgence of these methods of torture, we by no means seek to downplay the significance of other types of mistreatment more commonly employed in the interrogation process -- forced standing, forced exercises, death threats, threats against family or friends, confinement in overcooled or particularly tiny rooms, and deprivation of food, water or sleep. These persist, they are objectionable and they should not be permitted to continue. What is most troubling at present, however, is government forces' increased reliance upon more drastic forms of mistreatment. Whereas in 1987 we expressed concern regarding "*sporadic* reports of electric shock, hanging by arms and legs and use of the *capucha* (a rubber hood used to induce suf-

---

*   "[F]rom 1979 through 1983, . . . virtually every prisoner taken into custody by the Salvadoran security forces [was] tortured." Americas Watch, The Continuing Terror (Seventh Supplement to the Report on Human Rights in El Salvador), September 1985, at 99.

focation),"* today the number of reports we and other human rights organizations are receiving of gross abuses in detention is far more frequent.

Torture most frequently occurs during the limited period of administrative detention permitted under the Constitution,** which in practice is *incommunicado* detention. This administrative detention takes places in security force centers or in military barracks or even in the field, when it is the army that makes the arrest. After the expiration of the administrative detention period, detainees must be either consigned to the order of a judge for trial, or released. The judge usually remits the prisoner to the penitentiary system for the three-day period the law allows him to review the file before determining whether to hold the defendant for further investigation and ultimately trial.

At the time the prisoner appears before the judge, he is asked to ratify his extrajudicial confession or statement, given to the security forces; although the army may arrest the prisoner, such statements can only be taken by the security forces. Many prisoners refuse to do so at that time, on the grounds that the statement was coerced from them.

The detained say that torture and mistreatment occur during the period of administrative detention, not while in the penitentiary system (where they are more likely to experience problems from common criminals also confined in jail).

At times, this constitutional limit is itself exceeded; however, reports of torture suggest that interrogators have ample opportunity to subject detainees to extraordinary abuses within the formal legal time limits.

---

*   Americas Watch, The Civilian Toll, August 30, 1987, at 18 (emphasis added).

**   Prior to the November offensive and the government's declaration of a state of siege, administrative detention could not exceed 72 hours. Constitution, Article 13. From November 12, 1989, when President Cristiani declared a state of emergency later ratified by the Legislative Assembly, until March 12, 1990, when most constitutional guarantees were reinstated, the period of administrative detention was fifteen days. Constitution, Article 29. On March 12 the 72-hour period of administrative detention was reinstated.

Much mistreatment occurs in the course of interrogation and serves the systemic objectives of interrogators: compelling detainees to provide information or accept accusations of guerrilla involvement. Extrajudicial "confessions," which can be neither knowing nor voluntary, are commonly obtained from detainees who may be blindfolded or coerced to sign blank sheets of paper. Even when, as sometimes occurs, such statements are discredited by reviewing judges and detainees are released,* the physical and psychological effects of torture endure long afterward.

Torture is objectionable and illegal notwithstanding the guilt or innocence of the detainee. Universal standards of human decency do not tolerate the extremes of pain, cruelty and moral degradation to which torture subjects its victims, as a means of extracting information from a prisoner. Although the concept of what constitutes torture is somewhat elastic, there can be little question that the practices described herein are precisely the "cruel, inhuman or degrading treatment or punishment" specifically prohibited by the Universal Declaration of Human Rights, Article 5, the American Convention on Human Rights, Article 5(2), and other international instruments.

The following cases of torture are a small, representative sample of the kinds of mistreatment which detainees in El Salvador increasingly suffer.**

A. Reina Noemi Alfaro Ramos (Atlacatl Battalion)

Alfaro Ramos, a 23-year-old resident of Jayaque, La Libertad, went to San Salvador early in the morning of January 12, 1989, to visit some priests. She got off the Route 101 bus at a factory en route, located at the Santa Tecla intersection of the roads to La Libertad and San Salvador, in order to seek employment.

While she was walking towards the factory, an armed, uniformed soldier of the Atlacatl Battalion stopped her a short distance from the Senorial

---

* Article 12 of the Constitution of El Salvador expressly invalidates declarations which are not given freely, and provides, in theory, for the punishment of persons who obtain such statements.

** In Carnage Again and Update on El Salvador, our two reports on the November offensive, we offered testimonies of foreigners who had been subjected to unusually harsh treatment when detained by Salvadoran security forces. See Carnage Again, November 24, 1989, at 34-37; Update on El Salvador, Dec. 16, 1989, at 27-29. We also reported on a death from beating in National Police custody. Update on El Salvador, at 24.

Motel, and asked to see her personal identity documents. The soldier looked at her documents, said they were not valid, and whistled to three other Atlacatl soldiers who were standing in front of the motel. The four soldiers climbed into a dark beige pickup truck, forced Alfaro inside, blindfolded her and stuffed a dirty rag in her mouth.

After driving for about 45 minutes, the soldiers stopped the car, took Alfaro out and placed her in a dark room. The soldiers tied her hands in front of her and left her alone. About 6:20 p.m., the same four soldiers reentered the room. The soldier who had asked to see her documents pulled off her clothes, including her blindfold. Until about 11:00 p.m., the four took turns raping her. She received blows and marks in different parts of her body.

Alfaro said that if the soldiers let her free, she would denounce them. The soldiers laughed, saying no one could do anything to them because they were military personnel. After a while, all four soldiers slept. At about 4:45 a.m., they woke up and raped her again. Then they put the blindfold back on her, told her to put her clothes on, and drove off with her. When the car stopped in Ciudad Merliot, La Libertad, the soldiers threw her to the ground and kicked her in the back before driving away.

Tutela Legal denounced the incident publicly. Some time later, soldiers visited the house where Alfaro lived in Jayaque and threatened the townspeople not to associate with her.

B. Teenage Girl* (Fourth Military Detachment, National Police)

A 17-year-old girl was detained on January 20, 1989, by soldiers of the Fourth Military Detachment while attending a U.S. AID-funded food distribution event in *caserio* Las Crucitas, *canton* La Estancia, jurisdiction of Cacaopera, Morazan. (See Chapter on U.S. Role) She was taken with other detainees to San Francisco Gotera, where she was interrogated that night and the following day in the Fourth Military Detachment barracks. On the afternoon of January 21, an interrogator told her that, because she would not admit to being a guerrilla, she was being taken to the National Police in San Miguel. She arrived there about 7:00 p.m. on January 21.

---

* For reasons of security, this person wishes to remain anonymous.

At the National Police, she was taken to a room where she was interrogated and, after a time, blindfolded. At one point, while she was blindfolded, a man entered the room and raped her. After he had finished, he told her not to report what had happened to anyone, particularly to "los gringos." Following her rape, she was interrogated further.

On the morning of January 23, police photographed her and placed her thumbprints on a document she could not read. They instructed her not to complain about her treatment and to say, if anyone asked, that she had been treated well. She was released that morning without being consigned before a judge. On January 25, the girl reported her rape to a physician and received treatment for a vaginal discharge.

C. Carmen* (Treasury Police)

Four armed plainclothesmen captured Carmen at about 8:30 a.m. one Wednesday morning in May 1989, when she was on her way to work in San Salvador. Without identifying themselves, they shoved her into a van and took her to a basement, which she later discovered to be the Treasury Police headquarters.

Her captors placed her in a cubicle and interrogated her, handcuffed and blindfolded, for three days and most of each night. She received virtually no food or drink.

On the first day police beat her and refused to let her go to the bathroom, obliging her to relieve herself standing in her cell, handcuffed and blindfolded.

The next day, Thursday, they told her that her mother and children had been killed. She felt the tip of a knife in her side and stomach and the barrel of a gun at her temple as they plied her with questions, demands and threats.

The police hung her by her handcuffs, with her hands in back, "like a *pinata*," she said. They swung her back and forth, pushing and kicking her. Her feet did not touch the ground. They said they would let her down if she told the truth, and laughed at her as they kicked her repeatedly. When the pain was too much, she would say she was ready to tell the truth, and they would let her

---

* For reasons of security, this woman wishes to remain anonymous.

down. She would then repeat her denials, only to be strung up again and batted back and forth.

They made her crouch down, knees bent, for hours on end, while they interrogated her. They beat her and stepped on her stomach several times with their boots. Her interrogators tortured her with a plastic *capucha*,* which, tied at the neck, made her feel as though she were drowning. Her throat still hurt when she was interviewed two months later. At one point a man identified as an FMLN deserter interrogated her. He beat her with his fists and kicked her for about one day. He placed a *capucha* on her for the second time.

The police did not let her sleep. Between interrogations she was taken, blindfolded and handcuffed, to a cell. People repeatedly hit the door and yelled and cursed at her.

On Saturday, the fourth day, she was drugged, and felt disoriented for about two days. On Monday, still feeling the effects of the drug, she was made to sign a piece of paper.

She was consigned to court later that day, where she denied the charge of being a health worker for the FMLN. She was held at Ilopango Prison for five days, and then released.

D. Pablo** (Fourth Military Detachment)

On June 7, 1989, the FMLN ambushed a group of soldiers near *caserio* El Rodeo, *canton* Estancia, jurisdiction of Cacaopera, Morazan. Eleven soldiers from the Morazan Battalion of the Fourth Military Detachment were killed in the attack. When Battalion troops returned two days later to collect the bodies, they mistreated numerous villagers, threatening to kill everyone and blaming them for the ambush. Soldiers threatened to leave the people in the same condition as the cadavers. One man, Pablo, in his mid-thirties, was particularly badly treated.

Soldiers stripped Pablo to his underwear and tied his hands and feet to a mango tree near the decaying bodies. As villagers watched, they fired a

---

* The capucha is a hood, of plastic or other material, which is placed around the head of the victim and closed at the neck to induce suffocation. At times the inside of the hood is lined with lime, which burns when inhaled.

** For reasons of security, this man wishes to remain anonymous.

gun right over his head, and at his feet, but did not hit him. The soldiers took eighteen men, including Pablo, to a nearby hill for questioning. They put the detainees face down with guns to their heads, and asked who wanted to die first.

In the late afternoon, the soldiers left the hamlet, but took Pablo with them to Cacaopera, where he spent the night lying on a floor, tied and blindfolded. The next morning, June 10, a lieutenant interrogated him and repeatedly slapped him on the head and kicked him in the chest. At 3:00 p.m., Pablo was taken to the Fourth Detachment in San Francisco Gotera by foot, a four-hour trip. Having received no food or water in nearly two days, still blindfolded, Pablo had to strip to his underwear. Soldiers struck him with an iron rod on the back when he took off his shoes.

The soldiers handcuffed Pablo and took him to another room, where they placed him in a large tank filled with water up to his neck. While interrogating him, soldiers dunked him again and again and held him under water. They accused him of killing the soldiers in El Rodeo. They grabbed him by his ears, pulled him part way out of the water, and beat him behind the ears with a stick for a long time. A soldier put a pistol to his neck and cocked it. A cigarette was put under his nose until he started to feel drugged.

At 1:00 a.m., after nearly ten hours, the soldiers took him from the water tank and left him to lie on a floor throughout the night. He received a tortilla and some water on June 12, his fourth day of detention.

The following day, June 13, Pablo was made to sign a paper without knowing its contents, and was released without charges.

E. Gang Rape By Army Soldiers*

At 11:00 a.m. on Sunday, June 11, Blanca, 42, was at home in the department of San Miguel with her crippled 18-year-old son and several younger children, when three uniformed soldiers came by, asking if she had any weapons. They demanded that her son, crippled since age two, hand over his weapons as well. She told them there were no weapons.

The soldiers dragged her out of the house and into the woods. The soldiers had detained another man from the neighborhood, whom they brought

---

* For reasons of security, the woman who was raped has asked that neither her name, her town, nor the unit to which the soldiers belonged be identified.

with them. When she could not find any guns in the woods, they started beating her and the young man.

A soldier threw her on the ground and raped her twice. The other two soldiers then took turns raping her. When she did not answer their questions about weapons, they beat her with a large stick. This ordeal continued until 4:00 p.m.

Upon letting her go, the soldiers told her not to report what had happened to human rights groups, because they no longer existed. Now, the soldiers said, there was ARENA.

When interviewed six days later by Americas Watch, Blanca had two discolored bruises on her buttocks, each more than six inches in diameter.

F. Juan* (Fourth Military Detachment)

Juan was arrested by soldiers of the Fourth Military Detachment in a village in Morazan while he was working in his corn field at 9:00 a.m. one day in June, 1989. The soldiers, who carried a list of names, accused Juan of collaborating with the guerrillas. Juan was taken to the Fourth Detachment barracks in San Francisco Gotera. He was in detention for four days.

At the barracks, soldiers blindfolded Juan and made him take his clothes off. He spent one day and one-half lying naked and blindfolded on the floor of a cell. On the evening of the second day, someone put a gun in his mouth. On the third day, interrogations began. He was asked if he had a son in the guerrillas, and he said he did. He was told nothing would happen to him if he turned over his weapons.

His interrogators put handcuffs on his wrists and fastened them to a horizontal bar running along the wall. They tied his legs and pulled them up behind him, leaving him suspended in the air, face down, and still blindfolded, in a "hammock" position. The soldiers took turns sitting on his back.

Electrical shocks were applied to his left wrist and hand for half an hour. When interviewed nine days later, his hand still bore small, black spots where the shocks occurred.

---

*   For security reasons, the victim has requested that his name and village not be identified, and that the exact date of his detention not be revealed.

Twice soldiers placed a *capucha* over Juan's head. Each time, soldiers found it too loose, so they sent for another size. This *capucha* was then applied twice.

While Juan was still in the hammock position, soldiers accused him of participating in a recent guerrilla attack on an army unit in the area. One soldier said, "Let's leave him useless." Soldiers accused him of knowing where there were hidden arms caches and took turns sitting and standing on his back.

In pain from the torture, Juan finally said he had seen a place where the guerrillas hid firearms. He was taken to a cell, still handcuffed, where he spent the night.

On the fourth day, soldiers took Juan out of the barracks and dressed him in army uniform, instructing him to lead them to the alleged arms hiding place. Juan took them to a spot, but there were no weapons there. The soldiers became angry and threatened to kill him. They took him back to the barracks.

Juan was released the next day, on the condition that he return within fifteen days with a guerrilla weapon or some information. Before he was released, the soldiers made him place his fingerprints on a paper of whose contents he was ignorant. He did not return to the barracks.

G. Three Cooperative Members* (Artillery Brigade)

Artillery Brigade soldiers captured Alfredo, Roberto, and Joaquin, all in their thirties, from their homes in *caserio* Quebrada de Agua, Nueva Concepcion, Chalatenango, at 6:00 a.m. on July 21, 1989. All three are affiliated with a cooperative in Chalatenango that works with the cooperative association FEDECOOPADES.

The soldiers made the captives walk all day through the hills of Chalatenango, while they repeatedly beat and questioned them, they told Americas Watch. They tied Alfredo's feet and hands, and threw him into the Lempa River. They pulled him out with a rope tied to his waist. This was repeated three times. They did not arrive at the Artillery Brigade until 10:00 p.m.

---

*   For reasons of security, these persons wish to remain anonymous.

There soldiers blindfolded and handcuffed the three men. They hit Roberto in the stomach, the back of the neck, and the head several times during the two days he was there.

The three were sent to the National Guard on Sunday night, July 23, 1989, and were consigned to the court in Tejutla, Chalatenango on Monday, July 24.

H. Torture of Seven Peasants Captured near Tres Ceibas (Atlacatl Battalion, First Brigade)

Between July 1 and 3, 1989, soldiers from the First Brigade and Atlacatl Battalion arrested seven young men from the Tres Ceibas and Camotepeque farming communities around Apopa, a northern San Salvador suburb. As they were interrogated in the field, the young men were brutally mistreated by soldiers -- they were beaten, kicked, hung from trees, whipped with branches, smothered with a *capucha*, stabbed with a bayonet, and dunked in a river. Two of the men, Lucio Parada Cea and Hector Joaquin Miranda Marroquin, were killed. (See Chapter on Government Violations.)

I. Jose Tomas Mazariego (Treasury Police)

Four armed plainclothesmen seized Jose Tomas Mazariego, 39, a member of the Executive Committee of ASTTEL (Association of Telecommunications Workers) and Secretary of Relations of FEASIES (Federation of Independent Associations and Unions of El Salvador), as he was walking in downtown San Salvador at about 6:40 p.m. on June 12. A blue van with darkened windows pulled up. The plainclothesmen blindfolded Mazariego and forced him onto the floor of the van. One man sat on top of him and another put his shoe on Mazariego's neck. They took him to Treasury Police headquarters and placed him in a cell.

The police made Mazariego disrobe and put on underclothes. They interrogated him for about two hours, accusing him of belonging to the FMLN. They hit him in the chest and slapped him in the head.

During the second day of his interrogation, June 13, police applied a *capucha*, but he did not lose consciousness. Removing the *capucha*, they pulled his hair. They applied the *capucha* a second time, and this time someone held his nose and mouth as well, and he lost consciousness. When he began to revive, they sat him down and asked if he was ready to accept their accusations. Mazariego told them he had already said all that he knew.

His interrogators put what he believed to be acid on his knees, which burned. Five minutes later they put the *capucha* on him a third time. This time the *capucha* was lined with lime, and he fainted, he told Tutela Legal.

He was again interrogated and beaten repeatedly, and told he would have to admit his terrorist links, or they would kill him. He was offered food for the first time at about 6:30 p.m. on June 14. About 4:00 p.m. on June 15, he was driven blindfolded in a car to a place where he was set free.

A medical examination conducted June 21 reported that Mazariego had abrasions in the right forehead, four lacerations in the back of the palate, and abrasions on the right elbow and both wrists. He exhibited first degree burns and abrasions on both knees, and additional abrasions and burns on the internal face of the right leg. He had diminished feeling in both thumbs.

J. Daniel Maradiaga Jovel (Fifth Brigade)

About ten uniformed soldiers of the Fifth Infantry Brigade captured Daniel Maradiaga Jovel, 19, farmer, as he was walking to work in the fields at 6:00 a.m. on June 20 in *canton* La Esperanza, jurisdiction of San Sebastian, San Vicente. At the moment of his capture, Jovel's hands were tied and he was interrogated on the street regarding his alleged links to the FMLN. He denied involvement, was blindfolded, and brought to Fifth Brigade headquarters in San Vicente, where he was placed in a cell.

Soldiers held Jovel for six days. During virtually the entire period, he was blindfolded and handcuffed. They interrogated him about his alleged guerrilla ties, and punched and kicked him in the chest, stomach and legs. Three times they forced his head into a trough of dirty water to simulate drowning. In addition, they applied a *capucha*. They placed a hood over his head so that he could not breathe; he suffocated and fell unconscious. The hood was removed and, after he had revived, the process commenced all over again. On three separate occasions during the course of his detention, this process lasted for between one-half hour and one hour.

On three nights soldiers awakened him, interrogated him, then picked him up, beat him with their fists, and threw him head first against a wall.

On the fourth, fifth and sixth days of detention, soldiers placed Jovel in a chair, blindfolded, and applied electric shocks to the outer sides of both knees. Each time the shocks were applied in the course of interrogations in which he refused to accept the accusations of guerrilla involvement. Finally, on June 25, he relented and signed a piece of paper. He said that his blindfold was lifted just long enough for him to sign, not so that he could read the words written on the page.

On June 26, soldiers transferred Jovel to the National Police, who consigned him before the Judge in San Sebastian. He was remitted to San Vicente Prison.

K. Former Union Leader (Treasury Police)

Plainclothesmen grabbed from behind a former union leader who does not wish to be identified in Planes de Renderos, just outside San Salvador, where he had gone to eat *pupusas*, stuffed tortillas, on August 5, 1989. They blindfolded him, handcuffed him and put him into a vehicle with darkened windows. His captors immediately began hitting him on the legs with pistols and on his face next to his left eye. The eye began to bleed. They accused him of being a guerrilla, and he responded that he was a unionist.

They took him to Treasury Police headquarters (he learned that he was there because he saw the Treasury Police identification on someone's shirt). They took all his things -- chains, rings, shoes, money -- and left him naked. They accused him of being a member of the FMLN, burning telephone exchange boxes, blowing up electric posts, and participating in the killing of Edgar Chacon and Jose Antonio Rodriguez Porth. He denied all these accusations. They said they would kill his family if he did not accept the accusations.

The first night they put the *capucha* on him seven times. He was kicked in the back and stomach. Someone held a hand up to his nose and told him to inhale. When he refused he was hit in the stomach, which forced him to inhale. A substance on the hand put him to sleep. He was later subjected to continued questioning and then to a procedure known as the *avioncito* ("little plane"). One interrogator sat on his back while another hit him in the head. They hit his head against a wall. By Sunday night he was bleeding from the mouth and nose. He was assured that this was nothing, that they had only begun. That night they applied the *capucha* seven times and told him to admit to terrorist acts.

They took him to a dark room with blue walls and removed his blindfold. He saw blood, both fresh and dry, in the room. They told him they had a machine to cut fingers, and that they would cut off his finger to make him talk. His interrogators' faces were masked. They turned on a motor and showed him how they were going to cut his finger. Instead of cutting his finger, however, they took him out and again applied the *capucha*. They told him they had captured his mother, his brother and his 13-month-old daughter, and would kill them.

He was given no food or water, was not permitted to sleep and had to drink from the toilet. He said that drinking the foul water gave him a throat infection so that he could hardly talk when he appeared in court. At the time of his interview (September 16), he had small scars on his hand from the handcuffs, his left hand was numb, and his legs were bruised. Police forced him to sign approximately six documents, and took eight photos of him.

On August 9 at 3:00 p.m., he was taken to the Fourth Criminal Court in San Salvador. There he learned that his extra-judicial confession admitted to burning buses and telephone boxes, blowing up light posts and vehicles, and placing bombs in officials' houses. He denied all the charges before the court. He was remitted to Mariona Prison, and was transferred to San Vicente prison on August 15.*

L. Jose Adolfo Lima (Probably Second Brigade)

Jose Adolfo Lima,** student leader of the western branch of the University of El Salvador (CUO), was driving in a university pick-up truck with university driver Santiago Martinez Centeno about 4:30 p.m. on Friday, August 11, 1989, near Santa Ana, when their car was intercepted by four armed men in civilian clothes. The men, who did not identify themselves, took them out of the pick-up and put them in a red Toyota jeep at a spot very close to the Santa Ana toll booth, a place of frequent military presence. Lima was blindfolded and his hands were tied. After about two hours driving, they were taken into a house. His captors placed Lima in a room where he remained, blindfolded, for twenty days.

During the first five days, he was interrogated and tortured. Interrogators accused him of belonging to a subversive organization and of using

---

* Testimony given to Human Rights Institute, Central American University (IDHUCA).

** The victim is the son of Marco Tulio Lima, president of the Confederation of Cooperative Associations of El Salvador (COACES).

the student organization SECUO to recruit students for subversive associations. He insisted he was a university student who was a member of SECUO, and that he had no ties to any subversive organization.

The first night, he was made to take off his clothes except for his underwear. His interrogators tortured him with electric shocks in his ears that night and the next morning.

On the third day, his interrogators took all his personal data, and discovered that he was the son of Marco Tulio Lima. They said COACES was an FMLN front and threatened his family.

On the fourth day, August 14, Lima was given shocks in his testicles. His interrogators accused him of working with other students in the FPL. They told him he would be given some time, and if he still refused to admit the charges, he would be killed. They left him alone until 11:00 p.m., when they woke him and told him he had one hour to accept the charges or he would be killed. He insisted he was not involved in anything illegal.

On August 15, they applied electric shocks in the ears, testicles, legs and back. He was also given water which seemed to contain some form of drug. After drinking it he started seeing double and felt bewildered. At some point, his captors burned him on both hips, particularly the right hip, with what he thought to be cigarettes. They then had him sign a document saying he was an active member of the FPL, that he had been treated well, and that he would be freed on the condition that he provide information in the future. He signed it under threat that he and his family would be killed. Once he signed the document, the torture ended. Subsequently he was kept in the room, blindfolded, barefoot, and shirtless. He received food and was generally treated better.

Despite being blindfolded, Lima believed he was being held by the military because he was able to see a military poncho and military dishes for food. One interrogator identified himself as a member of the National Guard. During his detention, Lima heard radio stations from Guatemala as vehicles passed by the house, one of which announced a dance in Ahuachapan, which led him to conclude he was being held in that city.

On August 31, Lima was given back his documents and keys and, at about 10:00 p.m., he, along with Martinez, was placed in the same vehicle he had been driving when captured. He was still blindfolded. They were driven for about an hour, then transferred to another vehicle. After two more hours of driving, their vehicle stopped. With a gun pressed against his back, Lima was told to walk and get into their pickup, parked directly in front. The blindfold was removed, and he was told not to look back or he would be killed. His captors then drove off, leaving Lima and Martinez in the pickup in the middle of the night. They discovered they were in San Juan Opico, and drove to Santa Ana, according to testimony given to the UCA Human Rights Institute (IDHUCA).

M. Unionist (National Police)

National Policemen arrested a unionist who does not wish to be identified as he left his house in San Marcos, San Salvador, at about 10:00 a.m. on August 14. The police hit him and a co-worker told them to confess to the burning of a Route 21 bus nearby. The two were taken to the San Marcos police station, and that evening to the National Police headquarters in San Salvador. He was blindfolded and taken to a small cell. The police threatened to kill his family.

They picked him up by the collar and hit him against the wall. Someone hit him with a stick-like object above the left shoulder and kneed him in the stomach. They asked him where he hid weapons. He denied having weapons. They beat him repeatedly. At one point he was made to kneel, as one interrogator stood on his shoulders while another hit him on the thighs. When he fainted and fell down, they ordered him to get up and picked him up by his shirt. They sat him down in a chair, boxed his ears and kicked him in the ribs. They hit his head against the wall so much that it swelled up.

During his third night in detention he was pushed in a pool of water. They pushed his head under, and told him to admit to being a member of the FMLN. While he was in the water they applied four electric shocks to him. He was then taken out.

On the fourth night, as his interrogation continued, he was made to stand up and was struck with a gun on the right side of his head. He was kicked in the leg. He said that he did not admit their accusations, but that they could write down whatever they wanted. They produced a document of eight to ten pages, which he finally signed, as one interrogator cocked a pistol.

On August 17, he was consigned before the Fifth Criminal Court, where he denied the charges. He was remitted to San Vicente prison, according to testimony given to the IDHUCA.

N. Jose Antonio Serrano (Treasury Police)

Armed plainclothesmen arrested Jose Antonio Serrano, Secretary of Conflicts of ANTMAG (Association of Employees of the Ministry of Agriculture), on Friday, September 8, at 7:00 a.m. in a parking lot near his home in San Salvador. They struck him in the face and forced him into a blue Toyota van. In the van, he was punched in the head and back and told he would be killed. He was brought to Treasury Police headquarters.

Upon arrival at the Treasury Police, Serrano was blindfolded and taken to a room where he was hit repeatedly until his face was bloody. He was made to take off his clothes except his underwear. Accused of being a terrorist, he was interrogated while standing for about two hours, while he was hit with fists and sticks.

At what he estimates to have been about 3:00 a.m. on September 9, Serrano was taken to another room, where he was again blindfolded and handcuffed. Police placed a plastic hood filled with a substance which burned when he inhaled over his head. After a minute, they removed it. The police repeated the process. The third time they placed the hood over his head, he lost consciousness. Police threw water on him to revive him.

Twice they placed a larger plastic bag over his head and neck; afterward, he regurgitated.

That night, Serrano was brought into a room with a concrete floor where a fan was blowing directly on him. Still handcuffed and blindfolded, he was made to stand for about four hours as his captors interrogated him about his alleged activity as an urban commando leader. Interrogators threatened to kill his wife. They hit him repeatedly with open hands on both ears. Someone pulled on his testicles. He was slapped, punched and hit with sticks in the chest and back. He was given karate-chop-like hits to the front of his neck.

Before his release, Serrano was made to sign a blank sheet of paper as his head was forcefully held. During the course of his detention, his interrogators told him not to believe that the International Committee of the Red Cross or any humanitarian agency would help him. He was consigned before the First Criminal Judge in San Salvador at 2:00 p.m. on September 11. He denied being an urban terrorist and was sentenced to Mariona prison. He urinated blood during his first three days in prison. When interviewed on September 21, Serrano had pain in the back, lower legs and ankles.

Serrano is still in jail as of mid-March.

O. Inmar Rolando Reyes Flores (Third Brigade)

Inmar Rolando Reyes Flores, 32, Treasurer of AGEMHA (Association of Treasury Ministry employees), works in the Rent Administration office in San Miguel and is a fourth-year law student at the eastern branch of the University of El Salvador. On September 7, the death squad "ARDE" issued a death threat over Radio Chaparrastique in San Miguel against Reyes and several other persons. On September 15 Reyes was returning on the Route 301 bus to San Miguel after participating in a march held by the Permanent Committee for the National Debate. Soldiers from the Cavalry Regiment stopped the bus at around 4:20 p.m. at the turn-off for Nueva Granada, Usulutan. Despite his protestations and those of the bus driver, the soldiers forced the driver to head to Villa El Triunfo, where their lieutenant was waiting. Reyes was taken off the bus and brought to the Third Infantry Brigade at about 6:40 p.m.

A sergeant from the intelligence section (S2) brought handcuffs and a kerchief that said "FMLN." He made Reyes take off all his clothes except his underwear and put him in a cell, blindfolded and handcuffed. At 9:00 p.m., the interrogation began. His interrogators accused him of being an urban commando, which he denied. They put the *capucha* on him once, then hit and kicked him in the stomach and back. They lit matches and burned him on various parts of the chest and back. At least six such marks and a large bruise on the back of his right calf were visible during his September 23 interview with a human rights monitor. In addition, at the time of the interview with the ID-HUCA, he had a large bruise on the back of his right calf.

He was interrogated, threatened with death, hit and accused of guerrilla involvement for six days. When he was finally released at 12:30 p.m. on September 21, he was warned that if he did not collaborate with the Army he and his family would be captured and killed.

P. Andres de Jesus Sanchez Henriquez (National Guard)

Andres de Jesus Sanchez Henriquez, 22, was sleeping in the Santa Mercedes textile factory, the site of an ongoing labor dispute since late 1988, when the National Guard entered early in the morning of September 18 and arrested him and four other unionists. After conducting a search of the premises, the guardsmen ordered all five to come with them. They handcuffed and beat Sanchez and brought him in a vehicle to National Guard headquarters. They forced him to put his head down and blindfolded him as he entered.

Inside the National Guard, Sanchez was kicked in the side and boxed in the ears. He was accused of being an urban commando and told to turn over his weapons. He said he had none. Someone stood on his fingers. His captors applied electric shocks in both ears, more than fifteen times, he estimated. They put a string around his neck and tightened it. He was told to tell the truth about the organization he belonged to. They applied electric shocks to the back of his heel and the sole of his foot. They hit him in the head and the buttocks. Someone climbed on top of him, took off his handcuffs, and had him do knee bends with the interrogator on his back until they both fell over. Cold water was thrown on him. His ears were boxed repeatedly, and his head was banged against the wall, he told IDHUCA.

On September 21, he was taken to court. En route he was hit hard in the chest with a stick and pushed; he was told he would be killed later. In court, he denied the charges against him. He was sent to Mariona prison, and was released on September 25.

Q. Tatiana Mendoza Aguirre (National Police)

National Policemen arrested Julia Tatiana Mendoza Aguirre, 21, on Monday, September 18, from the Central American Mission Church in downtown San Salvador after her participation in a march by the FENASTRAS labor federation. Police hit her in the head and back as she and others were forced from the church and onto a bus which brought them to the National Police.

Upon arrival at National Police headquarters she was blindfolded and accused of belonging to the FMLN, which she denied. The National Police held her for three days. Twice in the course of her detention she smelled a marijuana-like substance. At one point she was told to stand against the wall of a room. One man opened her shirt and grabbed her breasts while he accused her of belonging to the FMLN.

During what she believes was her third day in detention, Mendoza was taken to a room where a man with a soft voice told her to collaborate with the police, and accused her of being a subversive. He forced her to take down her pants and underwear, and raped her.

She was later taken to a shower, where she cleaned her face and parts of her body, trying not to wipe away the signs of the rape. Later that evening, a man with the same voice as the man who had performed the rape again interrogated her. He made her lean forward over a chair and sodomized her.

On September 21, Mendoza was consigned before the First Penal Judge in San Salvador, where she accepted the charge of belonging to FENASTRAS but denied involvement with the FMLN. She told the judge that she had been raped. Examination by a forensic physician revealed a bruise of six by six centimeters in the back right thigh and lacerations in the area of the anus.

Her testimony was taken by Americas Watch before she was killed in the October 31 bombing of the FENASTRAS offices.*

R. Maria Juana Antonia Medina (National Police)

Maria Juana Antonia Medina, 37, was also arrested after participating in the FENASTRAS march. She was detained at the National Police for three days. Her daughter, Sara Cristiani Chan-Chan, an employee of FENASTRAS, was captured and disappeared by the Air Force on August 19, 1989. (See the Chapter on Government Violations)

During her interrogation, policemen accused Medina of belonging to the National Resistance (RN) of the FMLN. She was blindfolded throughout her detention. She spent much of one afternoon and evening being interrogated as she was lying face down on the floor. Interrogators struck her repeatedly in the lower back with objects which felt like the butts of rifles. They kicked her in the chest and hit her with open palms in the face. For one hour she was taken to a separate room where a man raped her. She says that as a result of the continuous beating her abdomen suffered, her appendix became inflamed and she experienced hemorrhaging.

S. Rogelio Diaz Martinez Barrera (National Police)

On September 18, National Police arrested Rogelio Diaz Martinez Barrera, 19, a member of the STIRGAS restaurant workers union, after he participated in the FENASTRAS march. He was blindfolded when he arrived at

---

*   Rogelio Diaz Martinez Barrera, Maria Juana Antonia Medina, and Blanca Frasedi Diaz Rivera also reported that they were raped; all were part of the same mass arrest.

the National Police and was taken down to the basement, where water was thrown on him. Police kicked him in the stomach and back. They grabbed him by the hair and threw him on the ground. His interrogators accused him of belonging to the FMLN, a charge he denied.

For much of his first day in detention, Martinez was alone in a room with a few men interrogating him. Each time he denied belonging to the FMLN, someone struck him in the head, back and stomach.

On Tuesday, they took him to another room where electric shocks were applied to his right elbow. Four shocks were applied for three or four seconds each, one after another. A small laceration of the skin could be seen when he was interviewed several days later.

Police placed a plastic bag over his head for a few seconds. It contained a substance which burned upon inhalation. He fainted. When he regained consciousness, the process was repeated.

On Tuesday night, he was taken to a room where, from their sounds, he divined there were five men. They took off his clothes and, as one of the men held his hands, another man raped him. The man who raped him told him he was doing so because Martinez would not admit that he was an FMLN member. Afterwards, Martinez was told not to tell anyone he had been raped. If he talked, they said, they would kill his family. Martínez was released on September 21.

T. Santos Faustino Fabian (Seventh Military Detachment)

Santos Faustino Fabian, administrative coordinator and member of the Administrative Council of FEDECOOPADES and member of the Administrative Council of the Salvadoran Institute for the Promotion of Cooperatives (INSAFOCOOP, a government institute), and another man were driving in a Suzuki jeep along the road from Atiquizaya to San Lorenzo in Ahuachapan at 6:00 a.m., September 18, when soldiers from the Seventh Military Detachment stopped them. As Fabian was blindfolded and his thumbs were tied together, the soldiers forced his companion to drive to their headquarters in the Suzuki. They were handcuffed upon arrival.

Fabian was accused of participation in a guerrilla attack on Atiquizaya several months before. His interrogators asked him what FMLN organization he belonged to, where his weapons were, and what his pseudonym was. That afternoon they took his shoes, pants and shirt, wet his legs, put wires in both his ears, and gave him electric shocks. He estimated that this lasted about one minute. He said he felt everything turning into flames. Afterward, one interrogator hit him in the arms and stomach, and boxed his ears. He was made to stand all night and was interrogated with breaks of no longer than one-half hour. Around dawn an interrogator put a grenade to his chest, a knife to his neck, and something else to his earlobe as if it were being cut. The knife blade was moved up and down on his throat, he later told IDHUCA.

He was offered money if he would return to FEDECOOPADES and provide information to the army. He was urged to think of his children and their need to eat. At about 3:00 p.m. on September 19, an official came and asked if he had said anything. The interrogator reported that he had not, and the official said, "You'll have to put a bullet in him." The interrogator then asked Fabian if he wanted a bullet put to him. He said he did not. At 5 p.m., he was released.

VI. THE CLOSURE OF POLITICAL SPACE: VIOLENCE AGAINST CIVILIAN OPPOSITION

The final years of President Duarte's Christian Democratic government were marked by gradually, if precariously, expanding opportunities for political expression. Observers hailed as signs of progressive democratization the return from exile of opposition politicians Guillermo Ungo, Hector Oqueli, Ruben Zamora, Hector Silva and others, and their participation, through the newly-formed Democratic Convergence, in the March 1989 presidential elections.* In the Duarte years labor unions, cooperative associations, and community organizations fought persistently and with some success for the ability to operate openly.

By the end of 1989, however, a dramatic change had been wrought. Pursuant to the state of siege put into effect when the FMLN offensive started, constitutional freedoms of speech, association, press and communication through the mails and telephones, as well as procedural due process rights, were suspended. Opposition politicians once again left the country in fear for their lives. Prominent labor and human rights activists went into hiding, and the offices of most popular organizations were closed. The assassination of six Jesuit priests by the military, the issuance of hostile threats against other church

---

* The Democratic Convergence is composed of the National Revolutionary Movement (MNR) (Guillermo Ungo, and Hector Oqueli, before his assassination), the Popular Social Christian Movement (MPSC) (Ruben Zamora, Hector Silva), and the Social Democratic Party (PSD) (Reni Roldan). Ungo was the presidential candidate, and Roldan the vice-presidential candidate.

leaders, and the arrest and deportation of numerous international humanitarian and religious workers sent a chill through the religious communities. For all intents and purposes, independent political activity came to a halt for at least two months.

With notable exceptions, including the spate of assassinations of conservative figures, the April mass arrests and searches of popular organizations following the assassination of Attorney General Garcia Alvarado and the shooting of four members of the press on election eve and election day, the political climate remained relatively stable through the first half of 1989. Although the Legislative Assembly in June began consideration of a proposed "anti-terrorist" law that threatened to criminalize human rights reporting and much peaceful opposition activity, the legislation was scuttled following energetic protests within El Salvador and abroad.* All in all, the first few months of ARENA government failed to fulfill the most dire predictions of worsening political violence and repression of dissent. Indeed, overall levels of human rights deaths continued on a course of moderate decline through October

---

*   On June 23, 1989, three weeks after President Cristiani's inauguration, the ARENA Party introduced into the Legislative Assembly legislation entitled the "Bill for the Protection of Democracy," which contained 26 reforms to the criminal code and four reforms to the criminal procedure code.   The proposed reforms would have criminalized an impressive range of peaceful opposition activities. Among them were promoting, by "any" means, the "intervention" of "international organisms" in "the internal affairs of El Salvador"; organizing or directing "associations that have as their objective the teaching ... of doctrines that subvert the public order"; organizing or directing "sections or branches of foreign organizations ... that subvert the public order"; spreading or promulgating "propaganda that subverts the public order"; to "knowingly rent or lend houses or locations destined to assist in the spreading or propagation" of doctrines to "subvert the public order"; peaceful occupation of work places, churches or universities, where -- as will be presumed absent indications to the contrary -- such actions are intended to provoke terror in the population; and painting "public or private goods" in order to provoke disorder.   In the face of substantial protest in El Salvador and the United States, the proposal was not acted upon.   In late November, however, following the FMLN offensive, the Assembly approved virtually identical reform legislation and submitted it for President Cristiani's signature. The President returned the legislation to the Assembly, indicating that he considered portions to be unconstitutional. The proposal seems to be dead, for the time being.

1989.*

Nonetheless, even during the earliest months of the new government there were troubling indications of a growing intolerance of independent political expression and activity. The rate of arrests by government forces through October 1989 for "subversive" crimes -- i.e. political crimes -- increased 12.5% over the 1988 rate.** By mid-year, Americas Watch and other monitoring organizations noted a substantial increase in reports of severe torture by the Army and security forces, as reported above. A shooting incident at the National University in July reflected the long-simmering tensions between students and soldiers on that campus. On July 22, bombs seriously damaged the printing press of the Central American University, a favorite target of right-wing and military violence and threats.

At the same time, a string of FMLN assassinations of prominent government and right-wing figures in the first half of the year certainly discouraged professionals from accepting government positions in the new ARENA administration and others from becoming involved in politics. In March, Dr. Francisco Peccorini, a prominent conservative theorist affiliated with the National University, was killed. His killing was followed by the assassinations of Attorney General Garcia Alvarado in April, Minister of the Presidency Rodriguez Porth in June, and the anticommunist civilian organizers

---

* According to Tutela Legal investigations, there were 34 deaths resulting from government forces (excluding acts of drunken soldiers) from January through May 1989 and 10 such deaths from June through October. These figures were about half the nearly eight civilian deaths per month attributed to government forces by Tutela Legal throughout 1988. Similarly, death squad killings as recorded by Tutela Legal declined progressively from five per month throughout 1988 to 3.8 per month from January to October, 1989; excluding the FENASTRAS bombing that killed 10, that total would have been only 2.8 per month. See Appendix C. Over the same period, FMLN killings declined somewhat. According to Tutela Legal, FMLN assassinations averaged almost four per month in 1988 (44 for the year), and were near that level in January to May (23 assassinations, or 4.6 per month), decreasing in June to October (11 killings or 2.2 per month). Over the same period, FMLN killings declined somewhat. According to Tutela Legal, FMLN assassinations averaged almost four per month in 1988 (44 for the year), and were near that level in January to May (23 assassinations, or 4.6 per month), decreasing in June to October (11 killings or 2.2 per month). Due to the high profile of some of the FMLN targets, however, the impression was of increasing FMLN killings. There remain unsolved killings that ultimately may be attributed to the FMLN as well.

** Statistics published in the monthly bulletin of the governmental Human Rights Commission show an average of 321 arrests per month in all of 1988, increasing to 363 per month from January through May 1989, and holding at 360 per month from June through October 1989. This represents an increase of 12.5%.

of a new paramilitary group Edgar Chacon and Gabriel Payes in June and July. The FMLN was responsible for the killings of Peccorini and the Attorney General and probably for the others as well.

The situation worsened markedly in September and October, when the government and the FMLN held their first two meetings --in Mexico City and San Jose, Costa Rica -- to begin a process of negotiation. Arrests of union members and bombs thrown at union headquarters alternated with attacks on military targets and relatives of the military. By the end of October, tensions were running high, culminating in the October 31 bombs that destroyed the offices of COMADRES and FENASTRAS, killing ten and wounding more than 30, one day after an FMLN attack on the headquarters of the Army General Staff. Despite government promises to investigate the FENASTRAS bombing, the FMLN announced on November 2 that it would not attend the next scheduled negotiation session in Caracas.

Throughout the pre-offensive period a disturbing pattern emerged in which FMLN attacks against civilians and on military targets were followed by arrests, searches or bombings of civilian opposition groups or members. On April 19, 1989, following the assassination of the Attorney General, 75 persons were arrested when Treasury Police agents raided and searched the offices of CRIPDES/CNR (Christian Committee for Displaced Persons of El Salvador and National Coordinator for Repopulation), the trade union federation FUSS, a coalition of unemployed and laid off workers (CODYDES), and a women's organization (ADEMUSA).

Following an FMLN attack on the First Brigade and other targets the evening of May 25, 1989, several offices -- the Confederation of Cooperative Associations of El Salvador (COACES), the Federation of Independent Unions of El Salvador (FEASIES), CRIPDES, FENASTRAS, and the nongovernmental Human Rights Commission -- were searched for arms of war on May 26. The searches were undertaken purportedly to discover links between the popular movement and the FMLN. No weapons or other evidence of urban commando activities was found.

On October 19, the houses of Ruben Zamora, former Vice-Presidential candidate of the Democratic Convergence, and Aronette Diaz, his sister-in-law and leader of the opposition Nationalist Democratic Union (UDN) party, were bombed. The bombings followed by two days the killing of Ana Maria Casanova, daughter of an army colonel. The October 30 FMLN mortar attack on the headquarters of the armed forces high command was followed on October 31 by the bombings of the FENASTRAS and COMADRES offices.

If a sense of fear and intimidation among opposition leaders and popular organizations increased in September and October, it was little compared to what followed in the wake of the November offensive. The Salvadoran government and military responded to the offensive -- the most serious military threat in years -- by slamming shut what political space had been opened since the mid-1980's. The list of humanitarian, religious, and social service organizations whose officers were arrested or deported or whose offices were searched in the weeks of and following the offensive includes the United Nations, Medical Aid for El Salvador, Doctors Without Borders, the Lutheran Church, the Episcopal Church, the Mennonite Central Committee, Catholic Relief Services, the Popular Social Christian Movement, the National Revolutionary Movement, the Council of Marginal Communities, COMADRES, the Confederation of Cooperative Associations of El Salvador (COACES), the National Coordinator of Repopulation (CNR), the National Coordination of Women of El Salvador (CONAMUS), and the Foundation for Community Organization Development (PADECOES). Between November 11 and December 15, 1989, Army or security force soldiers entered and searched more than 50 churches, refugee centers or homes of religious workers.

The death squad-style January 12, 1990 killing in Guatemala of Hector Oqueli Colindres, deputy secretary-general of Guillermo Ungo's National Revolutionary Movement, which followed the December 6 capture and beating of MPSC leader Jorge Villacorta by Treasury Police, have put all opposition activists on notice that their lives are still very much at risk. Opposition political leaders Reni Roldan, of the Social Democratic Party, and Hector Silva, of the Popular Social Christian Movement, are still outside of El Salvador, for security reasons.

Human rights documentation by Salvadoran organizations slowed considerably in the weeks after the offensive. Tutela Legal and Socorro Juridico remained open, but their activities were greatly constricted. The nongovernmental Human Rights Commission closed entirely for several weeks, as did the Human Rights Institute of the Central American University, following the murder of its director, Father Segundo Montes, along with five other Jesuits, on November 16.

It appears that about 1,000 persons were arrested in the month after the offensive began. The majority were released, but at least 130 were consigned to the judge and sent to prison to await trial, most charged with crimes such as subversive association and acts of terrorism. As of February, there were 370 persons in jail for such crimes. Following the arrest and imprisonment of Jennifer Casolo, a U.S. church worker,* foreigners have been barred from visiting the jails without express permission from the prison system administrator. There appears to be no rational relationship between this regulation and the welfare of the prisoner or the security of the state. Rather, this change from a more open policy allowing visits twice a week seems intended to prevent foreigners from making humanitarian gestures and investigating allegations of mistreatment.

A state of siege declared November 12 suspended freedom of expression, freedom of movement, freedom of association and the inviolability of correspondence and telephonic communications. Certain due process guarantees for detainees were suspended, and the security forces were authorized to hold prisoners *incommunicado* for 15 days before charging them with a crime. The state of siege was renewed every month through early February, when several constitutional guarantees were reinstated, but the suspensions of freedom of association and due process guarantees were continued.

In March, the 72-hour limit on administrative detention regained legal force, although the constitutional provision guaranteeing free association remained suspended.

By early 1990 many unions, cooperatives, human rights and community organizations were beginning to test the political waters, as some returned to their old offices and others rented new ones. President Cristiani promised members of Congress in February that religious workers who had been deported could return freely to El Salvador and that damaged offices would receive compensation.

For the first time ever the head of the General Staff, Colonel Ponce, granted the long-standing request of the nongovernment Human Rights Com-

---

* See Update on El Salvador at 32-35.

mission (CDHES) for a meeting, and promised to investigate the cases it brought to him. While Colonel Ponce has met with literally hundreds of foreigners concerned about human rights in an effort to improve the image of the army, which we as foreigners appreciate, he still had never met with this legitimate Salvadoran human rights organization. Unlike the foreign visitors, several of the CDHES representatives at the meeting had been arrested and tortured by the security forces. Colonel Ponce promised to investigate the cases of human rights violations presented by the Commission and to respond to them at another meeting. We will be watching this development with interest.

The understanding and acceptance by the military of the watchdog role of human rights organizations is not complete, however. After the Air Force rocketed a house in Corral de Piedra, Chalatenango, on February 11, 1990, killing five and wounding 16 civilian repatriatees, the Army prevented Tutela Legal from reaching the scene of the incident for several days. Although the Army finally admitted its responsibility, when Tutela Legal director Maria Julia Hernandez urged that those individual soldiers and pilots responsible be criminally tried for the indiscriminate attack on a civilian village, the Army press office reacted angrily, characterizing Tutela's attitude as "confrontative insensitivity."*

In addition, in early 1990, the General Staff of the Army promulgated new guidelines, more stringent than ever, regarding access by human rights, humanitarian, and press organizations to "the interior of the country" as well as to "zones of conflict." Human rights organizations would be required to have two interviews with the General Staff before being issued a safe conduct pass, and would be required to return to the General Staff afterwards for a third interview, presumably to debrief the army on their investigations! These guidelines constituted nothing less than unconstitutional legislation by the military, unconstitutional because the Assembly reinstituted the constitutional right to freedom of movement in February.

---

* Diario Latino, February 21, 1990; Diario de Hoy, February 21, 1990.

A. Bombing of FENASTRAS Office, October 31, 1990: 10 Dead

At 12:30 p.m. on October 31, 1989, a powerful bomb destroyed the FENASTRAS headquarters, killing 10 persons and wounding more than 30. The explosion killed eight people affiliated with FENASTRAS, including Febe Elizabeth Velasquez, a member of the executive committees of both FENASTRAS and the UNTS and a leading spokesperson for the most militant sector of the Salvadoran labor movement.* Clearly intended to kill, the bomb exploded as many of the Federation members were having lunch inside the offices. Much of the office was turned to rubble.

The bombing marked a qualitative escalation in the use of political violence in the urban war, and served as the catalyst for the FMLN offensive launched 11 days later.** Shortly after the bombing, President Cristiani announced the appointment of a high-level investigative commission to identify those responsible for the bombing. In addition to representatives of the government and international organizations, the commission was to include Jesuit Father Ignacio Ellacuria, killed with five other priests November 16 by Army soldiers, and representatives from FENASTRAS. FENASTRAS declined to participate in the proposed commission, as did opposition political leaders, absent certain guarantees.***

---

* Those who died were Luis Edgardo Vasquez Marquez, 26, leader of the bank workers union SIGEBAN; Vicente Salvador Melgar, 42, Secretary of Social Assistance for the SETA water workers union; Ricardo Humberto Bestoni, 35, SETA Secretary of Acts; Rosa Hilda Saravia de Elias, 30, a FENASTRAS employee, formerly of the STITAS textile workers union; Jose Daniel Lopez Melendez, 42, a leader of the SOICSCES construction union and FENASTRAS Secretary of Conflicts; and Julia Tatiana Mendoza Aquirre, 22, FENASTRAS press secretary, who was raped in National Police custody in September; Carmen Catalina Araujo de Hernandez, 24, a FENASTRAS employee; Maria Magdalena Rosales, 9; Ana Patricia Chacon, 13; and Velasquez. Among the injured was Gerardo Diaz, Secretary General of FENASTRAS.

** The FMLN underlined this link by calling the offensive, "Out With the Fascists! Febe Elizabeth Lives!"

*** In a November 6 meeting with Bernard Aronson, Assistant Secretary of State for Inter-American Affairs, opposition political and union leaders said they would not participate in any commission unless, among other things, the Armed Forces were made subject to civilian authority and the investigation be thorough and complete enough to find and punish all responsible parties. "We are not going to play the game of the government," declared Ruben Zamora upon leaving the meeting. Diario Latino, November 7, 1989.

On November 8, FENASTRAS officials permitted the judge in the case, Nelson Ulises Umana Bojorquez, visiting FBI agents and members of the Special Investigative Unit* to examine the premises and collect evidence. Following the FMLN offensive launched November 11, attention was diverted to the investigation of the Jesuit killings, among other things.

Interviewed in early November, First Brigade commander Colonel Elena Fuentes, echoing the line of other military and ARENA party officials,** suggested that the bombing of FENASTRAS was undertaken by the FMLN and FENASTRAS itself to galvanize the population in preparation for a planned military offensive. Noting that the bomb had been placed in between the outer office entryway and the inner one, the colonel told Americas Watch that the unionists themselves were responsible for the bombing, because "no authority could enter into that union without permission."

In fact, the outer door at the FENASTRAS headquarters was frequently left open during the day, and only the inner door was secured. Thus, it would have been possible for anyone to enter as far as the inner door -- into the area where the bomb detonated -- without the permission of persons inside the office. One witness told Americas Watch that, shortly before the explosion, he was standing in the corridor which runs between the inner and outer doors, when he saw a man in plainclothes enter the outer door and quickly place a smoking burlap bag on the floor of the corridor before leaving. The witness said he walked to within a few feet of the bag before he realized the danger. He returned to the inner door and rushed inside the office to give a warning. Seconds later, the bomb exploded.

Other witnesses reported seeing a vehicle drop two men off at one corner of the block on which the FENASTRAS headquarters was located. The

---

* This investigative unit is funded by U.S. AID under the Administration of Justice Act.

** "At a peasant meeting, Major Roberto D'Aubuisson, deputy and leader of the ARENA party, declared yesterday that 'there are strong suspicions that the bombing was produced by the manipulation of explosive artifacts that the unionists were making." Diario de Hoy, November 7, 1989.

men ran to the entrance, and one of them, carrying something, briefly went inside. The two then ran to the far corner of the block, where the vehicle had driven and was waiting for them.

Visiting El Salvador in early November, Assistant Secretary of State for Inter-American Affairs Bernard Aronson surmised that "violence by the extreme right is a credible idea" in seeking a suspect for the bombing.* Indeed, suspicion of FENASTRAS is long-standing among government and military figures who have consistently characterized the federation as nothing more than a "guerrilla front."** Since October 1988, FENASTRAS has experienced four bomb or grenade attacks, the August disappearance of two members, and the arrest and mistreatment of dozens of members in September by the National Police and National Guard. This recent history of official and quasi-official violence against FENASTRAS raises a presumption of military or death squad responsibility for the October bombing which only a thorough and satisfactory investigation might rebut. To date no such investigation is in evidence.

In January 1989, a member of President Cristiani's staff said that the investigation was going nowhere because of FENASTRAS's refusal to cooperate. On January 10, the Treasury Police reported that a detainee, Pablo Salvador Carcamo Centeno, had implicated the FMLN in the FENASTRAS bombing, as well as in numerous other murders in 1989.***

On January 23, 1989, FENASTRAS Secretary General Gerardo Diaz wrote to President Cristiani that FENASTRAS sought an independent investigation conducted under the auspices of international observers from the U.S. Congress, American or European labor unions, the Organization of American States or the United Nations. FENASTRAS also sought protection outside El Salvador for all witnesses to the massacre, and the release of all imprisoned unionists, among whom, it contended, were witnesses.

Currently, there are complaints on the bombing pending before the human rights commissions of the United Nations, the Organization of

---

*   Douglas Farah, "3 Salvadoran Politicians Found Dead," The Washington Post, November 8, 1989.

**   The U.S. Embassy has, shamefully, endorsed these life-threatening characterizations.

***   Diario de Hoy, January 11, 1990.

American States, and the International Labor Organization. The National Police and the U.S. FBI are said to be investigating the case.

B. Bombing of COMADRES Office, October 31, 1989

On the night of October 30-31, 1989, several hours before the FENASTRAS bombing, four persons were injured when a bomb exploded in the San Salvador office of COMADRES, a human rights organization of relatives of the disappeared, assassinated and political prisoners. Thirteen people were sleeping in the office that night. Two of them were members of COMADRES. A U.S. citizen working with the organization, Brenda Hubbard, 41, was sleeping near the front door when, at about 2:40 a.m., she was awakened by what she believed to be an explosion. Other persons there described the sound as a gunshot. Hubbard crawled toward the back of the room away from the door. She stood up, saw a burst of light, and then heard a loud explosion as the quarter-inch interior steel door flew toward the back of the room and crashed into a wooden desk, splitting it in half.

Hubbard was slashed by flying glass. Her head was cut in a line from her forehead down over her nose to her left cheek and ear. She received more than twenty stitches for her ear, which was sliced in half.

Pablo Mejia, 25, the office caretaker, was lying in between two desks at the time of the big explosion. He was cut by flying glass, and received three stitches in his knee. Mejia's life was apparently saved by the protection one of the desks offered against the flying door. Julia Leiva, 44, who was a visitor in the office that night, was injured when an object fell on her chest. A 3-month-old child was also slightly injured.

The explosion produced substantial damage to the office, damaging the outer brick wall, the garage door, and the doorbell apparatus, as well as several inner doors. Most windows were shattered, and several interior objects -- including an incubator, a photocopy machine, a sewing machine, two file cabinets, and a desk -- were damaged.

C. Other Attacks on Union Offices and September 1989 Mass Arrest of FENASTRAS Marchers

On the night of February 8, 1989, several armed men in a vehicle shot at the headquarters of the National Unity of Salvadoran Workers (the UNTS, the principal opposition labor coalition) and damaged the front of the building without harming any persons.

At 3:50 a.m. on February 15, 1989, a high-powered bomb exploded in the door of the UNTS, destroying part of the office and damaging some nearby houses. In a communique left at the site, the "Comandos Urbanos Maximiliano Hernandez Martinez," an anti-communist organization, took responsibility for the explosion and said it would not rest until it had exterminated the communists.

During the evening of September 4, about 25 union members were in the FENASTRAS offices in downtown San Salvador. At about 12:30 a.m., September 5, several armed persons walked by and threw stones at the office for about five minutes. They returned at about 1 a.m., calling those inside guerrillas and screaming at them to leave. About 1:20 a.m., a large explosion was heard, and it is thought that a grenade was thrown over the outer office wall, damaging the upper part of the main entrance door and the wall dividing the office from the house next door.

On the night of September 17 and early morning of September 18, National Guardsmen raided four houses and the Santa Mercedes textile factory in Ilopango and arrested ten persons associated with FENASTRAS. The Santa Mercedes factory had been occupied by workers following an employer shutdown in December 1988.

On September 18, FENASTRAS held a march to protest the arrests of the previous night. During the march, participants obstructed traffic, and two buses were burned. National Policemen chased the marchers into the Central American Mission Church and then forced them out by throwing tear gas through the windows. Sixty-four persons were arrested by the National Police. Many of them alleged that they were kicked and struck as they were forced from the church into a bus which took them to the National Police headquarters.

At the National Police, many of the detainees were hit and forced to stand or do exercises. Of 37 persons examined by the forensic physician of the First Criminal Court of San Salvador on September 21, 19 exhibited marks or bruises indicating they had been beaten. Several alleged that they had been severely beaten, and at least four contended they had been raped during interrogation. Tatiana Mendoza's rape was confirmed by a court physician. She died in the October 31 bombing of the FENASTRAS headquarters.

Of the 74 persons arrested in the two sweeps, the majority -- not charged at all or charged with belonging to a union, which is not a crime -- were released within 72 hours. By March 1990, three FENASTRAS leaders arrested on September 17, Juan Jose Huezo, Francisco Javier Martinez, and Susana Dolores Rodriguez, remain in prison, charged with subversion or engaging in terrorist acts.

D. January 1990 Killing of Opposition Politician in Guatemala

Hector Oqueli Colindres, 45, the deputy secretary-general of the National Revolutionary Movement and Adjunct Secretary General of the Socialist International for Latin America and the Caribbean, was abducted by heavily armed men in civilian dress as he headed for the airport in Guatemala City between 6:30 and 7:00 a.m. on January 12, 1990. He was kidnapped along with Gilda Amparo Flores Arevalo, an attorney and member of the Socialist Democratic Party of Guatemala, who was driving Oqueli to the airport. Several witnesses reportedly saw the abduction, which occurred within one block of the Air Force Tactical Unit, which normally has soldiers posted in front.

Both of their bodies were reportedly found by late that afternoon in a pickup truck parked on the Pan American Highway near the Salvadoran border. Oqueli and Flores were both shot in the head.* Oqueli's passport was found in his shirt pocket, according to an MNR source interviewed by Americas Watch.

Oqueli had arrived from Mexico the day before his kidnapping. Upon arrival at the Aurora airport in Guatemala City, Oqueli was detained by immigration and his passport taken away for 15 or 20 minutes, according to a western diplomat. This, combined with the fact that Oqueli's colleagues in the Social Democratic Party in Guatemala (with the exception of Gilda Flores) did not know he was visiting the country, raises suspicions of involvement of immigration officials in the crime.** Oqueli, who was to leave Guatemala the same afternoon of his arrival, reportedly changed plans at the last minute and decided to stay overnight. He was on his way to catch the early morning COPA flight to Managua when he was abducted.

---

*　　"Two Activists Killed in Guatemala," The Washington Post, January 14, 1990.

**　　See Americas Watch, Messengers of Death: Human Rights in Guatemala, November 1988 - March 1990, March 1990, at 41-44.

It has been reported that Oqueli's murder may have been related to a secret meeting between U.S. Senator Christopher Dodd and two representatives of the FMLN, Ana Guadalupe Martinez and Roberto Canas, held in Guatemala City January 10. The meeting was apparently undertaken to discuss prospects for ending the civil war in El Salvador. Some observers have suggested that the murder of Oqueli was intended as a signal to the FMLN that Guatemala is not safe territory for them.*

Following a meeting in a private room at Guatemala City's airport, Senator Dodd reportedly left the country and the two FMLN leaders were taken to a West European Embassy. Martinez reported that the Embassy began receiving threatening phone calls from self-proclaimed "Salvadoran commandos" within two hours. She told The Los Angeles Times:

> We think it was the Salvadoran right operating with its network in Guatemala.... It was a warning from the right and the Salvadoran army that we were in their rear guard, in forbidden territory.**

After seven years in exile, Oqueli had returned to El Salvador in 1987 to help reactivate the leftist political party founded by his mentor, Guillermo Ungo. Oqueli left El Salvador for security reasons after the FMLN's November offensive started, imagining that he would be safe from right-wing reprisals abroad. On January 29, 1990, the Bush Administration sent an agent of the Federal Bureau of Investigations to lend technical help in the investigation.

E. October Bombing of Homes of Opposition Leaders

In the early morning hours of October 19, 1989, a powerful bomb damaged the home of Ruben Zamora, leader of the opposition Popular Social Christian Movement (MPSC). Two of Zamora's personal security guards were injured in the attack on his home. However, Zamora, his wife, and their five children escaped injury. Seconds earlier, three grenades were thrown into the

---

*   "Meeting Is Linked to Murder," The Miami Herald, January 26, 1990.

**   Marjorie Miller, "Rebels See Leftist's Murder as Warning," The Los Angeles Times, January 25, 1990.

house of Zamora's sister-in-law, Aronette Diaz, leader of the opposition National Democratic Union. She and her two children were unharmed. Shortly afterward, another bomb was placed in a building belonging to the Lutheran Church, causing damage but no injuries.*

F. Shooting and Other Incidents at the National University, April 1989-March 1990

On April 23, 1989, soldiers entered and searched the private San Salvador homes of the vice-rector Dr. Wilfredo Barillas Acosta, and another staff member, Flor Canales, of the University of El Salvador in San Salvador, the country's principal public university. No search warrant was presented.

On May 2, 1989, an unidentified gunman fired at Dr. Barillas's car near the Basilica Guadalupe in San Salvador. A bullet destroyed the windshield, but did not hit him.

A soldier beat a university watchman near the main entrance gate on May 15, 1989. On May 23, soldiers at the entrance to the dental school detained a youth around 8:00 p.m. and cut his hair off. Two other students received the same treatment at another campus entrance.

On May 16, 1989, there was a dispute at the University entrance. Colonel Juan Orlando Zepeda, then commander of the First Brigade (currently Vice Minister of Defense), claimed that "terrorist groups in the National University threw Molotov cocktails at the soldiers."**

At about 6:00 p.m. on July 17, 1989, First Brigade soldiers shot at a group of protesting university teachers, students and employees at the university, wounding eight students, including a North American. Colonel Elena Fuentes, commander of the First Brigade, said students had provoked the troops by tossing Molotov cocktails and fragmentation grenades at them from within the campus. Student leaders denied there was any provocation.

---

*   The Washington Post, October 20, 1989.

**   El Diario de Hoy, May 18, 1989.

President Cristiani and Minister of Defense General Rafael Humberto Larios Lopez said that this incident typified the provocations against the Armed Forces at the campus, but affirmed that the army would not intervene in campus activity. University officials denounced this and other incidents of violence at the university as "part of a plan of intervention.... The new government wants students and university authorities to abandon the campus."*

This incident reflected the heightened tensions between soldiers and students throughout the year.** These are not new. The Army has long accused the FMLN of using the university as a recruiting ground, a training center and weapons depot, and has a long history of having shut and opened the university during the 1970s and from 1980 to 1984, seriously disrupting higher education for students who cannot afford to attend the private institutions that cropped up in the awake of its closure.

Many students contend they have been harassed by soldiers who maintained a constant cordon around the university entrance in December 1988 and then again from March 1989 on. In early November 1989, Colonel Elena Fuentes told Americas Watch that between 30 and 50 soldiers were around the university on a daily basis, checking the bags of persons as they enter.

Following the November offensive, First Brigade soldiers took over the campus, and all academic activities ceased. Classes of the various faculties have been held in other buildings throughout the city ("in exile").

On March 13, 1990, an inventory was commenced as a step toward turning the university campus back over to the university administration. The purpose of the inventory was to establish the damage done after the military occupation of the campus. In attendance the first day of the inventory were about 100 persons, including representatives of the Court of Claims, Ministry of Education, administration of the university, and the First Brigade.***

---

*   Advertisement, El Mundo, July 19, 1989.

**   There were also tensions within the University. In 1988, the Committee to Rescue the University was formed by conservatives to regain control of the University from alleged communist dominance. In March, one of the members of the committee was executed by the FMLN and the car of another attacked, as described above.

***   Diario Latino, March 13, 1990.

G. July Bombing of UCA Printing Press

About 1:50 a.m. on July 22, 1989, four bombs exploded in the Central American University (UCA) -- two in the computer and photocopier area of the printing press, one in the transformer just outside the printing press, and one under a nearby bus. Three other bombs were deactivated by the National Police. Computers, photocopy machines, office equipment, transformers and printing machines were destroyed. Damages was estimated at between 400,000 and 500,000 *colones* (roughly $62,500 to $77,500). No one was injured.

H. April Mass Arrests at CRIPDES

At 7:30 a.m. on April 19, 1989, Attorney General Jose Roberto Garcia Alvarado was assassinated. That day Treasury Police agents raided and searched the offices of the Christian Committee for Displaced Persons of El Salvador and National Coordinator for Repopulation (CRIPDES/CNR) and a house shared by the trade union federation FUSS, a coalition of unemployed and laid off workers (CODYDES), and a women's organization (ADEMUSA). By midnight 75 persons -- the overwhelming majority from CRIPDES/CNR -- had been arrested and taken to Treasury Police headquarters.

Treasury Police agents surrounded the CRIPDES/CNR office at about 3:15 p.m., but CRIPDES members would not let them enter. Sixty persons were inside, including 20 children, and several elderly or handicapped persons. By 5:30 p.m., a riot squad arrived at the scene. By 9:30 p.m., the police claimed they had obtained a judicial search warrant but refused to show it to CRIPDES members. They were not accompanied by a justice of the peace. At 11:00 p.m., the police forcibly entered the building, searched the office, and arrested its occupants, who were brought to Treasury Police headquarters in a military truck. Police agents stayed behind and continued their search of the office. CRIPDES members later contended the police took Salvadoran and U.S. currency totalling more than $10,000, two radio-tape recorders, a megaphone, a video camera, a photographic camera and eight albums of photographs. Police said that from the various offices they seized sticks used at demonstrations, metal spikes used to flatten tires, and one pistol.

That morning, Treasury Police also arrested fifteen others, members of COMADRES, FUSS, ADEMUSA, and CODYDES. Most of the detainees were released within two days. Some of them reported being beaten, kicked, thrown to the ground, and threatened with a knife placed at the throat. Ten were consigned to the Second Criminal Court and sent to prison. CRIPDES members were charged with possession of arms of war, but released on August 8 for lack of evidence,* as were two ADEMUSA members. Several of the detained were tortured while in Treasury Police custody.**

While the six CRIPDES/CNR members were still in prison, the Army took out unsigned paid advertisements in the local press asserting that each of the six belonged to FMLN organizations. Under the title, "S/He is a Terrorist," appeared a purported guerrilla biography of each and the slogan, "FMLN = CRIPDES."

The absence of any evidence to support the charges of "terrorism" or "possession of arms of war" against those detained, as well as the mass nature of the arrests, raises the strong suspicion that these actions were intended to intimidate members of mass-based organizations opposed to government policies and to lash out at alleged FMLN "sympathizers" for the assassination of the Attorney General.

I. Recent Bombings and Other Threats to Religious Workers

At 9:00 p.m. on December 27, 1989, a bomb exploded in front of the garage of the San Salvador home of Hazel Browning, an evangelical lay church worker from New Zealand living in El Salvador for the past 15 years. Nobody was injured, but the explosion seriously damaged the home.***

In December, Americas Watch reported the November 20, 1989 arrest of Father Luis Serrano Lorente and seven other members of the Episcopal Church of El Salvador for allegedly covering up the possibility that a catapult bomb used in an earlier FMLN attack on the headquarters of the Army General Staff had been assembled in the church yard. On January 5, 1990, all but one of eight persons arrested were released from prison; the last detainee was released February 26 by the court.

---

*   The "arms" found at the CRIPDES office were home-made devices used to commit acts of petty sabotage during street demonstrations, called "miguelitos" (for flattening tires) and "mechugas" (pipes). They were not arms of war nor did they contain explosives or projectiles.

** See Human Rights Watch, The Persecution of Human Rights Monitors, December 1988 to December 1989: A Worldwide Survey, December 1989.

*** El Rescate, El Salvador Chronology, December 1989.

Father Serrano left El Salvador on January 6. On January 10, armed, uniformed soldiers entered and searched the residence of Father Serrano.*

In December, Americas Watch reported that on November 21, the National Guard emptied the contents from the residence and office of representatives of the Mennonite Central Committee (MCC). On December 8, the Guard returned some, but not all, of the property taken.

On January 23, 1990, two Salvadoran lawyers and a member of the MCC went to National Guard headquarters in San Salvador to retrieve still more, though still not all, of the items confiscated. In December 1989, photographs of two MCC workers which had been taken were seen on the National Guard bulletin board with a caption reading, "Terrorists infiltrated in the Mennonite Church."**

In the December 16, 1989 Update, Americas Watch reported that on November 22, a woman in Teotepeque, La Libertad, saw a uniformed soldier or civil defense member drop a flyer in front of her house. The flyer, and others found the next morning around the town, charged that six local church workers were "enemies of the people" and urged residents to "reject them."

On December 17, 1989, and again on February 3-4, 1990, new anti-church flyers were found on the streets of Teotepeque. The February leaflet was the eighth anti-church leaflet circulated in the area since August 1989.***

---

*   Churchworker Report, "Attacks on the Churches in El Salvador," December 16, 1989 - February 10, 1990.

**   Church Worker Report, "Attacks on the Churches in El Salvador," December 16, 1989 - February 10, 1990.

***   Churchworker Report, "Attacks on the Churches in El Salvador," December 16, 1989 - February 10, 1990.

VII. DUE PROCESS AND AMNESTY

Although the case of the assassinated Jesuits has been the subject of much international attention and even investigation by Salvadorans and foreigners resulting in the revelation that a colonel ordered the murders, many other human rights cases have languished not only in international attention but also in the judicial system.

During the FMLN offensive of November 1989, a state of emergency was declared. Under El Salvador's constitutional provisions for state of emergency, cases alleging "acts of terrorism," "sabotage," and "subversive association" and other politically motivated crimes are tried in military courts while the military, as always, is tried in civilian courts. As of this writing the military courts continue to have jurisdiction over political cases arising after the November 1989 state of emergency, while older political cases are still being tried in the civilian courts. Curiously, the assassination of the six Jesuits and the two women was never considered an "act of terrorism" although it arose after the state of emergency, thus a civilian court has always had jurisdiction over it.

On December 8, 1989, 82 prisoners forming a Committee of Prisoners of Ex-Members of the Armed Forces presented a signed petition to the Pardon and Amnesty Committee of the Legislative Assembly, asking that military and ex-military members who were being tried for crimes as well as those who had been condemned be amnestied.*

Several popular organizations are now raising the demand that political prisoners be amnestied as a means of demonstrating good will in connec-

---

* Lindsey Gruson, "Salvadorans Consider Sweeping Amnesty for Military," The New York Times, March 18, 1990.

tion with negotiations the government and the FMLN should hold soon under the auspices of the United Nations.

Americas Watch opposes all amnesties of serious violations of human rights, such as summary executions, disappearances, and torture. We especially oppose "self-amnesty" laws, which constitute a violation of the state's obligation to investigate, prosecute and punish crimes, particularly those committed by its own agents.

The existence of the prisoners' petition did not even come to light until March 13, 1990. The petition is said to cover about 2,000 prisoners.* There are about 6,000 prisoners in El Salvador's prisons, including 370 prisoners accused of politically motivated crimes. Many military offenders awaiting trial are not detained in the prisons but are under supervision at their respective bases or in the security forces.

Those accused in important human rights cases could be freed under the overbroad petition. The ARENA Assembly President said that they will not touch the Jesuit case, on the grounds that the defendants were not named until after the date of the petition. However, the specific intention of the petition is to free those military who defended their country against communism and are being tried for crimes that "resulted from the violence that El Salvador suffers."**

Based on press descriptions of the petition, the military or ex-military defendants in the following cases might be amnestied:

1. Four US church workers, killed December 1980: five National Guardsmen convicted in May 1984, not amnestied before.***

2. Archbishop Oscar Romero, killed March 1980: Captain Alvaro Saravia, still residing in the US, was identified as a defendant in 1988 but the Supreme Court held that the warrant for his arrest should be withdrawn in December 1988. Roberto D'Aubuisson, a former major in the National Guard,

---

*   El Diario de Hoy, March 15, 1990. Copies of such proposals, although introduced for debate in the Assembly, are not available to the public.

** El Diario de Hoy, March 15, 1990.

*** They are Daniel Canales Ramirez, Salvador Rivera Franco, Francisco Orlando Contreras Recinos, Carlos Joaquin Contreras Palacios, and Jose Roberto Moreno Canjura.

was accused (not judicially) by then President Duarte of being the intellectual author of the crime. As a member of the Assembly, he has immunity unless the Assembly decides to lift it.

3. San Sebastian case, 10 peasants killed, September 1988: Major Mauricio Beltran Granados and Corporal Rafael Rosales Villalobos are to be tried; their indictment of February 1990 is being appealed by their attorneys. At the same time, the Attorney General is appealing the dismissal of the case against nine of the soldiers and lower-level officers who allegedly participated in the massacre.*

4. Kidnapping for profit case, arrests in April 1986: National Guard major Rodolfo Isidro Lopez Sibrian, implicated in the Sheraton Hotel killings of the head of the agrarian reform institute and his two US AIFLD advisors in 1981, is awaiting trial in jail in San Vicente. Also in custody is Army Major Jose Alfredo Jimenez. Army Lieutenant Colonel Joaquin Zacapa Astasio is a fugitive from justice; there is allegedly a warrant for his arrest. Some or all of these defendants may actually have been dismissed from the service.

5. Lutheran pastor David Fernandez, killed November 1984: ex-Army Sergeant Jose Adan Cruz Bustillo and ex-soldier Manuel Martinez Segovia were convicted in 1987.

6. Reuters photographers Roberto Navas, killed, and Luis Galdamez, wounded, March 1989: Air Force junior officers and soldiers accused and under judicial investigation: they are Lieutenant Saul Solano Reyes, Subsergeant Efrain Guardado Moraga, and soldiers Cesar Caballero Pleites, Francisco Cesar Gonzalez, and Felix Rivas Gomez.

7. Channel 12 soundman Mauricio Pineda DeLeon, killed, March 1989: a corporal or sergeant of the ARCE Battalion was allegedly detained, and is allegedly under judicial investigation in San Miguel.

8. Tres Ceibas, two peasants tortured and killed, July 1989: Corporal Salvador Alcides Gomez Gomez, of the Atlacatl Battalion, supposedly detained by the National Guard, and Cesar Vielman Joya Martinez, First Brigade (a fugitive from justice seeking political asylum in the US; he has

---

* Diario Latino, February 27, 1990.

denied guilt in this case but admitted that he participated under First Brigade orders as part of a death squad in many other cases).

There are many other cases in which military and ex-military personnel are in jail convicted or awaiting trial, many for common crimes. The 1990 convictions of 19 members of the San Agustin, San Pedro Perulapan, Cuscatlan civil defense (for killing 23 peasants in March 1982)* and seven Armenia civil defense members (for killing an engineer and former university professor, with three others, in 1984 at a checkpoint)**, and the 1989 conviction of a lieutenant Jorge Alberto Rivas Aguirre (triple assassination on the road to Santa Ana in August 1987 of young men captured by the military in San Salvador)***, would all have been for naught if this proposal were to pass. There are also countless cases of drunken soldiers throwing grenades into parties; these too might be amnestied if the proposal were passed, although some ARENA deputies have opposed amnestying this category of prisoner.

One justification offered for the proposed legislation is that FMLN combatants have been freed in amnesties, but that the military has not been amnestied. This is not true.

There was a broad amnesty in October 1987 that covered not only FMLN combatants and collaborators (about 400 political prisoners were freed from jail) but also absolved all military, security forces, paramilitary groups and death squads. The amnesty forgave a wide range of political crimes and those that were committed prior to October 22, 1987, "with the motive, reason, or as a consequence of the armed conflict" or were committed by more than 20 persons. The law favored the military much more than it did the FMLN, whose combatants had only 15 days to turn themselves in and receive amnesty, while the military who had not even been accused of any crime were absolved in the unlikely event they might be prosecuted sometime in the future. In addition, about 400 leftist political prisoners were freed from jail.

---

*   Diario Latino, March 9, 1990; El Mundo, March 9, 1990.

**   El Mundo, March 9, 1990.

***   El Mundo, May 6, 1989; Diario de Hoy, May 8, 1989.

As a result of the 1987 amnesty, the following well-known human rights cases, among others, were amnestied, in which military were defendants:

1. Sheraton murders of the head of the agrarian reform institute and his two US advisors in 1981; two National Guardsmen were convicted in 1986 and freed by the amnesty.

2. Las Hojas massacre of 74 peasants, 1983: the proceedings against subordinates of Colonel Elmer Gonzalez Araujo, then head of the Sixth Military Detachment in Sonsonate, were dropped after the amnesty. This case is now being pursued before the Inter-American Commission of Human Rights of the Organization of American States, seven years after the massacre.*

3. Battalion killing of five peasants in San Miguel in May 1987: proceedings in Ciudad Barrios, San Miguel court were dropped even though no individual defendants in the Battalion were identified and the army denied responsibility.

Some notorious cases were not amnestied: the killing of four US churchwomen in December 1980, for which five National Guardsmen had been convicted,** and the Zona Rosa killing by the FMLN of four US Marines and nine civilians in June 1985.*** The Romero assassination was specifically exempted from the amnesty legislation, as was any case of kidnapping for profit.

Recently there were amnesties given to FMLN wounded ex-combatants who were never arrested. Thirty-one ex-combatants were able to leave the country in October 1989 and 48 in February 1990. Although the FMLN maintains that they were not amnestied but that the first group was given political asylum by the Mexican government, and that the government had the obligation under international humanitarian law to permit them to leave the country for medical care, there were two amnesty decrees passed in connection with these two groups of wounded ex-combatants by the Legislative As-

---

* El Mundo, February 20, 1989.

** The judge determined that the killings were common crimes to which the amnesty law did not apply.

*** Judge Jorge Alberto Serrano Panameno, later assassinated, granted amnesty but on appeal through the military justice system, President Duarte, as Commander in Chief, overruled him. The three Zona Rosa defendants are in jail today, awaiting trial since 1985.

sembly, one in October 1989 and the other in February 1990. Both groups of wounded immediately left the country for medical treatment abroad.

Other cases in which defendants were not investigated but where there is evidence of military involvement are:

1. June 1987, Los Degollados: Jose Antonio Lopez Cruz, 28, Jose Bertilio Alvarado Lopez, 28, and Jose Antonio Ortega Orellana, 26, were separately captured by soldiers in and near their homes near La Laguna, Chalatenango. After interrogation, the soldiers cut their throats, leaving them for dead, but they survived. The case is pending in the court in Dulce Nombre de Maria, Chalatenango.

2. Puerta del Diablo, January 1988: witnesses recognized members of the National Guard and First Brigade who captured Jose Luis Cornejo Calles, 27, Manuel de Jesus Santamaria, 25, and Javier Santamaria, 16, on January 31, 1988 near San Jose Guayabal, Cuscatlan. Their bodies were found the next day at the infamous death squad dumping ground Puerta del Diablo, with signs of torture. General Adolfo Blandon, then head of the General Staff, promised to investigate. This case is pending in the Third Penal Court, San Salvador, where in May 1988 the First Brigade through the Minister of Defense provided to the court the names of hundreds of soldiers who were on duty that day.

3. Tepemechin, Morazan, February 1988: soldiers captured three young men in front of witnesses from their homes in *caserio* Tepemechin, *canton* El Tablon, Sociedad, Morazan on January 31, 1988. The bodies of two, Mario Cruz Rivera, 16, and Felix Antonio Rivera, 25, were found later the same day, with ears and noses missing as well as some fingers, and signs of their feet and legs having been burned. The third man, Sebastian Gutierrez, 18, was missing. An exhumation of the two bodies was conducted by the First Trial court of San Francisco Gotera, Morazan, in May 1988.

4. Soyapango Sand Diggers, April 1988: Jose Arnoldo Cerritos, 25, Vicente Cerritos Torres, 56, and Arturo Navarro Garcia, 31, were captured in and near their homes in Soyapango, San Salvador, on April 14, 1988, by the Air Force, according to some witnesses, and were disappeared until their bodies were exhumed on April 21 by order of the justice of the peace of San Juan Talpa, La Paz, in whose jurisdiction the bodies were found.

5. Military Judge Serrano, May 1988: Jorge Alberto Serrano Panameno was assassinated in San Salvador on May 11, 1988, by unknown men. He was First Military Judge of First Instance. His predecessor had also been assassinated. There is no direct evidence of military involvement in this case, but although most of his caseload consisted in persons accused of being FMLN collaborators or members, the kidnapping for profit case (see above) was pending before him at the time of his death; three witnesses had earlier been killed in that case.

VIII. U.S. ROLE

A. Ten Years Later: U.S. Policy in El Salvador

In the past decade the United States has granted vast amounts of military and economic assistance to successive Salvadoran governments. The figures (in millions of dollars) are as follows:*

	Economic**	Military***	Total
FY 1981	113.6	35.5	149.1
FY 1982	182.2	82.0	264.2
FY 1983	245.6	81.3	326.9
FY 1984	212.4	64.8	277.2
FY 1985	425.4	136.3	561.7
FY 1986	310.8	121.8	432.6
FY 1987	457.3	111.5	568.5
FY 1988	328.0	86.5	418.5
FY 1989	313.4	86.4	430.1
FY 1990	228.98	86.0	314.98
Total	**2,817.68**	**892.10**	**3,709.78**

*   Source: U.S. State Department, Agency for International Development.

** Economic assistance includes Development Assistance (DA), Economic Support Funds (ESF), PL-480 Title I, PL-480 Title II, Section 416 (in Fiscal Year [FY] 1987 and FY 1988), and Disaster-OFDA (in FY 1987).

*** Military assistance includes funding under the Military Assistance Program (MAP), military training, and, in FY 1985, Foreign Military Sales (FMS).

The striking resemblance of the Jesuits' slaying to equally infamous atrocities committed at the very beginning of the decade should have have shocked American policymakers into a thorough reevaluation of the U.S. role in El Salvador: what it has accomplished and where it is headed. Yet as intensive United States involvement in the Salvadoran war and in Salvadoran society enters a second decade,* U.S. policy --and the rhetorical tools employed by Administration officials to justify it -- remains remarkably consistent.

In the face of the continuing tragedy of El Salvador, however, Bush Administration officials offer the same arguments in support of the existing position as their predecessors throughout the 1980's. On the whole, these arguments are no more persuasive today -- after the U.S. government has had a decade to end the terror in El Salvador -- than they were in earlier years.

U.S. officials, today as in the early 1980's, put forth three principal claims in support of their contention that U.S. military assistance to El Salvador is essential in promoting human rights and the rule of law: 1) human rights abuses by the Salvadoran government and military have progressively declined; 2) to the extent they persist, such abuses are not the responsibility of the elected civilian government of El Salvador; and 3) U.S. military training and assistance offers the surest means of eliminating remaining abuses by inculcating in the Salvadoran Armed Forces greater respect for human rights. A review of these rationales suggests they remain as weak now as at the dawn of U.S. military involvement.

Argument 1: *Things Are Getting Better*

On January 24, 1990, appearing at a hearing before two subcommittees of the House Foreign Affairs Committee, Bernard Aronson, Assistant Secretary of State for Inter-American Affairs, stated the conventional ad-

---

* Although on a far smaller scale than in the past decade, the U.S. government has been providing military assistance to El Salvador since the end of World War II. The U.S. sent its first military mission to El Salvador in the mid-1940's. Between 1950 and 1979 the U.S. trained 1,971 Salvadoran officers. See Americas Watch/ACLU, Report on Human Rights in El Salvador, January 25, 1982, at 178-81. See also M. McClintock, The American Connection: State Terror and Popular Resistance in El Salvador (1985).

ministration wisdom: "Every year in which we've been engaged in El Salvador, political violence has gone down ... steadily, dramatically down -- every year."*

If it is true that, given the cumulative effect of political violence over time, fewer murders in later years may achieve a "desired" level of popular fear and intimidation, it is also the case that the assassination of a few selected individuals may have a more lasting impact than the slaughter of hundreds of peasants. The recent murder of six Jesuit priests is illustrative. By murdering the first priests in El Salvador since 1980 -- men who were intellectual leaders and among the most prominent and respected opponents of government and military policies -- the armed forces sent a powerful and unmistakable message to the rest of the population. If six such important religious figures, one of whom was on friendly terms with President Cristiani, could be killed, who could be safe?

Numbers of political murders have undeniably declined since 1982, but that in itself unfortunately does not evidence greater respect for human rights within the Armed Forces, or enhanced freedom to express political dissent. Political murder is undertaken to terrorize a civilian population and to discourage political organization and the expression of dissent. The killing of 30,000 civilians over the course of three years -- the toll for 1980-82 -- is bound to have constrained opposition in later years. Declining numbers may measure popular adjustments to political violence at least as well as they gauge the shifting attitudes of Army soldiers.

Moreover, as Americas Watch noted during the height of the violence in 1982,

> there is only a finite number of people in El Salvador to be killed. At some point, the number of political murders ought to decline if for no other reason than that there are fewer politically suspect persons who remain alive to be killed and have not left the country. Should the numbers decline for this reason ... it would be the height of cynicism to interpret such

---

*   Testimony of Assistant Secretary of State Bernard Aronson, U.S. House of Representatives Subcommittee on Human Rights and Subcommittee on the Western Hemisphere, Hearings, January 24, 1990, as transcribed by Federal News Service, Washington, D.C. [hereafter "Hearings"], at 12, 29.

a decline as an indication that the government of El Salvador has become more respectful of human rights.*

This is not to say, of course, that the human rights climate has not improved since 1982, but rather that a mere recitation of a numerical decline does not alone show that. Indeed, to the extent that Bush Administration officials have ventured beyond numbers to argue that the military in El Salvador today tolerates a greater range of political expression than was heretofore the case, their arguments have proven similarly unconvincing. In his testimony last January Mr. Aronson stated:

> I think you also have to give this armed forces credit. . . . [T]his is an institution that, when I went to El Salvador [in 1983], the former leaders of it, who are no longer there, published a list of 113 people who were considered traitors, including Ruben Zamora and Guillermo Ungo. The last few years, this same military has been protecting their security and allowing them to campaign, even though they haven't severed an alliance with the FMLN that's tacit. So I think things have changed; I think the military has become committed to guarantee the democratic process.**

In fact, although both Zamora and Ungo returned to El Salvador in October 1987 and campaigned under the umbrella Democratic Convergence in the March 1989 presidential elections, they have been frustrated by obstacles to political expression and participation. In October 1989, Zamora's house was bombed and two activists of his Popular Social Christian Movement were killed. In November, following the FMLN offensive, death threats against Zamora and Ungo were broadcast over the government-controlled radio station, and President Cristiani on November 12 issued a warning to all leftist politicians that they would have to break formally with the rebels or leave: "We can," he declared, "no longer allow there to be political parties that doubt whether the FMLN is trying to restrict the freedom of the Salvadoran people." On November 22, the government-controlled radio broadcast an interview with ARENA party leader and legislative assemblyman Roberto D'Aubuisson, in

---

* Americas Watch. First Supplement to the Report on Human Rights in El Salvador, July 20, 1982, p. 14.

** Hearings, at 56.

which he said that the offensive was a joint action of the FMLN and the Democratic Convergence. As a result, D'Aubuisson said, there existed "the moral justification to annihilate" the Convergence. Popular Social Christian Movement leader Jorge Villacorta was arrested at the airport returning from Guatemala on December 6 by the Treasury Police and beaten overnight. Ungo and Hector Oqueli, his deputy at the National Revolutionary Movement, left the country in November in fear for their lives. Oqueli was murdered in Guatemala in January. Since the offensive, government forces have entered and searched offices of the MPSC and the MNR on more than one occasion. Ungo's home was searched at least four times. These and other actions suggest that, contrary to Bush Administration hopes, it is not at all clear that the military has grown committed to guaranteeing any "democratic process" that includes genuine dissent.

Nor have the raw numbers shown all that the U.S. administration hopes. While the numbers in recent years do not approach the carnage of the early 1980's, the trend, as measured, by Tutela Legal, has not been toward steady improvement. In fact, targeted government and death squad killings increased from 96 in 1987 to 152 in 1988. Combined government and death squad disappearances increased from 39 in 1986 to 101 in 1989.

In pointing to alleged numerical "improvements" in the human rights situation where the evidence simply does not support the claim, Bush Administration officials have a long tradition -- the practice in the Reagan years -- upon which to draw. On September 24, 1981, Assistant Secretary of State Thomas O. Enders told the House Foreign Affairs Committee that "the level of violence has apparently decreased over recent months, we believe, in part due to the effort of the Government to end the abuses that have occurred in that country."* In early 1982, the State Department noted a "downward trend in political violence"** and reported to Congress that the Salvadoran government was making a "concerted and significant effort" to protect human rights -

---

* Quoted in Americas Watch, Managing the Facts, December 1985, at 28.

** U.S. Department of State, Country Reports on Human Rights Practices for 1981 (1982), at 424.

- this at a time when, according to the human rights office of the Catholic Archdiocese of San Salvador, government forces and their paramilitary allies killed more than 13,000 civilians. *

Argument 2: *The Elected Government Is Not Responsible*

Throughout the course of U.S. involvement in El Salvador, U.S. officials have consistently sought to absolve the Salvadoran government and military of responsibility for human rights violations, pointing instead to runaway "death squads" and "vigilante" elements who allegedly operate without the approval of the authorities. This responds to the fear that the U.S. is funding a military which systematically violates the human rights of its citizens.

At the same time, the U.S. government has portrayed civilian leaders of El Salvador as exercising control over the reins of governmental power. This addresses the concern that the U.S. not be seen to be supporting a mere civilian facade for military rule. The two contentions -- responding to competing needs -- frequently come into conflict.

As in earlier years U.S. officials sought to dissociate President Duarte from the crimes of the Salvadoran Armed Forces, so today the administration builds on that habit, asserting both that President Cristiani is in control of his government and military forces, and that he bears no responsibility for the atrocities they commit. When pushed to reconcile these contradictory premises, U.S. officials argue that President Cristiani is gradually gaining control over those elements in the Armed Forces which have yet to respect democracy and human rights. Thus, once again, as throughout the past decade, we are led to believe that unrestrained rogue elements are running riot within the Armed Forces, committing unsanctioned acts of terror and thereby tainting an Army and a government which, in large part, respect human rights and the rule of law.**

---

* Managing the Facts, at 29.

** The contrasting responses of President Cristiani and Salvadoran military officials to the Jesuit massacre led some observers to conclude that President Cristiani does not exercise genuine control over the army. When Salvadoran military officials contended in December, even as President Cristiani was promising a thorough investigation, that the FMLN had committed the murders, Senator Patrick Leahy was moved to note: "It makes me question who is running the government -- the elected president or, what appears more likely, the rightist elements within the military." Lee Hockstader, "Salvadoran Murder Probe Now Focuses on Military," The Washington Post, December 10, 1989.

U.S. officials have engaged in this contradictory two-track rhetorical strategy for much of the last decade. As early as December 1, 1981, U.N. Ambassador Jeanne Kirkpatrick told the United Nations that, "in Salvador, murderous traditionalists confront murderous revolutionaries -- with *only* the government working to moderate murder and attempting to pacify adversaries."*

The State Department's Country Reports on Human Rights Practices for 1982 attributed political murders to "extremes of the right and the left." In May 1984, President Reagan attributed the political violence in El Salvador to the guerrillas and to "a small, violent right wing" that is "not part of the government."**

As Administration officials were attempting to divert responsibility for thousands of murders from the government to allegedly independent death squads, they simultaneously contended that civilian authorities exercised increasing authority in El Salvador. On January 28, 1982, and on three successive occasions through 1983, the Reagan Administration certified that "the Government of El Salvador is achieving substantial control over all elements of its armed forces."***

The Administration's evolving responses to developments in the investigation into the November 1989 murders of six Jesuit priests have followed a similar logic. Following the killings, but before President Cristiani announced that the military was responsible, U.S. officials consistently asserted that, despite persuasive circumstantial evidence pointing to army involvement, anyone could have done the deed.

---

*   Quoted in Managing the Facts at 15.

** Quoted in Cynthia Brown, ed., With Friends Like These: The Americas Watch Report on Human Rights and U.S. Policy in Latin America (1985), at 131. The State Department is now more willing to admit that death squads did in the past operate out of the Army. The 1989 Country Report for El Salvador states, "As the insurgency gathered strength in the early 1980's, members of the security forces repeatedly violated the human rights of their fellow citizens and were unquestionably involved in widespread death squad activities." U.S. Department of State, Country Reports on Human Rights Practices for 1989 (1990), at 570.

*** This semi-annual statutory certification requirement ended following a November 1983 presidential pocket veto of legislation which would have extended it.

Four days after the murder of the Jesuits, when the investigation barely had begun, President Bush said "he was sure that El Salvador's government was not involved."* After U.S. officials mistreated the lone eyewitness in the case and discredited her testimony that Army soldiers were shooting at the Jesuits' residence the night of the murders, Ambassador William Walker stressed that, "Even if her first version was completely accurate, the fact that she saw five guys in camouflage suits doesn't prove army involvement."** As late as January 2, the Ambassador told congressional investigators that the FMLN might have undertaken the killings dressed in army uniforms.***

After President Cristiani's announcement in January that the military had committed the murders, U.S. officials sought to limit the blame to an isolated group of soldiers inexplicably acting out of control. The day after the announcement, White House spokesman Marlin Fitzwater reportedly said that the United States "has no information that the government itself was involved with the murders."**** At the January 24, 1990 House subcommittee hearing, Assistant Secretary Aronson observed:

> I don't think that it indicts the armed forces if a unit committed an atrocity.... It seems to me the test is, is this the norm, is it tolerated, and is it investigated. I don't think it's the norm. I don't think it's tolerated. +

---

* "Bush Vows to Keep Aid for Salvador," The Miami Herald, November 21, 1989.

** Elaine Sciolino, "Witnesses in Jesuit Slayings Charge Harassment in U.S.," The New York Times, December 18, 1989.

*** Robert Pear, "Salvador Evidence Escaped U.S. Envoy," The New York Times, January 16, 1990.

**** Al Kamen, "U.S. Praises Salvadoran Death Probe," The Washington Post, January 9, 1990.

\+ Hearings, at 27-28. President Cristiani employed similar reasoning when he appeared on the MacNeil/Lehrer News Hour on public television on January 18, 1990: "Well I don't think that the military as an institution is going its own way.... [T]here might be individual elements in the armed forces that might go the wrong way in to [sic] committing such [sic] crime as the one of the Jesuit priests but not the institution in itself. I think that the institution deserves some understanding that they have during this entire process have evolved and they evolved into an institution that does support the democratic process in the country and they have been doing that for some time now." Transcript, MacNeil/Lehrer Newshour, January 18, 1990, at 4.

More generally, the State Department continues to attribute much political violence in El Salvador to "individual acts of rightwing vigilantism."* Yet the Jesuit killing was not an "individual act of rightwing vigilantism." The massacre was, like so many others, a military operation conducted by troops at the direct order of their commander. In this case, the commander was not just a lieutenant in the field but a colonel, the head of the Military School, the former head of military intelligence and part of the General Staff of the Army and a member of the powerful *tandona* military class of 1966. And since the investigation is not over, it is not possible to say with certainty that this high-ranking officer, who had no record of known human rights abuses or of acting on his own, was the only colonel involved.

One suspects, however, that even if the entire General Staff of the Army pulled the trigger, the Bush Administration would continue to maintain that it was not the action of the "government." Under its view, nothing the military does is the action of the government, despite the disproportionate influence the military has in the political life of the country.

The contention that the great majority of political crimes in El Salvador are committed by unauthorized bands of outlaws would be plausible if the "outlaws" were regularly identified and punished. To the contrary, however, the great majority of killings of noncombatants in El Salvador have never been investigated. In case after case where prosecutions were brought, they have stalled under the weight of Army pressure. In 1987 a broad amnesty that covered military, security force, and death squad killings as well as FMLN crimes made a joke of the rule of law and accountability. Even before that date, the only criminal convictions involved a handful of enlisted men and civil defense members, often made to pay solely because the victims were North Americans. Five low-level National Guardsmen were imprisoned for the December 1980 killing of three U.S. nuns and a lay worker, but senior officers implicated in a cover-up were never indicted. Two officers charged in the "Sheraton case" -- the 1981 killing of two American land reform advisers and the head of the Salvadoran land reform program -- were released for a supposed lack of evidence. The convicted triggermen were released as a result of

---

*   U.S. Department of State, <u>Country Reports for Human Rights Practices for 1989</u> (1990), at 572.

the October 1987 amnesty. The most infamous crime of the decade, the assassination of Archbishop Romero, has never been resolved, despite evidence linking ARENA leader Roberto D'Aubuisson and others to the crime.

Under the spotlight of international scrutiny, President Cristiani and the Armed Forces have identified a colonel and eight other soldiers as those responsible for the Jesuit massacre. To date, however, President Cristiani has yet to mention, let alone investigate, other atrocities committed by units of the Salvadoran Armed Forces in the wake of the November offensive: the November killings by Army soldiers of seven young men in Cuscatancingo, the November murders by a Second Brigade unit of as many as nine persons -- some of whom appear to have been captured guerrillas and civilians -- outside Santa Ana; the murder of Norma Guirola de Herrera and possibly others by soldiers of the Instruction Center of the Armed Forces; and the death in National Police custody of Yuri Edson Aparicio Campos.* Although the case is still a long way from a satisfactory conclusion, punishment of the killers of the Jesuits would signify a new and important development in El Salvador. However, it alone could not bring about civilian control over the military, absent equally vigorous and thorough prosecutions in a host of other cases. If only one out of numerous human rights violations by government forces were investigated, how could it possibly be argued that punishment, rather than toleration, represents the "norm," as Assistant Secretary Aronson's own test requires?

Those who assert that President Cristiani has substantial control of the military, and that the military respects human rights, have the burden of answering the following concerns, in addition to the overwhelming question of why they killed the Jesuits:

* If President Cristiani is in control of a government and military which respect human rights, why did the national radio hookup broadcast after the offensive started in November 1989 myriad death threats against opposition political leaders, Father Ignacio Ellacuria, Archbishop Rivera Damas, Lutheran Bishop Medardo Gomez, leaders of the UNTS labor coalition, and other prominent critics of government policies?

---

* See Chapter II. See also <u>Carnage Again</u> at 28-29; <u>Update on El Salvador</u> at 17-22, 24.

* If President Cristiani is in control of a government and military which respect human rights, why did the Air Force that same month distribute leaflets, with the approval of Armed Forces Chief of Staff Colonel Ponce, which encouraged "patriotic Salvadorans" to "kill FMLN terrorists as well as their internationalist allies," at a time when international humanitarian and church workers were regularly branded as "terrorists" and "guerrillas?"*

* If President Cristiani is in control of a government and military which respect human rights, why has he not been able to control the public warnings issued by the Attorney General that Archbishop Rivera Damas, Auxiliary Bishop Rosa Chavez and other clergy sympathetic to the poor might do well to leave the country, or at least avoid appearing in public places, as well as prevent the Attorney General from making a series of other inflamatory and irresponsible statements?

* If President Cristiani is in control of a government and military which respect human rights, why did he fail to speak out in November and December, when Salvadoran troops entered, raided, searched and, in some cases, ransacked, more than 50 homes and offices of religious and humanitarian workers, and arrested dozens, and why did Salvadoran government forces arrest eleven more church workers from mid-December through early February, 1990?

* If President Cristiani is in control of a government and military which respect human rights, why can he not guarantee that the military will not commit a repeat of the Jesuit massacre in the future?**

* Finally, if President Cristiani is in control of a government and military which respect human rights, why, despite all the fanfare surrounding the Jesuit case, has he failed to date to mention, let alone commence investigations or prosecutions of, numerous other gross human rights violations com-

---

*   See Update on El Salvador, at 30-31.

**   In a recent television interview following the identification of the Jesuit case defendants, President Cristiani was asked how he could assure members of Congress that "this sort of thing will not happen again." "Well," he replied, "all we can assure of is that any new incident that might arise with actions such as the one in the murder of the Jesuit case there are extremes in the country that might commit new crimes in the future. All we can assure them is that we are going to investigate with the same enthusiasm as we investigated this one and hopefully these people will understand that the Government is not willing to accept and let anybody go free without being held responsible for their actions." Transcript, MacNeil/Lehrer Newshour, January 18, 1990, p. 4.

mitted by the Salvadoran Armed Forces and detailed in this and two prior reports?

The sheer number of violations committed by Salvadoran Armed Forces over the past year belies the notion that a few rogue bands are responsible for all the terror. In all likelihood, President Cristiani does not exercise substantial control over the Armed Forces. But he is the Commander in Chief of the Armed Forces and thus he must be held responsible for human rights violations which continue to emanate from within the military. In any event, the Bush Administration cannot have it both ways. The "government" cannot stand so completely apart from the military that it has no responsibility for the excesses of these government employees. If President Cristiani is not responsible for military abuses and if he cannot control them, then civilian government in El Salvador is a misnomer.

Argument 3: *U.S. Military Aid Breeds Human Rights Improvement*

The belief that U.S. training and military assistance will lead to a disciplined, professional military more respectful of human rights has guided U.S. policy toward El Salvador since the inception of the civil war. One element of that policy supposedly has been to convince the military that its practice of mass killing of civilian supporters of the FMLN is not a winning strategy. It does not appear that all have been convinced, as recent cases demonstrate.

In justifying U.S. training of soldiers in 1982, a State Department official noted that a "central theme" of the courses offered "is the importance of human rights and the need to avoid abuses against the civilian populace, particularly in a counterinsurgency situation."* At hearings before a subcommittee of the House Foreign Affairs Committee in May 1984, then-Assistant Secretary of State for Human Rights and Humanitarian Affairs Elliott Abrams argued against legislation prohibiting aid to foreign police forces on the grounds that, "To inculcate in police and security forces more professional standards of conduct is one way, I think, of improving rights performance..."**

---

* Letter from Powell A. Moore, Assistant Secretary of State for Congressional Relations, to Representative Patricia Shroeder, received March 5, 1982, quoted in Americas Watch, July 20, 1982 Supplement to the Report on Human Rights in El Salvador, at 217.

** Cynthia Brown, ed., With Friends Like These (1985), at 11.

In 1986, Assistant Secretary Abrams contended:

> The treasury police were at one time among the most notorious abusers of human rights in El Salvador. They have changed, at least in part as a result of pressure from America and others stemming from that notoriety. . . . [T]he treasury police are acutely conscious of the American embassy's insistence upon humane treatment of all prisoners.*

More recently, at January, 1990 hearings before two House subcommittees, Assistant Secretary Aronson stated:

> The death squads, in part, used to operate out of the armed forces, and [the fact that members of the armed forces have been implicated in the murders of the Jesuits] proves that some still do. And that has to be rooted out vigorously. So nobody is saying the institution has been cleansed and everything is perfect *and that's what we want to use our aid for.***

Archbishop Romero was among the first to recognize the dangers of granting unconditioned aid to a military which viewed winning the war at any cost, and maintaining its own institutional power, as more important objectives than protecting the rights of its citizens. On November 4, 1979, Romero declared:

> It seems to me that the best way the U.S. can help El Salvador at this time is to condition its aid to purification of the security forces, a satisfactory resolution of the problem of the disappeared, and punishment of those guilty. If it doesn't set these prerequisites, the military assistance the U.S. might give would only be strengthening those who oppress the people, even if it is providing tear gas and protective jackets. This will mean more confident repression of the people.***

Rather than apply the specific conditions advocated by Archbishop Romero, the U.S. instead has attempted to create a "professional" army, which

---

*   Letter to The Sunday Times of London, quoted in Settling Into Routine, May 1986, at 133.

** Hearings, at 29 (emphasis added).

*** Quoted in Americas Watch, Report on Human Rights in El Salvador, January 25, 1982, at 181.

has done as Romero feared: it has strengthened those who oppress the people and enabled them to engage in more confident repression.

But the U.S. has not even succeeded in the limited goal of "professionalization": no one has yet explained why, in a supposedly professional army, promotion is made not on merit but by class. In the Salvadoran Armed Forces, everyone in a particular military graduating class is promoted simultaneously, down to the last and grossest alleged human rights abuser and incompetent, since none are ever tried or dismissed from the service. This system promotes insularity and uncritical class loyalty and surrounds accused human rights abusers with an unbreachable wall of fraternal silence. The history of gross abuses committed by the army over the years has only reinforced officers' perception of the need for solidarity.

A lengthy analysis in The New York Times Magazine last November also concluded that the millions thrown at the Salvadoran military over the past ten years have served primarily to strengthen the Armed Forces' ability to ignore pleas to respect human rights, whether they come from the U.S. Embassy or the Salvadoran government:

> One billion dollars in American military aid seems to have bought an army big enough to survive its own mistakes, and powerful enough to resist any effort to reform it -- to end pervasive corruption or weed out corrupt officers. Instead of fostering reform, the American money has been absorbed into a network of corruption and patronage that has grown up over half a century, and has made the Salvadoran military an empire unto itself.... After more than a year spent studying the empire ... a picture emerges of an already powerful institution grown virtually untouchable on the spoils of a lucrative war.*

U.S. officials consistently underline how little basic attitudes within the Salvadoran military have changed when they posit that a withdrawal of military aid will lead to increased abuses on the part of unrestrained military forces. The U.S., the closest ally of the Salvadoran Armed Forces, paints a very grim picture of its ally and pupil. Assistant Secretary Aronson stated recently:

---

* Joel Millman, "El Salvador's Army: A Force Unto Itself," The New York Times Magazine, December 10, 1989, at 95.

> [I]f we cut aid ... just suspended it, I think ... there would be renewed violence very quickly, and it would be even more savage violence than we've seen because both sides would think they've got to strike quickly because the situation could change.... We cut aid to Guatemala ... in 1980 for legitimate human rights grounds, but what followed over the next few years was not peace or human rights. It was savagery and a bloodbath.

How sincere can the Salvadoran military's commitment to human rights be, if, after ten years, it is still being held in place by U.S. dollars? Has any change of heart ever taken place?

Perhaps the central example of the failure of U.S. assistance to improve the Salvadoran military's human rights performance is the history of the Atlacatl Quick-Reaction Battalion, whose soldiers professionally obeyed orders from their officers to kill the Jesuits in cold blood.

Created, trained and equipped by the United States, the Atlacatl -- named after a Salvadoran Indian chief -- is an elite grouping within the Armed Forces designed to serve as the very model of a clean, efficient weapon in the fight against the FMLN. In the past nine years, however, Atlacatl soldiers have committed some of the most prominent and horrifying atrocities committed in the course of the war, culminating with the murder of the Jesuits.

In March 1981, fifteen counterinsurgency specialists from the U.S. Army School of Special Forces were sent to El Salvador to provide training in patrolling, air mobile operations, individual soldier skills and counter-guerrilla tactics for the creation of a 2,000-strong infantry unit supported by helicopters for rapid mobility to points of conflict.* Almost from the start, the Atlacatl Battalion -- "the first Salvadoran army battalion to be created from scratch by U.S. funding and training"** -- was engaged in the murder of large numbers of civilians. A visiting professor at the U.S. Army School of the Americas in Fort Benning, Georgia, recently described the Atlacatl soldiers as "particularly fero-

---

* Cynthia Arnson, "Beefing up the Salvadoran Military Forces: Some Components of U.S. Intervention," in El Salvador: Central America in the New Cold War (1982) at 226.

** Michael McClintock, The American Connection, at 307.

cious": "We've always had a hard time getting [them] to take prisoners instead of ears."*

In December 1981, soldiers of the Atlacatl Battalion participated in a search-and-destroy operation which resulted in the killing of over 700 civilians in nine hamlets in Morazan -- collectively known as the El Mozote massacre, for the village of El Mozote, which was wiped off the map.** Men were gathered together, blindfolded and murdered; young women were raped and burned; old women were taken and shot. The vast majority of the dead were elderly, women and children.***

In September 1983, Atlacatl Battalion soldiers took part in an operation in which civilians were bombed from the air in Tenancingo. Dozens were killed and Colonel Domingo Monterrosa, commander of the Atlacatl, asked residents to "please understand the situation, it was an exception." In mid-November Atlacatl soldiers killed dozens more civilians in the towns of Copapayo, San Nicolas and La Escopeta. Twenty women and children were taken inside a house and shot; thirty more were drowned when troops firing automatic weapons drove them into Lake Suchitlan. U.S. Ambassador Thomas Pickering said he was prepared to believe that "troops of the Atlacatl Battalion had actually been involved in a massacre."****

In July 1984 soldiers of the Atlacatl Battalion murdered 68 civilians in the vicinity of Los Llanitos, Cabanas. Most of the dead were women, elderly and children. Troops burned the majority of the bodies. The governmental

---

* "Anatomy of a Murder Probe," Newsweek, January 26, 1990.

** Although survivors compiled a list of over 700 killed, evidence reaching the Catholic Church legal aid office by March 1982 indicated that more than 1,000 noncombatants were killed in the operation.

*** See Americas Watch/ACLU, July 20, 1982 Supplement to the Report on Human Rights in El Salvador, at 27-31.

**** See As Bad As Ever, Fourth Supplement to the Report on Human Rights in El Salvador, January 1984, at 18 - 22.

Human Rights Commission later admitted that the Army killed 80 non-combatants in Cabanas.

One month later, Atlacatl soldiers killed at least 50 civilians on the banks of the Gualsinga River, near Las Vueltas and El Tamarindo, Chalatenango. Families who were fleeing an August 28 mortar shelling were the next day gunned down or drowned when they jumped into the seasonally high Gualsinga River.*

Just in the last year, Atlacatl soldiers were implicated in three separate killings of civilians. On February 13, 1989, troops of the Atlacatl Battalion attacked an FMLN field hospital in El Chupadero, Los Encuentros, Dulce Nombre de Maria, Chalatenango, where they murdered ten persons, including a doctor, a nurse, three paramedics, and five wounded guerrillas.** In July, Atlacatl soldiers, along with two soldiers from the First Brigade, brutally tortured seven detainees near Tres Ceibas, Nejapa, San Salvador, resulting in the death of two men.***

The record of the Atlacatl Battalion is only the most glaring symbol of the overall failure of U.S. policy to produce an army which respects the human rights of the population it purports to defend. If this is lamentable, it ought not be surprising. U.S. officials have never pretended that human rights concerns should take precedence over the need to win the war, when, as they often do, the two goals conflict. In fact, successive administrations have fought at least as hard to prevent the imposition of conditions upon military aid to El Salvador as they have to teach Salvadoran soldiers to abide by the rule of law. So long as the U.S. government continues to fund the Salvadoran military no matter what atrocities they commit, the human rights performance of Salvadoran soldiers can hardly be expected to improve.

---

*   See Americas Watch, Draining the Sea, March 1985, at 3 - 18.

**   See Americas Watch, Human Rights in El Salvador on the Eve of Elections, March 1989, at 12.

***   See Chapter on Torture.

B. U.S. Officials' Interrogation of Pedro Antonio Andrade Martinez, Suspect in Zona Rosa Case

On August 29, 1989, the Toronto Globe and Mail published an article in which human rights monitors and others accused U.S. officials of "directing the police interrogation of a jailed rebel in El Salvador who says he was drugged and tortured."* The detainee was Pedro Antonio Andrade Martinez, commander of the Central American Workers Revolutionary Party (PRTC, one of the FMLN component groups), who was accused of directing the Zona Rosa operation in which four U.S. marines and nine Salvadorans were killed June 19, 1985.** The article quoted human rights monitors as saying that U.S. officials had ordered that Andrade be kept in detention so that they could interrogate him; that the officials knew that Andrade had been abused and drugged by Salvadoran security personnel; and that the officials had threatened Andrade with harm to his family.

Americas Watch spoke with Andrade, Andrade's wife, the present judge in the case, U.S. Embassy officials, human rights monitors, and one of Andrade's lawyers. We have concluded that one U.S. official may have issued a veiled threat regarding the welfare of Andrade's family in the United States. If this threat was in fact issued, it was highly improper, and the official should be sanctioned for his misconduct. With respect to the other allegations, Americas Watch has concluded that U.S. officials did not interrogate Andrade while he was under the influence of drugs. Moreover, Andrade's extended stay in the National Police was a product, not of U.S. coercion, but of his own decision. However, Salvadoran police were subjecting Andrade to sleep deprivation at the time he was questioned by U.S. officials; he thus was particularly vulnerable to psychological pressures, and the nature of his initial "consent" to speak with those officials is still unclear. Finally, this episode illustrates how the interrogation of suspects in the custody of Salvadoran

---

* Charlotte Montgomery, "U.S. Accused in Salvadoran rebel's torture," The Globe and Mail, August 29, 1989.

** See Americas Watch, The Continuing Terror, September 1985, at 115-119. In addition to his alleged involvement in the Zona Rosa case, Andrade was charged with committing acts of terrorism, possessing arms of war, and subversive association.

authorities may taint U.S. officials with the reputation for abuse so prevalent among Salvadoran security force personnel.

On May 28, 1989, Pedro Antonio Andrade Martinez and Ana Concepcion Rivera Valladares, his common law wife, were arrested by the National Police in their home in *Colonia* Guadalupe, Soyapango, San Salvador. In a search of another home which Andrade was renting, the National Police found arms of war. On May 30, Ana Rivera was released to the International Committee of the Red Cross.

From the time of his arrest until about June 20 or 21, Andrade was subjected to what he characterized as virtually continuous questioning in the interrogation section of the National Police. For the first week of his detention, this interrogation was around the clock, with no opportunity to sleep. He received enough food so that he would not starve. Andrade said that, in the course of his detention, he received no beatings, no *capucha* and no electric shocks. At various points between May 28 and June 20 or 21, he experienced what he called "self-control problems," a feeling of disorientation, which he said might have been the result of a drug, but might also have been the product of sleep deprivation.

On June 4 or 5, Andrade was visited by two men who identified themselves as Ronald Ward, assistant legal attache in the United States Embassy in Mexico City, and Richard Chidester, legal advisor in the United States Embassy in San Salvador. The officials told Andrade that they would like to question him about the Zona Rosa case. Andrade responded that he would first like to clarify his detention status in the case with the judge, but that afterward he would be happy to talk with them. They agreed and said they would return.

On June 6, six days beyond the constitutionally permissible time limit, Andrade was consigned before the First Military Judge, Dr. Cruz Cienfuegos,[*] who ordered that Andrade remain in National Police custody rather than be sent to a penitentiary, as is the custom. Andrade was not represented by counsel at this hearing and said that he did not understand everything that was hap-

---

[*] In late July Dr. Cienfuegos became the Second Military Judge in San Salvador. Dr. Guillermo Romero Hernandez, the newly appointed First Military Judge, took over this case.

pening. The Judge announced that Andrade would be remitted back to the National Police.

On about June 8, Ronald Ward returned alone and told Andrade he was going to interrogate him about the Zona Rosa case. Ward handed Andrade a piece of paper, which, Andrade believed, described his rights and the U.S. government's legal basis for questioning him. Ward remained for four hours, asking questions solely about the Zona Rosa case and Andrade's possible involvement in its planning. Andrade consistently denied having anything to do with the case. In the course of this session, according to Andrade, Ward asked Andrade, who has five brothers in the United States, "Where are your brothers in the United States? Of course, we're not going to let anything happen to them," and then laughed sarcastically.*

The next day, Ward returned, accompanied by Chidester. During this visit the questions were, according to Andrade, more accusatory in tone. During about four hours of interrogation, the two U.S. officials accused Andrade of planning the Zona Rosa attack and/or participating in it as leader. Andrade consistently denied the charges. At the end of this interview, Ward and Chidester asked if Andrade would agree to submit to a lie detector test regarding his involvement in the Zona Rosa case. He agreed, on the condition that the tests be performed and reviewed in an impartial manner.

During these two interrogation sessions, which were the principal substantive discussions he had with U.S. officials concerning his own alleged involvement in the Zona Rosa case, Andrade was, according to him, visibly exhausted while he was being questioned, because he had previously not been permitted to sleep and had been threatened by National Police interrogators. Andrade believed that both U.S. officials might have taken advantage of his deteriorated physical and mental state when they thrust a series of rapid-fire accusations at him. Andrade said that he was not under the influence of drugs while he was interrogated by U.S. officials. He was not asked to sign any document. Andrade said that U.S. officials did not hit or physically mistreat him.

---

* When interviewed, Chidester denied that any threat had been issued in his presence. Chidester said that the issue of Andrade's family in the United States had come up at one point, in order to verify whether Andrade might be a legal U.S. resident, a determination, Chidester contended, that would depend in part on whether Andrade had family there. Ronald Ward refused to answer any questions regarding the Andrade case.

On June 15, six days beyond the legal time period for the Judge to determine whether to hold Andrade or set him free, Judge Cienfuegos came to the National Police and read an act of provisional detention. Andrade's wife and a representative of Tutela Legal accompanied the Judge.

On June 20 or 21, Andrade was finally moved from the interrogation section of the National Police to a more spacious, if modest, cell. On June 27, Judge Cienfuegos, apparently responding to concerns raised by Andrade's counsel, again visited Andrade to ask whether he wanted to stay in the National Police or be moved to the men's prison at Mariona. Andrade signed a statement manifesting his desire to be transferred to Mariona. The Judge then asked Andrade whether he would consent to a lie detector test, and Andrade said he would.

About two days later Chidester returned alone to ask Andrade is he was still disposed to submit to a lie detector test, and Andrade again agreed.

On July 11, according to court files, the National Police sent a letter to the Judge confirming that Andrade would be transferred to Mariona. Just two days later, however, on July 13, Andrade wrote to the Judge saying that he had reconsidered and had decided to remain in the National Police. In all likelihood, Andrade had decided that his personal safety -- placed in jeopardy by the length of time he had been talking with U.S. and Salvadoran officials -- could better be protected at the National Police.

Not long afterward, Andrade was questioned for five hours while attached to a lie detector. He maintained throughout the examination that he was not involved in any way with the Zona Rosa assassinations. Neither Chidester nor Ward was present during the administration of the test. A few days later, Chidester visited Andrade to tell him that the results of the test had been sent to Washington to be studied. More than a week later, Chidester returned to say that the results had returned from Washington and had supported Andrade's denial of involvement.

At Chidester's request, Andrade submitted to a second lie detector test, which lasted about three hours. In mid-August, Chidester returned to say that the second test results were identical to those of the first. In September, according to Andrade, Chidester informed him that the U.S. Embassy in San Salvador had concluded that the results of the tests were reliable.

In October, Salvadoran officials were considering administering a third lie detector test to Andrade, who remained in detention at the National Police.

The role of U.S. officials in the Andrade case has been, at the very least, troublesome. If one U.S. agent did issue a veiled threat against Andrade's family members in the United States, this was clearly improper.

More generally, the performance of U.S. diplomats in this case highlights the dangers inherent in any U.S. participation in interrogations of persons held by Salvadoran security forces. Given that U.S. officials apparently questioned Andrade after he had been deprived of sleep by Salvadoran authorities for several days, there exists a genuine question as to how voluntary was Andrade's initial decision to speak with them. U.S. agents have a duty to ensure that the consent of a detainee to speak with them and any statement tendered are voluntary. Coerced consent or forced statements would make the U.S. government a party to mistreatment which is proscribed under international law. Here, it is not clear that U.S. diplomats ever questioned Andrade about the circumstances of his prior treatment to determine whether his agreement to speak with them was voluntary. If they did inquire, it is hard to imagine how they could have concluded that a week of virtually continuous sleep deprivation had not impaired the voluntary nature of Andrade's consent. If they did not inquire, they proceeded in conscious ignorance, and thus lost an opportunity to uncover -- and, perhaps, put an end to, or at least distance themselves from -- the prior mistreatment.*

Furthermore, by participating in the interrogation process, U.S. officials allow the impression to be given that they are aware of, and thus condon-

---

* It is not clear whether U.S. officials ever specifically informed Andrade of his right, under Salvadoran law, see Constitution Article 12, to have an attorney present during these interrogations. Even assuming that Andrade was so informed, any failure on the part of U.S. officials to ascertain the nature of Andrade's prior treatment might have undermined the voluntary nature of his waiver of this right as well. Andrade's physical and mental condition may have been such that he could not knowingly and voluntarily waive his right to have counsel present. Furthermore, U.S. officials first spoke with Andrade on June 4 or 5, after he had been held for 72 hours, but prior to his first appearance before the Judge on June 6. The very fact that they saw Andrade and asked to question him after the constitutional limit for administrative detention had expired, could well have been interpreted by Salvadoran authorities as acceptance, indeed approval, of their violation of this constitutional provision.

ing, abuses commonly committed in the course of detention. To the extent that officials consciously ignore what mistreatment may have taken place, or proceed to question someone knowing that past mistreatment may have affected the detainee's current condition, they are inappropriately taking advantage of the susceptibility to pressure which such mistreatment creates. Whether or not U.S. officials have participated in mistreatment of detainees, their mere presence as active interrogators inside Salvadoran detention centers where abuses commonly take place creates -- for the detainee, their Salvadoran counterparts, and U.S. and Salvadoran public opinion -- the appearance of impropriety.

C. Use of U.S. Economic Assistance: Las Crucitas, La Estancia, Cacaopera, Morazan, January 1989

On January 20, 1989, 27 persons were detained by soldiers of the Army's Fourth Military Detachment at a Combined Civic Action (CCA) event held in Las Crucitas, La Estancia, Cacaopera, Morazan. One of the detainees was held in the Army barracks in San Francisco Gotera, Morazan until January 25, two days beyond the constitutionally-mandated limit for administrative detention. In addition, five of the detainees were taken from Gotera to the National Police in San Miguel for further interrogation on the afternoon of January 21. All five, released January 23, reported that they were mistreated, and one woman was raped, while in National Police custody. None of the detainees was brought before a judge and formally charged with a crime.

The U.S. Embassy in San Salvador has acknowledged that the event at which these detentions occurred was a Combined Civic Action (CCA) supported by United States Agency for International Development supplies. According to AID officials in San Salvador, AID funds about forty CCA's per month throughout El Salvador. According to AID, it is common practice for the Salvadoran military to sign for the commodities and to transport them from the warehouse to the distribution site. Although civilian supervisors from CONARA* theoretically oversee the distribution of food, it is not uncommon

---

* The Commission for the Restoration of Areas, CONARA, is the the Salvadoran agency which administers much of AID's grants in El Salvador. It was originally designed to implement the civic part of the army's 1983 counterinsurgency strategy and to provide government services and reconstruct areas the army had "cleared" of guerrillas.

for soldiers to make speeches at CCA's stressing the military's commitment to democracy and the need for citizens to report guerrillas and guerrilla collaborators.

AID has come under criticism in past years for allowing military considerations, rather than humanitarian needs, to determine the allocation of food and other goods and for enhancing the power of the military at the expense of civilian authorities in certain areas. In addition, some observers have in the past expressed concern that U.S. food aid was being used to prod residents into siding with the government.* In the case of Las Crucitas, U.S. food aid was used not merely as a means of enhancing military authority, but directly as a lever to attract community residents to a site from which they were picked off one by one -- detained, interrogated, tortured, and then set free, without any semblance of judicial process. U.S. Embassy officials in San Salvador agreed that the events in Las Crucitas were intolerable and contrary to the purposes for which U.S.-donated food is to be used. They argued that this was an isolated event, which we certainly hope is true, but cannot confirm. They further promised to investigate the allegations of mistreatment by Army soldiers and National Policemen and to bring them up with local military leaders. We await the results of these efforts.

The events at Las Crucitas unfolded as follows. The residents of Las Crucitas and surrounding communities were advised by army soldiers that there would be a food distribution on January 20. Colonel Roman Alfonso Barrera, then head of the Fourth Detachment, addressed the group, saying that the Army was collaborating with them and that they should collaborate with the Army by identifying guerrillas. He said that he would help the peasants and look after them. If anyone was captured, he noted, that was because they had done something wrong.

Food and clothing were then distributed. The food was in containers marked with the "Alliance for Progress" symbol of two shaking hands above an emblem of red, white and blue. Clowns, barbers and dentists were also present, and pinatas were brought out for the children.

---

* See Americas Watch, The Civilian Toll (1987), at 295-97.

As the distribution was winding down about midday, certain individuals in the crowd were pulled aside by soldiers and told to attend a meeting a distance away from the distribution site, under a mango tree. However, there was no meeting. When they arrived at the tree, these persons were told they were under arrest and were interrogated about alleged collaboration with the guerrillas. Twenty-seven persons who attended the event were placed in the back of the same military truck which had brought the AID food supplies and taken to the Army barracks in San Francisco Gotera. Some of the detainees were standing on top of the undistributed food on their ride to the garrison.

When they arrived in Gotera in the late afternoon, the detainees were blindfolded as they got down from the truck. Inside the barracks, most were made to stand off and on throughout the evening. At midnight most of the detainees were made to lie down, while soldiers nearby sharpened their knives and threatened to kill them. At times soldiers grabbed a detainee by his hair, yanked his head back, and put the point of a knife to the detainee's throat. The next day soldiers interrogated each of the detainees individually. In the late afternoon of January 21, all but six were released without being consigned before any judge. One of the detainees was held in the barracks until January 25, when he too was freed without being formally charged.

On the afternoon of January 21, five of the detainees -- four men and a 17-year-old girl -- were taken to the National Police in San Miguel. Upon arrival, police interrogated the girl. At one point, while she was blindfolded, a man raped her. She was interrogated further and released on January 23 without being consigned before a judge.*

One of the four men brought to San Miguel was blindfolded and interrogated at the National Police. For three hours during the course of his interrogation he was hit and kicked in the chest, as he was accused of collaborating with the guerrillas. He was denied food for the full three days of his detention. At one point a knife was put to his neck. He was released January 23, along with the three other men, and never formally charged.

---

* See Chapter on Torture.

D. Labeling Civilian Groups as FMLN Fronts

In the past year, the State Department and officials at the U.S. Embassy in San Salvador have continued their past practice of publicly referring to prominent civilian organizations opposed to Salvadoran government policies as "FMLN front groups" or "FMLN allies." Such open disparagement by the United States government undermines the already precarious position of some of these groups and legitimizes attacks against them or their members. By branding vigorous opponents of the government as supporters of the guerrillas, U.S. officials impede the very expansion of political space they claim to desire. Although it may be true that opposition organizations share some of the publicly-stated aims of the FMLN, U.S. officials contribute little to the cause of truth by branding whole organizations as FMLN fronts. In fact, in El Salvador the very act of labeling puts in jeopardy the lives of all an organization's members, many of whom are, in the eyes of U.S. officials, mere innocents unwittingly duped into joining.

The most common objects of this labeling tactic are unions and cooperatives, particularly those labor organizations which have expressed opposition to government policies most vigorously and vehemently. The FENASTRAS labor federation is perhaps the paradigm of a civilian organization which has been the target of U.S. officials' verbal onslaught.

The 1989 State Department <u>Country Report on Human Rights</u> is emblematic. In the Report on El Salvador the arrest of dozens of FENASTRAS members in September 1989 is justified as a necessary response to cynical provocation, and the torture and rape of several of the detained are completely ignored:

> FMLN-linked labor organizations regularly use ostensibly peaceful dissent to provoke government actions, then level charges of worker rights violations when the Government responds to street violence and occupations. For example, in September the FMLN-linked FENASTRAS union demonstrated in San Salvador, burning several buses and automobiles, and causing thousands of dollars in damage to other private property. The subsequent arrests of 60

demonstrators were characterized as a violation of worker rights.*

The State Department overlooks two essential facts. First, many of the 64 persons arrested by the National Police on September 18 were charged, not with bus burning, but with being members of FENASTRAS. Despite the attempt to brand FENASTRAS illegal by calling it "FMLN-linked," it is not a crime to belong to FENASTRAS or to any other labor association. Hence, most of those arrested were released in a matter of days. Second, many of those arrested asserted that they were beaten, subjected to electric shocks, and otherwise tortured in the course of their interrogations. Several persons alleged that they were raped, and one of those rapes -- that of Tatiana Mendoza -- was confirmed by a court physician. Ms. Mendoza was killed in the October 31 bombing of the FENASTRAS office. Torture is illegal and unacceptable under any circumstances, no matter who the detainee is, no matter what the charge.

Vice President Dan Quayle may have seriously undermined any human rights message he conveyed to government and military officials in his two trips to El Salvador in 1989 when, upon returning, he used the "pro-FMLN" label to belittle the detention and torture of union leader Jose Mazariego. Writing in The New York Times, the Vice President urged Congress not to "remain silent in the face of FMLN murders even as it expresses deep concern over the brief detention and alleged mistreatment of a pro-FMLN union leader that happened recently."** Once again, the political sympathies of Mazariego or his union -- whatever they may be -- do not justify his physical mistreatment by Salvadoran government forces.

Most recently, responding to an inquiry by the staff of Senator Edward Kennedy concerning the January, 1990 detentions of two members of the SICAFE coffee workers union, Jorge Alberta Sosa Landeverde and Adan Chacon Gutierrez, Ambassador William Walker went out of his way to note, "SICAFE is an affiliate of the FMLN affiliated group FENASTRAS."*** In

---

* U.S. Department of State, Country Reports on Human Rights Practices for 1989 (1990), at 587.

** Dan Quayle, "Get Tough on Salvador's Killers," The New York Times, July 16, 1989.

*** Unclassified Cable from William Walker to Senator Edward Kennedy.

1989 four SICAFE leaders were gunned down by death squads; two of them were killed. Given this record of violent hostility in a country where union leaders have long been thought of as nothing more than closet guerrillas, the explicit linking of SICAFE -- a labor union -- with the FMLN -- a political-military organization which employs violence to achieve its ends -- puts all SICAFE members in greater danger.

Placing the imprimatur of the U.S. government behind labels that are not supported by due process determinations, and which can cost persons their lives, is intolerable.

APPENDIX A: LIST OF 18 PRIESTS ASSASSINATED IN EL SALVADOR

The fact that church workers in El Salvador have been made to bear the brunt of repression in the wake of the November offensive lends a certain poignancy to this, the tenth anniversary of Archbishop Romero's assassination. Since the post-Vatican II transformation of the Catholic Church in Latin America and the diffusion of theologies of "liberation" advocating a preferential option for the poor, church workers have fallen under suspicion and have become targets of threats and attacks. The enmity felt for the Jesuits within certain sectors of the military and the far right has been matched by violence directed against catechists and other lay and clerical church workers throughout the country.

Archbishop Romero's explanation of why churches and churchworkers become targets of enmity and hostility in El Salvador still seems apt:

> While it is clear that our Church has been the victim of persecution during the last three years, it is even more important to observe the reason for the persecution. It is not that just any priest or just any institution has been persecuted. It is that segment of the Church which is on the side of the poor and has come out in their defense that has been persecuted and attacked. Here we once again encounter the key to understanding the persecution of the Church: the poor. It is again the poor who permit us to understand what has hap-

pened. That is why the Church has come to understand what persecution of the poor is. The persecution comes about because of the Church's defense of the poor, for assuming the destiny of the poor.*

List of 18 Priests Killed in El Salvador, 1972 - 1989

There have been 18 Catholic priests killed in the political violence in El Salvador, all by soldiers or unknown persons believed associated with the right. Three U.S. Catholic nuns and a U.S. lay worker were killed by the National Guard, and several other Salvadoran nuns were killed as well.

This list does not include the hundreds of catechists and lay workers assassinated, nor the thousands of persons of faith who have been killed during the conflict.

Some of the priests mentioned below died alone; others were accompanied by other persons of faith who were killed or disappeared along with them.

1. Father Nicolas Rodriguez- January 2, 1972

Father Nicolas Rodriguez was the parish priest of Chalatenango (town), and the first political martyr of the Church of El Salvador. He was arrested by National Guardsmen. A few days later, his dismembered body was found on the outskirts of the town. Bishop Arturo Rivera Damas, Bishop of Chalatenango at the time, said, "It was a political crime committed to intimidate the clergy."**

2. Father Rutilio Grande - March 12, 1977

Father Grande, 49, a Salvadoran Jesuit priest who was the parish priest of Aguilares, San Salvador, since 1972, was gunned down as he drove a jeep to give mass in his native town, El Paisnal. Also killed with him were Nelson Lemus, age 16, and Manuel Solorzano, age 72. Archbishop Oscar Arnulfo Romero sent President Molina a letter stating that until Grande's death was

---

*   Archbishop Romero, February 2, 1980, quoted in Margaret Swedish, Like Grains of Wheat (1989), at 23.

**   Penny Lernoux, Cry of the People (1980); Jorge Caceres Prendes, "Radicalizacion Politica y Pastoral Popular en El Salvador: 1969-1979," Estudios Centroamericanos, at 93-153, Sept.-Dec. 1982.

investigated, repression of the Church was ended and expelled priests were allowed to return, he would not attend government functions. An autopsy of Grande determined that he was killed by 9 mm. caliber bullets, the same used by the military in Manzer guns. His death was attributed to the Salvadoran Armed Forces.

Shortly before publication of this report, Americas Watch received the written testimony of a Salvadoran who witnessed Father Grande's assassination in 1977. The witness said three plainclothesmen were standing outside a large dark car, possibly a Cadillac, which was parked on the side of the road between El Paisnal and Aguilares. The witness recognized one of the men as a longtime police agent. When Father Grande's car drew near, the men fired, causing the priest to lose control. The car hit a post on the side of the road and turned over, leaving the priest hanging from the car.

The witness stated that another resident of El Paisnal named Ernesto also saw the killing. Ernesto was himself murdered by unknown men shortly after the First Brigade established a barracks in El Paisnal in the middle of 1987.

3. Father Alfonso Navarro Oviedo - May 11, 1977

A 35-year old Salvadoran diocesan priest, Father Navarro was killed by a right-wing vigilante group (death squad) which called itself the White Warriors Union. He and a 15-year old youth were killed in his home in *Colonia Miramonte*, San Salvador, using the same ammunition and guns as those issued to government troops. The White Warrior Union also announced they would murder all the country's 47 remaining Jesuits if they did not leave the country by July 21, 1977.*

4. Father Rafael Ernesto (Neto) Barrera - November 28, 1978

Father Barrera's tortured body was found inside a house in *colonia* Divina Providencia, San Salvador, after a feigned skirmish nearby. Security agents fired on the building, killing the priest and others inside. Monsignor

---

*   Lernoux, Cry of the People.

Romero wrote of his death, "Father Neto was found shot to death, but, by some conjectures, he had been killed in another place and was carried to that place (the house where his body was found)." The funeral wake was held in the parish of Mejicanos, where his brother, Manuel Barrera, was the parish priest.*

5. Father Octavio Ortiz - January 20, 1979

Father Tavo, a 34-year old Salvadoran diocesan priest originally from Morazan, was killed when National Guardsmen and police agents violently entered the El Despertar retreat center in San Antonio Abad, San Salvador around 6:00 a.m. The police entered with a tank, killed Father Ortiz and four youths who were attending a retreat at El Despertar, and arrested 46 other persons who were there, including 20 youths ages 9 through 15 who were also attending the retreat, two assistants of Father Ortiz, the retreat center caretaker, and the cook and her two children. They were taken to National Guard headquarters in San Salvador, and were eventually released. There was no judicial investigation of the incident.

6. Father Rafael Palacios - June 20, 1979

Father Palacios worked with the base communities in Santa Tecla (Nueva San Salvador), La Libertad. He was shot to death in the morning. Monsignor Romero went to the courts where the forensic medical examination was being performed; Father Palacios had been shot in the face and other parts of the body.**

7. Father Alirio Napoleon Macias - August 4, 1979

Father Macias, age 38, was the parish priest of San Esteban Catarina, San Vicente. He was actually inside the parish church when assassinated; his body was found about one meter from the altar.***

8. Monsignor Oscar Arnulfo Romero, Archbishop of San Salvador - March 24, 1980

---

*   Monsenor Oscar Arnulfo Romero: Su Diario.

**   Monsenor Oscar Arnulfo Romero: Su Diario (San Salvador, 1990).

***   "Otro Sacerdote Asesinado," in UCA/Editores, El Salvador: Entre el Terror y la Esperanza: Los sucesos de 1979 y su impacto en el drama salvadoreno de los anos siguientes (1982).

9. Father Cosme Spezzotti - **June 14, 1980**

Father Spezzotti, a 57-year old Italian Franciscan priest, was assassinated on June 14, 1980, as he was inside the church in San Juan Nonualco, La Paz. He had been the parish priest there for 27 years. It is not clear who killed him.*

10. Father Manuel Antonio Reyes Monico - October 6, 1980

A diocesan priest of the Archdiocese of San Salvador, Father Reyes Monico was assassinated on October 6 after his home was surrounded by National Police agents and they arrested him. The following day, October 7, his body was found on the outskirts of the capital city, with a bullet wound in the mouth and another in the chest.**

11. Father Jose Ernesto Abrego - November 23, 1980

Father Abrego, a diocesan priest of the Archdiocese of San Salvador and the parish priest in San Benito, San Salvador, left Guatemala City on November 23, 1980, to return to San Salvador. He was travelling in a private car with three relatives. Witnesses later said they saw the car pass the border station at "Las Chinamas" and enter El Salvador. But they never arrived in San Salvador and were reported as "disappeared."

Upon learning of the disappearance of the four, two relatives of Father Abrego travelled to San Salvador to look for the missing four. They left San Salvador, heading back to Guatemala City on November 29, 1980, but were never seen alive again. Their two bodies were found in Juayua, department of Sonsonate, about 70 kilometers west of San Salvador.

---

*   UCA/Editores. 1982. La Iglesia en El Salvador. Coleccion "La Iglesia en America Latina", Volumen 7 (Universidad Centroamericana Jose Simeon Canas, San Salvador).

** Socorro Juridico, Arzobispado de San Salvador. 1982? El Salvador: La Situacion de los Derechos Humanos: Octubre 1979 - Julio 1981.

Another relative of Father Abrego living in Guatemala City, Carlos Abrego, received a telephone call summoning him to meet someone at the bar of the Hotel Camino Real in Guatemala City, saying he would receive information about the whereabouts of his brothers. Carlos Abrego subsequently disappeared and was never seen again.*

The brutally tortured body of Father Abrego was found in November 1980. The other three relatives who had been travelling with him were never found, alive or dead.**

12. Father Marcial Serrano - November 28, 1980

All of the information available indicates that Father Marcial Serrano, the parish priest of Olocuilta, department of La Paz, was abducted by National Guardsmen around 4:00 p.m. as he left *canton* Chaltipa, jurisdiction of Santiago Texacuangos, San Salvador, after celebrating mass there on November 28, 1980. His vehicle was later found in the garrison of the National Guard. It was said that the cadaver of Father Serrano was tossed into the Ilopango Lake, near San Salvador; the body was never recovered.

A communique released by the Archbishopric of San Salvador in December 1980, stated, "Father Marcial Serrano, parish priest of Olocuilta, was, by all available evidence, assassinated on November 28, 1980. Father Serrano was travelling from celebrating a mass in canton Chaltipa and was returning to his parish; however, instead of celebrating a mass in his parish, witnesses saw him travelling along the road in the company of members of the army. After that, he did not appear. His pickup was found at the National Guard command post, with the license plates changed, in San Miguel Tepezontes, La Paz. Members of the National Guard affirmed they had recovered the pickup truck from a place where it was abandoned. Eye-witnesses, however, contradicted this version, saying they did not see the pickup truck in the place

---

*   Socorro Juridico, Arzobispado de San Salvador. 1982? El Salvador: La Situacion de los Derechos Humanos: Octubre 1979 - Julio 1981.

** UCA/Editores. 1980.

named by the National Guard, nor did they see the National Guard looking for it."*

13. **Father Ignacio Ellacuría - November 16, 1989**

14. **Father Ignacio Martín-Baro - November 16, 1989**

15. **Father Segundo Montes - November 16, 1989**

16. **Father Juan Ramon Moreno - November 16, 1989**

17. **Father Amando Lopez - November 16, 1989**

18. **Father Joaquin Lopez y Lopez - November 16, 1989**

These six Jesuit priests were assassinated by soldiers of the Atlacatl Battalion and other members of the Armed Forces on November 16, 1989. Two women, their cook Elba Ramos and her 15-year old daughter Celina, were killed with them.

Four U.S. Churchwomen and a Lutheran Minister

Four U.S. churchwomen were sexually abused and assassinated by the National Guard on December 2, 1980, after capture on the road from the international airport in La Paz department. They were working with the displaced in the departments of La Libertad and Chalatenango.

1. **Dorothy Kazel, Ursuline nun - December 2, 1980**

2. **Ita Ford, Maryknoll nun - December 2, 1980**

3. **Maura Clarke, Maryknoll nun - December 2, 1980**

4. **Jean Donovan, Catholic lay worker - December 2, 1980**

Five National Guardsmen were eventually charged and sentenced for the murders in May 1984, after defense attorney Salvador Antonio Ibarra resigned, saying the case was being framed. Senior officers implicated in a cover-up were never indicted. This was the only case where any military, police or paramilitary defendants were tried and convicted for the murder of priests or nuns, however, until the case of a Lutheran minister.

---

*   Socorro Juridico, Arzobispado de San Salvador, 1982.

5. Rev. David Ernesto Fernandez - November 21, 1984

Rev. Fernandez, a Lutheran minister, was killed in San Miguel. His body was found that day by peasants in a ditch about five kilometers outside the city of San Miguel. On June 17, 1987 a sergeant of the Third Brigade and his brother-in-law, a former soldier, were convicted.

APPENDIX B: PARTIAL CHRONOLOGY OF HUMAN RIGHTS EVENTS IN EL SALVADOR, 1979-1990

October 15, 1979: A group of younger military officers overthrows the government of General Carlos Humberto Romero and forms a ruling junta with prominent civilian politicians. The Junta declares its intention to restore the rule of law, bring peace and respect the 1962 constitution.

October 16, 1979: The Junta issues Decree No. 3, granting amnesty to all political prisoners and Salvadorans in exile.

October 26, 1979: The Junta issues Decree No. 9, establishing the Special Commission to Investigate Missing Political Prisoners to discover the fate of the "disappeared" under the Romero and Molina regimes.

November 23, 1979: The Special Commission recommends the prosecution of former Presidents Molina and Romero, as well as several high-ranking officials in their administrations, for human rights violations. However, formal charges are never brought against these individuals. The Commission fails to locate any of the "disappeared" alive. Although there are almost no political disappearances while the committee operates, they begin again after its final report in January, 1980.

1980

January 3: Two of the three civilian members of the Junta, Guillermo Ungo and Ramon Mayorga, resign along with all the civilian cabinet members after the military rejected civilian control.

January 22: The largest demonstration in the country's history takes places in San Salvador in commemoration of the 1932 rebellion. Sharpshooters

1981

January 3: The President of the Salvadoran Institute for Agrarian Reform (ISTA), Rodolfo Viera, and two top U.S. officials of the American Institute for Free Labor Development (AIFLD) officials, Mark Pearlman and Michael Hammer, are assassinated in San Salvador's Sheraton Hotel under orders from National Guard Majors Lopez Sibrian and Aviles, who are absolved of the murders while their bodyguards, convicted in 1986 of the killings, are amnestied in the general 1987 amnesty.

January 10: The FMLN launches a final offensive nationwide but does not succeed in overthrowing the government.

January 10: The Junta imposes a 7:00 p.m. - 5:00 a.m. curfew. By February 18, Socorro Juridico (the legal aid office of the San Salvador archdiocese) estimates 168 people have been shot by the government during the curfew.

January: *El Independiente*, the last independent newspaper in El Salvador, closes after eight of its employees are imprisoned and army tanks and trucks surround its office. It had been attacked on three other occasions and its editor was the target of several assassination attempts.

January 17: US president Jimmy Carter invokes special executive authority to send $5 million in emergency military aid to El Salvador despite the killing of the churchwomen.

February 26: Decree No. 603 ratifies the closing of the University of El Salvador.

March 17: As thousands of Salvadoran refugees attempt to flee by crossing the Lempa River, the Salvadoran Air Force bombs from helicopters while the Army fires mortars and machine guns. Twenty to 30 are killed and 189 are reported missing.

April 7: In the "Massacre of Monte Carmelo," more than 20 people are taken forcibly from their homes in a suburb of San Salvador and shot, apparently by police and others collaborating with them.

May 29: The armed forces issues a list of 138 persons deemed responsible for the "chaos" in the country, including prominent civilian politicians.

July 10: The Junta enacts the Provisional law for the Formation and Registration of Political Parties, requiring that new parties identify the names and addresses of at least 3,000 members.

October 15: Martial law and the curfew are formally lifted. However, abductions and killings by security forces still occur at night, leading many Salvadorans to continue observance of the curfew.

October 20-29: A counter-insurgency operation by security forces on the southern bank of the Lempa River results in the murder or kidnapping of 147 non-combatants.

November: The Human Rights Commission reports that at least 400 bodies have been dumped at the El Playon lava bed over the past two years. The area 15 miles from San Salvador is frequently patrolled by government troops. U.S. Embassy officials encounter six fresh bodies on a November 14 visit.

November: During an Armed Forces counter-insurgency operation in the department of Cabanas, approximately 1,000 fleeing civilians are trapped by helicopter and ground fire while Honduran troops block the border for 13 days. Fifty to 100 refugees are killed.

November: As the Salvadoran/Honduran border becomes increasingly militarized, refugees and relief workers in Honduras are assaulted by Honduran and Salvadoran armed forces. Relocation of refugees from the border area to the Mesa Grande site in the interior of Honduras begins despite insufficient facilities and against the wishes of the refugees themselves.

December 11: Massacres take place in the hamlet of El Mozote and nine other villages in the department of Morazan in what comes to be known as the Mozote massacres. At least 700 non-combatant peasants, including many children, are murdered by government troops.

1982

January 15: A U.S. Embassy cable acknowledges that armed civilian auxiliary forces, *patrulleros*, are responsible for numerous cases of murder and torture and have become "a law onto themselves".

January 28: President Reagan certifies that El Salvador has complied with the human rights conditions for receiving foreign assistance. The President makes this certification every six months until late 1983, when he pocket vetoes a bill that would have extended the certification requirement.

January 30-31: Uniformed troops conduct operations in the San Antonio Abad neighborhood of San Salvador in which 32 civilians are killed and others are detained.

January 31: Army troops kill 150 civilians at the Nueva Trinidad Canton, Chalatenango.

March: At least 11 hamlets in the San Vicente department are attacked by air during military "pacification programs" which include blanket bombings of inhabited villages. On March 10, 5,000 peasants from the San Esteban Catarina jurisdiction of San Vicente begin to flee army troops and bombings and are pursued by helicopter and mortar fire. Later they are caught in a surprise bombing in the area where they have taken refuge.

March: Repression escalates prior to the elections for the Constituent Assembly. The Commission on Human Rights in El Salvador documents 761 political murders March 1 - 19.

March 10: A death-list of 35 Salvadoran and foreign journalists is issued by a group calling itself the "Anti-communist Alliance of El Salvador."

March 17: Four Dutch journalists are killed in what may have been an army ambush. One of them had been detained by Treasury Police on March 11.

March 28: Elections for the Constituent Assembly are held in an atmosphere of intimidation and violence. The electorate is presented with a limited choice because the parties of the left cannot participate freely and safely. The turnout is reported to be high but the figures are likely exaggerated. The right-wing receives the most support and the National Conciliation Party (PCN) and the Nationalist Republican Alliance (ARENA) put together a governing coalition.

March - May: Immediately after the elections, political murders rise in urban areas. The military then shifts its attention to the countryside. Socorro Juridico reports 1,034 documented political murders from March 20 - May 7.

April 22: Roberto D'Aubuisson, ARENA leader reportedly implicated in the murder of Archbishop Oscar Romero, is chosen as president of the Constituent Assembly.

April 27: The Constituent Assembly issues Decree No. 3, recognizing the Constitution of 1962 as the basic law of the Republic and abrogating previous government statutes of exception to the Constitution, including parts of the land reform program. However, Decree No. 507, which denies many due process rights, remains in effect.

April 29: The Presidency of El Salvador goes to Alvaro Magana, a banker with close ties to the military. Three vice-presidents are selected, representing the PCN, ARENA, and the Christian Democratic Party (PDC).

May 18: Decree No. 6 is issued, suspending Phase III of the land reform, which gave land to tenant farmers.

May 31: The legal aid office of the Archdiocese of San Salvador is reorganized into Tutela Legal, with the mandate to compile statistics on violence by the guerrillas as well as the government. (Socorro Juridico continues to operate independently.)

May: The Christian Democratic Party issues a strongly worded statement accusing the military and security forces and paramilitary defense squads of killing party leaders, activists, and peasant supporters. In July, party leader Jose Napoleon Duarte charges the extreme right with the murders of hundreds of PDC mayors and other activists.

July 27: The Reagan administration again certifies that the Salvadoran government is meeting the human rights requirements for receiving U.S. aid. The State Department claims that 109 members of the Salvadoran armed forces and at least 20 civil defense *patrulleros* have been disciplined or remanded by civilian courts. However, closer examination of this statistic shows that at most 44 cases involved human rights violations and no convictions had been obtained.

August: During a military campaign in San Vicente, government troops massacre 300 to 400 civilian villagers.

August 3: President Magana and four of the five parties which participated in the March elections sign the Pact of Apaneca, establishing the government's basic platform. Respect for human rights is among the stated objectives, and a governmental Human Rights Commission is established to "protect, watch over, and promote" human rights.

October 8-17: Seventeen leaders of labor unions and the Democratic Revolutionary Front are kidnapped by heavily armed men. The Army later discloses that eight are held in military jails.

December 2: The governmental Human Rights Commission is inaugurated. From December 3, 1982 - June 21, 1983, the Commission processes 514 cases and resolves 91, playing a modest role in locating the "disappeared." However, the Commission does not initiate prosecutions or publish information about victims.

1983

January-June: The FMLN is responsible for at least 43 political murders of civilians. In early May, the FMLN summarily executes captured government soldiers on several occasions.

February 22: Uniformed army soldiers abduct men from the farming cooperative of Las Hojas and surrounding communities in the province of Sonsonate. Approximately seventy are killed. Some corpses are found with hands tied behind their backs, shot in the back of the head. The governmental Human Rights Commission later submits a confidential report to President Magana, but no significant disciplinary action is taken.

March 16: Marianela Garcia Villas, President of the non-governmental Commission on Human Rights, is killed in an army ambush of a group of displaced persons.

May 4: The Salvadoran Assembly issues Decree No. 210, declaring amnesty for certain political crimes by civilians, whether under prosecution or not. By June 24, 533 political prisoners are released. The law also applies to those who turn themselves in.

July 19: Americas Watch finds that "the manner in which the armed forces of El Salvador have used Cessna A37B Dragonfly aircraft indicates that they are not making an effort to minimize the harm to civilians. Indeed, it appears that when this plane is used against FMLN 'controlled zones,' no attempt is made to distinguish between military and civilian targets."

August 25: Treasury Police arrest Pedro Daniel Alvarado Rivera, who "confesses" to the May 25 FMLN execution of a U.S. military advisor, Lieutenant Commander Albert Schaufelberger. On November 12, the U.S. Embassy states that Alvarado was not involved in the killing and his confession was obtained under duress. Years later, he is freed by the military judge.

September: Following a September 25 confrontation between the army and the guerrillas in the town of Tenancingo, 25 miles northeast of the capital, the armed forces undertake a bombing raid that kills about 100 civilians.

October 7: Victor Manuel Quintanilla Ramos, the highest ranking FDR spokesman still in El Salvador, is found strangled. The killing indicates the impossibility of any FDR representative taking part in the electoral process in upcoming 1984 presidential elections.

November: President Reagan pocket-vetoes the bill that would have continued to make US military aid and arms sales to El Salvador conditional on certification that the government is "making a concerted and significant effort" to respect human rights and is achieving control over the armed forces. However, he allows legislation to take effect that withholds 30% of military aid authorized for El Salvador until a verdict is reached in the case of the four U.S. churchwomen killed in 1980.

November: Troops of the U.S.-trained Atlacatl Battalion kill several score civilians in the towns of Copapayo, San Nicolas and La Escopeta, about 45 miles northeast of the capital. Twenty women and children are taken inside a house and shot; at least 30 drown when soldiers firing automatic weapons drive them into Lake Suchitlan.

December 11: Vice President George Bush visits El Salvador and meets with top military leaders. He reportedly makes explicit threats that U.S. aid will end unless death squad activities and disappearances are curbed and the 1984 presidential elections are conducted without problems. The frequency of these abuses diminishes significantly in coming months.

1984

February 24: The Salvadoran Assembly enacts Decree No. 50, the "Law of Criminal Procedure Applicable During the Suspension of Constitutional Guarantees," formally replacing Decree. No. 507 of the Junta. Many provisions of the latter law are maintained. Incommunicado administrative detention is permitted for up to 15 days. Appeal proceedings for convictions by military courts are instituted.

April and May: Some 1,500 Salvadorans flee the rural areas in response to FMLN attempts to forcibly recruit their children in northern Morazan.

May 6: Christian Democrat leader Jose Napoleon Duarte is elected President of El Salvador, defeating ARENA's Roberto D'Aubuisson, whom Duarte in later years accuses of being the intellectual author of the murder of Archbishop Romero. Turnout is high and the vote count appears fair.

May 25: Five former National Guardsmen are convicted of the 1980 murder of the four U.S. churchwomen. They are given the maximum sentence, 30 years imprisonment. This is the first time members of the regular Salvadoran security forces are convicted of a politically-motivated murder. Evidence of higher orders and a cover-up is not investigated.

July 17-22: The Salvadoran army massacres 68 civilians in the vicinity of Los Llanitos, Cabanas.

August: President Duarte announces the establishment of a commission to investigate five well-known political killings, including massacres in the villages of Armenia and Las Hojas, the slaying of Archbishop Oscar Romero and the murder of several U.S. civilians.

August: Americas Watch concludes that "[t]housands of noncombatants are being killed in indiscriminate attacks by bombardment from the air, shelling, and ground sweeps [by the Salvadoran armed forces]. Thousands more are being wounded. And hundreds of thousands are being driven from their homes."

August 28-30: Killings of civilians by the Army occur in and around Las Vueltas, Chalatenango, culminating with a massacre on the bank of the Gualsinga River. At least 50 die and others are missing. Elliott Abrams, U.S. Assistant Secretary of State, denies that this massacre or the massacre at Los Llanitos has occurred.

1985

March: According to Americas Watch, "It is now plain that the Salvadoran armed forces are attempting to win the war by forcing civilians out of zones controlled by the guerrillas." By "terrorizing civilians to flee their homes," as well as by more humane methods, the armed forces seek "to deprive the guerrillas of access to a civilian population from which they may obtain food and other necessities."

March 1, 1985: Americas Watch opens a field office in San Salvador.

March 1985: the FMLN assassinates Colonel Cienfuegos, head of COPREFA, at a San Salvador tennis club, and kills military judge Araujo in his car after he dropped his daughter off at school.

March 31: The Christian Democratic Party wins a majority of seats in the Legislative Assembly and a majority of municipalities. The General Staff declines rightist demands to void the elections because of fraud.

June: The Legislative Assembly dismisses Attorney General Jose Francisco Guerrero, citing his failure to take convincing action in the assassinations of Archbishop Romero and Dr. Mario Zamora.

June: The new Minister of Justice, Dr. Santiago Mendoza Aguilar, announces plans for penal reform, including a special commission to investigate conditions at Mariona prison, where male political prisoners are held. At the end of June, he announces the dismissal of 20 employees of the Ministry of Justice for abuse of authority.

June 19: Members of the Central American Workers Revolutionary Party, part of the FMLN, attack off-duty U.S. marine guards sitting in a cafe in the Zona Rosa neighborhood of San Salvador. Four marines and nine civilians are killed.

July: The Salvadoran Legislative Assembly ratifies the Judicial Reform project agreement with USAID. The $9.2 million U.S.-funded project provides for a Revisory Commission for Salvadoran legislation; a Judicial Protection Unit to improve security for participants in criminal justice proceedings; a Commission for Investigations, consisting of an Investigative Unit and a Forensic Unit; and judicial administration and training.

September 10: Ines Guadalupe Duarte and a friend are kidnapped and held hostage by the FMLN. They and several mayors, kidnapped in prior months, are released on October 24 in exchange for political prisoners held by the government. The parties to the conflict agree not to target each other's family members.

October: the Central American University Jose Simeon Canas, run by the Jesuits, opens the Institute of Human Rights (IDHUCA).

November: Jose Vladimir Centeno and his brother Jaime Ernesto are subjected to a "media trial" for alleged involvement in the October 26 FMLN kidnapping of Colonel Omar Napoleon Avalos that illustrates the lack of effective due process. A video-taped confession is broadcast on November 18 and they are subsequently made to appear at a news conference. Later, they claim they were forced to rehearse their confession under torture. The telephone workers union, to which their father belongs, calls a strike in support of their release. Three union officials are arrested on November 23.

November 22: President Duarte makes a major statement on labor policy at a time of renewed union activity. While granting some of the public employees' economic demands, he also announces measures to prevent strikes threatening coercion.

December: The Salvadoran Supreme Court holds that the dismissal of Attorney General Guerrero by the Legislative Assembly was unconstitutional. He is reinstated.

1986

January 10: The Salvadoran armed forces launch "Operation Phoenix," an offensive to remove rebels from their traditional stronghold on Guazapa volcano. One of the stated objectives is to dislodge the "masas" - the civilian population that supports the guerrillas. Many civilians are captured and forcibly relocated by the army.

January 28: Fifty-six families begin resettling the town of Tenancingo, which was abandoned because of the war in 1983. Under the sponsorship of the Archdiocese of San Salvador and Fundasal (a Salvadoran non-profit organization), an effort is made to rebuild this town and secure guarantees by both sides in the conflict to stay away.

February: Three new death squads announce their existence with press communiques. In 1985 the number of death-squad killings recorded by Tutela Legal was the lowest in seven years: 136.

February: Two National Guardsmen, the triggermen, are convicted of the January 1981 "Sheraton" killing of two U.S. labor advisors and a Salvadoran agrarian reform leader. Captains Rodolfo Lopez Sibrian and Eduardo Avila had been indicted for planning the assassinations, but charges against them were dismissed for insufficient evidence.

March 14: The Legislative Assembly extends the state of siege, which has continued almost uninterrupted since 1980, for yet another 30 days, but excludes freedom of expression from restrictions.

April: At the petition of the armed forces high command, made by Vice Minister of Public Security Colonel Carlos Reynaldo Lopez Nuila, the National Assembly once again restricts freedom of expression in the extending of the state of siege.

May 1: two members of the coffee processer's union and their friend disappear in Santa Ana upon their return from a union march in San Salvador. Their mothers occupy the Cathedral in protest, but the boys remain disappeared.

May-June: 10 leaders of COMADRES and the nongovernmental Human Rights Organization are arrested and spend months in jail before being freed in prisoner exchange, at which time they return to their work.

June: peasants displaced in Operation Phoenix in January start to repopulate, returning to area of El Barillo, Cuscatlan, in the company of foreigner churchworkers who are deported from El Salvador.

July: displaced persons return to San Jose Las Flores, Chalatenango.

September 14: Monsignor Ricardo Urioste states in his homily at San Salvador's Cathedral that for the previous 45 days the Army has stopped food supplies from reaching some 600 civilians in San Jose Las Flores, Chalatenango. This is one of many instances in which the armed forces restricted food deliveries to civilians.

October 12: an earthquake strikes San Salvador at lunchtime, killing over 1,000 and causing extensive damage to government buildings and slum communities.

November 29: Miguel Angel Rivas Hernandez, 19, is abducted by uniformed men believed to be Air Force soldiers in Ilopango. Despite evidence that he was transferred to the National Guard in January 1987, his capture was never acknowledged by either or any authority.

1987

January: The state of emergency ends as 27 right-wing deputies "strike" the Assembly, making the extension of the state of emergency impossible.

February: Ten civil defense members who had been detained in connection with the 1981 killing of 23 civilians in the village of Armenia are released for lack of evidence.

February 28: Decree 50, which had established special procedures for those detained for "security" reasons, lapses by its own terms. The expiration of the state of siege prevented its renewal.

June 15: The Maximiliano Hernandez Martinez death squad, one of the most notorious paramilitary groups of the early 1980's, reappears with the publication of a death list naming 14 students and teachers from the National University.

July 28: The bodies of five young men are exhumed from a well in the village of Los Palitos, San Miguel, pursuant to a court order. They were killed on May 21, allegedly by members of the Arce Battalion.

August 7: President Duarte signs the Central American Peace Plan, obligating the government to negotiate with the FMLN, to allow FDR leaders to return to El Salvador, to facilitate the return of refugees, and to declare amnesty for political prisoners.

October: The Christian Democrat-dominated Assembly grants amnesty to more than 400 political prisoners. The law also absolves all military, security forces, and paramilitary groups for thousands of killings and other crimes attributed to them before October 22, 1987. The only politically-related crime not forgiven by the amnesty is the 1980 assassination of Archbishop Romero.

October: 4,300 Salvadoran refugees return from Mesa Grande, Honduras. Most move back to their original villages, many in eastern Chalatenango. This is a concession by the Salvadoran military, which had long opposed repopulation of conflictive zones.

October 22: a broad amnesty for all crimes connected with the conflict, or committed by groups of 20 or more (to cover military patrols), is passed by the Assembly. This amnesty is to cover all events, whether or not the subject of pending prosecutions, prior to October 22, 1987, with the exception of the Romero case. FMLN combatants seeking amnesty must apply within 15 days; death squad and military operatives have no such time limits.

October 26,: Herbert Anaya, head of the nongovernmental Human Rights Commission, is murdered by unknown gunmen near his home in San Salvador.

November 8: Days before the two principal leaders of the Democratic Revolutionary Front are to return from exile, the bodies of two young men are found on the road from La Libertad to San Salvador. The letters "FDR" are scrawled in red ink on the chests of both bodies.

November: Ruben Zamora, leader of the Social Christian Movement Party that split from the Christian Democrats shortly after Zamora's brother Attorney General Zamora was assassinated in early 1980, and in exile vice president of the FDR, returns from exile.

November: Guillermo Ungo, president of the National Revolutionary Movement and vice presidential candidate in 1972 when Duarte was presidential candidate, returns from exile to resume political activity inside El Salvador. In exile he was president of the FDR, allied to the FMLN.

November: on the day of Ungo's return, President Duarte announces that the Special Investigative Unit has uncovered an important witness in the Romero slaying: the driver of the getaway car, whose testimony he summarizes on TV.

1988

January 5: The government claims, also on TV, that the murder case of Herbert Anaya is solved, based on the confession of a 19-year old that he served as a lookout for FMLN assassins. His statement was made during 12 days of incommunicado detention, and on February 20 he recants the confession and denies any involvement.

January 8: The head of intelligence for the army high command writes to the heads of the Catholic and Lutheran churches in El Salvador, asking them to "impede" the visits of foreign religious workers in conflictive areas. This is part of a campaign by the Salvadoran military to obstruct the activities of international relief and church workers in conflict zones.

February 17: Six civilians are killed when an FMLN mortar falling short of its target lands on their house just outside the Sixth Brigade barracks in Usulutan.

May 11: Armed men in plain clothes kill Jorge Alberto Serrano Panameno, the military judge who had been presiding over the trial of alleged death-squad members engaged in a kidnapping-for-profit ring and the Zona Rosa case. On July 28, Justice Minister Julio Alfredo Samayoa reportedly announced that he has proof members of ARENA were involved in the killing.

July: U.S. Secretary of State George Shultz visits El Salvador and reportedly presses top Salvadoran military officials to curb human rights abuses.

July 18: The Salvadoran Supreme Court approves the lower courts' grant of amnesty to those charged with the 1983 massacre of peasants at the Las Hojas farming cooperative in Sonsonate murders, under the October 1987.

September 21: Soldiers from the Jiboa Battalion of the Fifth Military Detachment massacre ten villagers from San Francisco, San Sebastian, San Vicente. Army first contends the villagers were "subversives" killed by soldiers in "fierce combat," then claims guerrillas killed the victims in the hopes the armed forces would be blamed.

1989

February 3: Vice President Dan Quayle visits El Salvador and delivers a sharp warning on human rights and the need to resolve the San Sebastian case.

February: the General Staff investigates the San Sebastian case and turns over the head of military intelligence at the Fifth Brigade and other lower-ranking officers and soldiers to the order of the court, declaring them guilty.

February 13: Soldiers of the Atlacatl Battalion attack an FMLN field hospital in El Chupadero, Los Encuentros, Chalatenango, killing ten people, including two women, a Mexican doctor and a Salvadoran nurse, both of whom are apparently raped.

February 16: In San Salvador FMLN guerrillas kill Miguel Castellanos, an editor of the journal Analysis and ex-commander of the Popular Forces of Liberation who collaborated extensively with the government after capture in 1985.

March 15: Dr. Francisco Peccorini, a doctor of theology and leading critic of the administration at the University of El Salvador, is killed by the FMLN in San Salvador.

March 18-19: On the eve of national elections members of the Salvadoran armed forces kill two journalists -- Roberto Navas and Mauricio Pineda -- wound a third -- Luis Galdamez -- and fire on a vehicle carrying a fourth journalist -- Cornel Lagrouw -- who was wounded in cross fire and dies en route to the hospital.

March 19: Alfredo Cristiani, of the ARENA party, is elected president.

April 14: The FMLN throws dynamite at the house of Vice President-elect Jose Francisco Merino Lopez, slightly injuring a young girl and seriously damaging the house.

April 15: An Argentine doctor and a French nurse are killed at an FMLN field hospital after capture, along with several Salvadoran FMLN personnel and a wounded combatant, by Air Force soldiers in San Ildefonso, San Vicente. An autopsy performed later in France shows that the nurse had been tortured, mutilated and probably raped.

April 19: Attorney General Jose Roberto Garcia Alvarado is killed by the FMLN at an intersection in San Salvador by an explosive placed on top of his vehicle.

April 19: Treasury Police raid and search the offices of four organizations working with displaced persons, the unemployed, and women; 75 persons are arrested, and several detainees are tortured.

May 22: Nine bus passengers are killed when an FMLN mine explodes under the bus at El Leon Pintado, Nancintepeque, Santa Ana.

June 1: President Cristiani is inaugurated.

June 9: Dr. Jose Alejandro Antonio Rodriguez Porth, newly appointed Minister of the Presidency, is killed along with his driver and orderly by shots fired by two unknown men in front of his San Salvador home. The FMLN denies involvement, but remains the prime suspect.

June 21: Sister Mary Stanislaus Mackey, a U.S. citizen, is shot and wounded by armed men in a pickup truck who pulled up alongside her vehicle.

June 30: Edgar Chacon, a well-known conservative theoretician, is shot dead in his car in San Salvador.

July: Soldiers from the First Brigade and Atlacatl Battalion arrest seven young men from the Tres Ceibas and Camotepeque farming communities north of San Salvador and brutally beat them, resulting in the death of two. Cesar Vielman Joya Martinez, one of two soldiers charged in the killings, flees the country and alleges he was a member of a death squad operating out of the First Brigade.

August 19: two union members, Juan Francisco Massin and Sari Cristiani Chan-Chan, last seen in the custody of Air Force soldiers, disappear.

September 18: National Police and National Guard arrest 74 persons affiliated with the FENASTRAS labor federation and mistreat and rape some.

October 17: Ana Isabel Casanova, daughter of Colonel Edgardo Casanova Vejar, commander of the Military Training School and cousin of former defense minister General Carlos Eugenio Vides Casanova, is gunned down as she leaves her family home in Santa Tecla.

October 19: Explosions damage the homes of opposition leaders Ruben Zamora, leader of the Popular Social Christian Movement, and Aronette Diaz, leader of the National Democratic Union. Two of Zamora's bodyguards are injured.

October 30: Shells fired in an FMLN attack on the headquarters of the armed forces General Staff explode in nearby streets, killing a gas station attendant and wounding at least 15.

October 31: Four persons are injured when a bomb explodes during pre-dawn hours in the office of COMADRES, the Committee of Mothers of the Disappeared.

October 31: At 12:30 p.m. a powerful bomb destroys the headquarters of the FENASTRAS labor federation, killing ten persons and injuring more than 30.

November 2: The FMLN breaks off peace talks with the government.

November 11: FMLN guerrillas catapult six homemade mortars at the National Guard barracks in San Salvador, injuring three soldiers, killing two children and wounding five other civilians. That evening the FMLN launches the most powerful military offensive of the war with coordinated attacks nationwide. Hundreds of civilians die over the next few weeks, as guerrillas and Army soldiers wage pitched battles in major cities and Air Force firepower is deployed to dislodge guerrillas from densely populated neighborhoods.

November 12: Soldiers of the Second Brigade summarily execute several civilians and wounded or captured guerrillas in La Union, Santa Ana.

November 16: In pre-dawn hours soldiers of the U.S.-trained Atlacatl Battalion, under orders at least from Colonel Guillermo Benavides Moreno, head of the Military School, enter the Central American University. They burn offices at the Monsenor Romero Pastoral Center and as ordered kill six Jesuit priests and two women employees, including the rector and vice-rector of the University and the director of its Human Rights Institute. They attempt to blame the FMLN for the crime by leaving a note supposedly signed by the FMLN.

November 18: Soldiers summarily execute seven unarmed young men in Colonia San Luis, Cuscatancingo, a northern suburb of San Salvador.

November 23: Lucia Barrera de Cerna, who testifies that she saw uniformed men firing at the Jesuit residence the night of the murders, is brought to the United States, where she is interrogated for four days by Salvadoran and U.S. officials, who subsequently assert that her testimony is of no value.

November 25: Jennifer Jean Casolo, a U.S. citizen coordinator of delegations for Christian Education Seminars, is arrested after a large cache of weapons is found in her back yard.

November 29: Former Supreme Court president Francisco Jose (Chachi) Guerrero is shot dead on a street in San Salvador by the FMLN.

November 29: The FMLN kills five journalists after capture at the headquarters of the government news agency, from which the FMLN had received fire during its occupation of the rich San Salvador neighborhood of Escalon.

December 5: Mario Roberto Alvarez, Secretary General of the Santa Ana local of the SICAFE coffee workers union, is shot and severely injured by an unidentified man in plain clothes. This is the fourth SICAFE director to be shot -- two died -- in little more than a year.

December 13: Jennifer Casolo is released on grounds of insufficient evidence, and expelled from the country.

December 20: Colonel Carlos Armando Aviles tells a U.S. army major in El Salvador that the Salvadoran military and Colonel Benavides is implicated in the murders of the Jesuits.

1990

January 2: Ambassador William Walker tells a U.S. Congressman that FMLN guerrillas might have committed the Jesuit killings dressed in army soldiers' uniforms.

January 7: President Cristiani announces that the Salvadoran military was involved in the murders of the Jesuits.

January 12: Hector Oqueli Colindres, deputy secretary-general of the National Revolutionary Movement opposition party, and Gilda Amparo Flores Arevalo, a Guatemalan attorney, are kidnapped by plain clothes men in Guatemala City and found dead the next day.

January 13: President Cristiani identifies nine army soldiers, including Colonel Benavides, as those responsible for the murders of the Jesuits.

January 18: Fourth Criminal Court Judge Ricardo Zamora orders that eight soldiers be provisionally detained for their role in the murders of the Jesuits. A ninth soldier implicated remains at large.

February 4: It is reported that senior armed forces officers met twice within hours of the Jesuit murders, indicating they may have known far more about the massacre, far earlier than has been acknowledged to date.

February 8: The judge in the case of the San Sebastian army massacre dismisses charges against nine of the defendants, but orders Major Mauricio Beltran Granados and Sergeant Rafael Rosales Villalobos to stand trial.

February 11: Two rockets fired from a Salvadoran Air Force helicopter hit a house in Corral de Piedra, Chalatenango, killing five civilians and wounding sixteen.

February 23: Ex-President Duarte dies of cancer.

APPENDIX C: 1989 STATISTICS*

TUTELA LEGAL CASES FOR JANUARY-OCTOBER 1989
AS CATEGORIZED BY AMERICAS WATCH

	Jan-May	Jun-Oct	Total
*Army***	34	10	44
Sec.Forces	3	1	4
Civil Defense	0	2	2
Death squads	17	21	38
FMLN	23	11	34
Mines & explosives			
Army	1	4	5
FMLN	25	0	25
Unknown	12	6	18
Crossfire	7	3	10
Unknown/disputed	1	12	13
Totals	123	70	193

Total FMLN: 59
Total government forces: 55
Total death squads: 38

---

*   Statistics for earlier periods can be found in previous Americas Watch reports.

** This total excludes cases of abuse of authority by drunken soldiers killing civilians.

Human rights reporting experienced a setback during the combat started in San Salvador on November 11, and especially after the assassination of the Jesuits on November 16 and the crackdown on popular organizations, many of which were sources for human rights monitors. The actual deaths investigated after November 11 to December 31 by either Tutela Legal or Americas Watch were, by the Army and security forces, 36; by the FMLN, 8; by the death squads, 5; by crossfire, 36.*

We believe that this represents severe undercounting of the civilian casualties and executions of captured combatants.

A comparison of 1988 statistics with those from the first ten months of 1989, before the offensive began, reveals that until then the rate of killings was lower in all main categories.

COMPARISON OF MONTHLY RATE OF KILLINGS:
1988 TO JANUARY-OCTOBER 1989

	1988	88/mo.	1-10/89	89/mo.
Government forces, total	92	7.67	50	5.0
Mines and explosive devices	65	5.42	53	5.3
FMLN	44	3.67	34	3.4
Death squads	60	5.00	38	3.8
Totals	**261**	**21.76**	**175**	**17.5**

---

* Tutela Legal estimates that another 941 people were killed in combat from November 11-December 7, not being able to determine if these 941 were guerrillas or civilians.

AMERICAS WATCH PUBLICATIONS 1989

Brazil:

Prison Conditions in Brazil, April 1989, 41 pages, $5.00. Also in Portuguese.

"Notorious Jail Operating again in Sao Paulo," October 1989 (News from Americas Watch, Issue No. 10, $2.00.)

Chile:

Chile in Transition, November 1989, 93 pages, $7.00; Also in Spanish.

Colombia:

The Killings in Colombia, April 1989, 123 pages, $10.00. Also available in Spanish.

"Colombian Government Adopts Measures to Combat Paramilitary Death Squads," July 1989. (News from Americas Watch, Issue No. 5, $2.00. Also in Spanish)

Cuba:

Human Rights in Cuba: The Need to Sustain Pressure, January 1989, 137 pages, $10.00. Also available in Spanish

"Human Rights Activists Behind Bars in Cuba, January -July 1989," July 1989. (News from Americas Watch, Issue No. 6, $2.00. Also in Spanish)

Dominican Republic:

Haitian Sugar-Cane Cutters in the Dominican Republic, November 1989, 68 pages, $5.00.

El Salvador:

Update on El Salvador: The Human Rights Crisis Continues in the Wake of the FMLN Offensive, December 1989, 86 pages, $7.00.

Carnage Again: Preliminary Report on Violations of the Laws of War by Both Sides in the November 1989 Offensive in El Salvador, November 1989, 84 pages, $8.00.

Human Rights in El Salvador on the Eve of Elections, March 1989, 13 Pages, $2.00. (Available in Spanish)

"The Army Massacre at San Francisco," September 1989 (News from Americas Watch, Issue No. 9, $2.00. Also in Spanish)

Petition Before U.S. Trade Representative on Labor Rights In El Salvador, March 1989, 21 pages, free (Available in Spanish)

Guatemala:

Persecuting Human Rights Monitors: The CERJ in Guatemala, May 1989, 50 Pages, $5.00

Massacre at El Aguacate; An Interim Report of the Ongoing Investigation, February 1989, 20 Pages, $3.00

"Renewed Violence Against Students," October 1989 (News from Americas Watch, Issue No. 11, $2.00. Also in Spanish)

"Labor Activist Murdered as Rights Abuses Deepen," July 1989. (News from Americas Watch, Issue No. 7, $2.00. Also in Spanish)

Haiti:

The More Things Change...Human Rights in Haiti, February 1989, 126 Pages, $10.00

"Human Rights: One Year Under General Prosper Avril," with the National Coalition for Haitian Refugees. September 11, 1989 (News from Americas Watch, Issue No. 8, $2.00.)

Honduras:

Without the Will, July 1989, 83 pages, $7.00.

Nicaragua:

The Killings in Northern Nicaragua, November 1989, 85 pages, $6.00

A Human Rights Chronology: July 1979 to July 1989, July 1989, 21 pages, $4.00

"Americas Watch Visits Detention Centers," November 1989. (News from Americas Watch, Issue No. 12, $2.00.)

"Extrajudicial Executions in Nicaragua," April 1989. (News from Americas Watch, Issue No. 2, $2.00. Also in Spanish)

Panama:

"Conditions for Fair Elections Lacking in Panama," May 1989. (News from Americas Watch, Issue No. 4, $2.00. Also in Spanish)

Paraguay:

"Post-Stroessner Paraguay," April 1989. (News from Americas Watch, Issue No. 3, $2.00.)

Uruguay:

Challenging Impunity: The Ley de Caducidad and the Referendum Campaign in Uruguay, March 1989, 44 pages, $6.00.

General:

"Human Rights Monitors Persecuted in Honduras and Guatemala; Inter-American Court Renders Verdicts Disappearances; Notorious Jail Closed in Brazil," March 1989. (News from Americas Watch Issue No. 1, $2.00. Also in Spanish)

NEWS FROM AMERICAS WATCH IS AVAILABLE BY SUBSCRIPTION, $35 PER YEAR